Elizabeth of York

In that garden be flowers of hue:
The gillyflower gent, that she well knew;
The fleur-de-lis she did on rue,
And said 'the white rose is most true
This garden to rule by righteous law.'
The lily-white rose methought I saw
And ever she sang.

Contemporary song about Elizabeth of York

Elizabeth of York

Forgotten Tudor Queen

AMY LICENCE

AMBERLEY

for Rufus and Robin

This edition first published 2014

Amberley Publishing
The Hill, Stroud
Gloucestershire, GL5 4EP

www.amberley-books.com

British Library Cataloguing in Publication Data.
A catalogue record for this book is available from the British Library.

ISBN 978 1 4456 3314 5

Typesetting and Origination by Amberley Publishing.
Printed in the UK.

Contents

The Yorkist line of descent from Edward III.

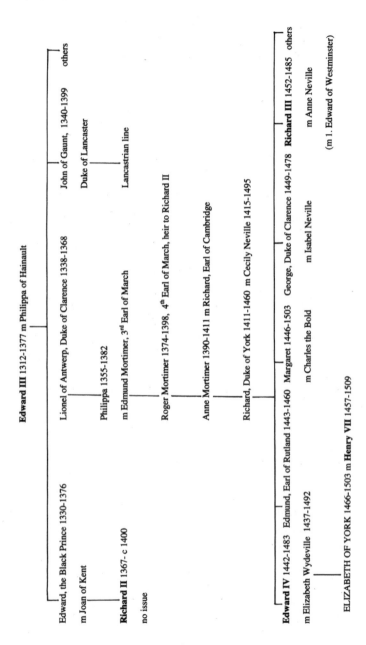

The Lancastrian line of descent from Edward III.

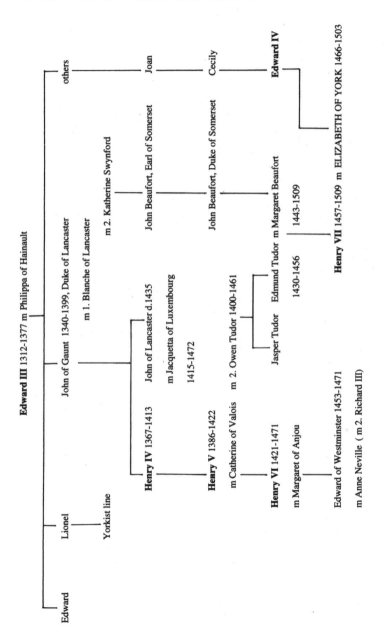

The descendants of Elizabeth of York and Henry VII.

Henry VII 1457-1509 m ELIZABETH OF YORK 1466-1503

Arthur
1486-1502

m Catherine of Aragon
1485-1536

Margaret
1489-1541

m 1. **James IV** of Scotland d. 1513

2. Archibald Douglas d 1557
   6th Earl of Angus

Margaret Douglas
1515-1578

m Henry, Lord Darnley
1545-1567

James V   others
1512-1542

m Catherine of Aragon

Mary, Queen of Scots
1542-1587

James VI of Scotland and I of England 1566-1625

Henry VIII
1491-1547

m 1. Catherine of Aragon d. 1536

m 2. Anne Boleyn d 1536

m 3. Jane Seymour d 1537

m 4. Anne of Cleves d 1557

m 5. Catherine Howard d 1542

m 6. Catherine Parr d 1548

Mary I   **Elizabeth I**   **Edward VI**
1516-1558   1533-1603   1537-1553

Elizabeth
1492-1495

Mary
1496-1533

m 1. Louis XII of France 1462-1515

m 2. Charles Brandon 1484-1545
1st Duke of Suffolk

Frances Grey, Duchess of Suffolk   others
1517-1559

Lady Jane Grey   others
1536-1554

Edmund
1499-1500

Edward
1501?

Katherine
1503

Elizabeth of York's maternal descent.

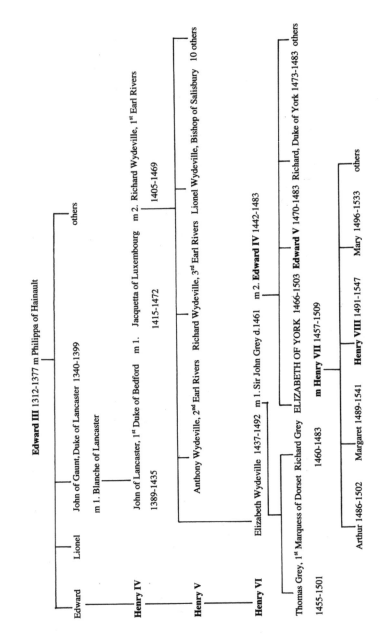

Introduction

The past is a foreign country; they do things differently there.

The opening sentence of L. P. Hartley's novel *The Go-Between* has been quoted many times since its publication in 1953. It has implications for the historical biographer that extend far beyond its original context and raise key questions for anyone in pursuit of the past. To try to understand the lives of those born over 500 years ago, to try to reconstruct their daily routines and draw theories from their experiences, is to attempt the translation of a sophisticated system of codes and beliefs that may be almost wholly lost to us today. Why people of the past behaved as they did is a far more challenging question than may first appear.

Basic human emotions do not change across time. Of course, the Tudors felt fear and desire, ambition and disappointment, love and hate, just as we do. They strove for success, cherished hopes for their marriages, raised their children and took great care to influence the way they were perceived in society, just like us. Many facets of their identities and existences strike us as surprisingly modern and remind us of the universality of the human experience. Because of this, it is possible to broach the divide of centuries and find common ground, even across different classes, genders, ages and events. Then we read that they did something which surprises us, something which we find totally incomprehensible according to modern sensibilities. Tudor people can sometimes seem very close and at others, their behaviour places them far from the twenty-first-century reader. To understand them, we have to try and get inside the Tudor mind, evaluate their actions according to their collective mentalité,[1] if such a thing exists.

Where the biographer and reader must be wary is in how their actions are interpreted. The late medieval 'environment' was very different from ours in social, cultural, political and religious terms. Thus the psychological backdrop of its inhabitants and the mechanisms by which they understood and acted on their emotions, indeed the very mental structures that produced them, differ widely from those of today. Put simply, our wallpaper has changed. The Tudors gave meaning to their experiences in different ways: a headache may have been seen as the result of witchcraft instead of dehydration, tiredness or eye-strain. Preparations for a journey might involve having an astrological chart drawn up as well as packing your bags. Superstition, fate and mysticism played a more significant part in the interpretive process then, along with a different set of communal mores and beliefs in the world's composition and extent. Different bodies of knowledge shaped meaning in areas where we would today look to science for explanation: medieval medicine encompassed astrology, alchemy, magic, superstition, morality and religion, while the inequality between the genders underpinned every aspect of male–female interaction.

To fully understand the lives of our own contemporaries is difficult enough. Individual identities are a function of the membership of social, religious, cultural and political groups, as well as variable influences such as family units, education, intelligence, experiences, regions and generations: there are more combinations of modern sensibilities and systems of belief than can be calculated. It takes a leap of imaginative faith and a degree of empathy to comprehend the motives and feelings of any other modern individual. This can only be exacerbated by the divide of centuries. One consequence of biography, therefore, is an unavoidable degree of distance and detachment which writers attempt to resolve with differing approaches, agendas and narrative structures. Two seem to emerge as most common. A biographer may recount the events of a person's life in a removed, linear manner, or try to recreate a recognisable human experience, with all the limitations this approach must imply. Often, out of necessity, the latter method becomes more of a study of the 'life and times', with heavy emphasis placed on the 'times'. It can be frustrating to tease out the individual from the events, especially when dealing with marginalised, relatively unrecorded figures such as children, the poor or women. Even the most important woman in the country, its queen, left few traces regarding her private thoughts and feelings.

It is impossible now, and misleading, to try to understand what it was like to 'be' Elizabeth of York or any other such historical subject. Her queenship alone makes her unique, even among other women of her time. Therefore, this study of her life must be one of constant questions, reasoned speculation and theories. Her reputation and that of her family have, to an extent, been determined by certain responses perpetrated by early historians. The authors of these are exclusively male. Elizabeth's actions as a princess, woman, wife, mother and queen need to be judged by the standards of regal, wifely and motherly behaviour of her time. Literary and historical sources can offer some sense of the ideals of contemporary conduct but these cannot present us with a full picture of the workings of late fifteenth-century society and take little account of personal response and reality. The careers of her predecessors, Margaret of Anjou and her own mother, Elizabeth Wydeville, are most clarified when they deviated from the regal behavioural models of the time. The questions raised by Elizabeth's life may outweigh the number of answers that can be given with any certainty.

Elizabeth of York's character is something of an enigma. Apparently quiet, long-suffering and dutiful, her history has been overshadowed by that of her husband and his mother. This study could have easily been dominated by the powerful figures of Henry VII and Margaret Beaufort, who undoubtedly played a huge part in Elizabeth's life, but ultimately it is not their story. In fact, I have deliberately restricted the amount of time each was allowed to feature. Equally, the lives of Elizabeth's children and grandchildren have received far more biographical attention, of both the academic and popular kinds. There is no doubt that some Tudors attract more interest than others and Elizabeth's impenetrability may have given her a less immediate appeal to the modern reader than her more obviously charismatic or colourful descendants. One irony of this lies in her popularity with her contemporaries and her identity as something of a Tudor Queen of Hearts: her portrait supposedly graces that image in a standard pack of playing cards. Historical novels have tried to recreate something meaningful out of her experiences by guessing at her emotions. Surviving portraits allow us direct access to her legendary golden beauty, even though ideals of beauty are notoriously subjective. In spite of this, her story still remains far more elusive than many of her contemporaries. Modern accounts of her life can present her as disappointingly one-dimensional, while historical sources emphasise her status; she is a construct of her femininity, beauty and fecundity; a distant iconic ideal. Yet she was also a real woman. Perhaps she may emerge as not so meek and mild after all, but rather an adaptor and survivor, operating within the limits of her choices. And they were severely limited.

Elizabeth is still very much a 'lost' Tudor. She has suffered by comparison with others of her dynasty. This is not to suggest she is any less of an interesting individual than her descendants or that colourful anecdotes and details of her life do not survive; she has simply received less direct treatment than her larger-than-life son and his marital exploits. 500 years on, the shadow of Henry VIII still looms large. Recently, Elizabeth has received more academic attention from American historians, notably Nancy Lenz Harvey in 1973 and Arlene Okerland in 2009, while the surge of British interest in her peaked in the Victorian era with Agnes Strickland and James Gairdner's short biography. Otherwise she appears in fictional form, as an appendage, part of a shared biography or study of queenship, such as those produced by Helen Castor, Sarah Gristwood or David Loades. More often she occupies a few paragraphs in the story of one of her relations. We glimpse the individual at various stages of her life but usually as the foil to her husband or her children. Her identity as something of the fifteenth-century 'trophy wife' reminds us of her importance in strengthening Henry's claim to the throne but her emotions amid times of war and peace remain elusive. As the mother of the dynasty, she must retain a central part in the Tudor story in spite of centuries of distance. The woman who paid her fool additional money while he was ill, who recompensed her servant when his house burned down and who bought her page's wedding clothes was a generous, empathetic individual whose experiences we can briefly glimpse from the outside.

This biography, therefore, will be an exploration of possible interpretations. The questions raised by Elizabeth's life address the nature of the female experience, universally and specifically. What did it mean to be a woman in the late fifteenth century? What changes did marriage bring for a woman? What constituted a wife's role and duties?

And what did it mean to be a queen? How did her status shape her experiences as a mother? Is it possible for the modern reader to find comparable experiences, common ground, and do we actually need to in order to appreciate her life? Perhaps the attraction of biography may lie as much in escapism and difference as in comparison. This is Elizabeth's story, as far as it can be told. It starts with her father, on the battlefield.

Prologue

Lette us walke in a newe wyne yerde and lette us make a gay gardon in the monythe of Marche with thys fayre whyte ros and herbe, the Erle of Marche.[1]

Two armies faced each other on a battlefield. It was early morning on Sunday 29 March 1461 and the driving rain and snow almost blinded the men lined up in anticipation of hand-to-hand combat. It seemed to come from all directions, blowing across the Yorkshire countryside in endless swathes. The field before them was sown with crops, bordered by forest, sodden ground and a river valley, barely visible under the heavy grey clouds. The medieval ridge and furrow ploughing would make it heavy going underfoot, while the unseasonable conditions had softened the soil into sludge. Many had endured a long march and were hungry; now provisions were running low and they would be fighting on empty stomachs. It was an important day in many senses: the bloodiest, most decisive battle of the Wars of the Roses lay ahead, but additionally it was a holy day, Palm Sunday. Soldiers on both sides would usually have been in church at this hour, praying in the flickering candlelight and receiving the all-important sacrament. Now they waited to fight, unshriven and shivering.

Yet there was no turning back. The day before, a skirmish had broken out over the bridge crossing the River Aire and both sides were keen to avenge their losses. They came from all walks of life, of all ages, and many had fought before in the battles that had raged through the countryside and towns of Middle England before this meeting, a short distance from the village of Towton. Both armies could claim to be fighting in the king's name, in defence of the realm, after six unpredictable years of civil war. However, they would have been referring to different kings. On a ridge to the south waited the eighteen-year-old Edward, Earl of March, tall for the era at six foot four, handsome, athletic and charismatic. He had headed the Yorkist forces since the death of his father three months earlier and had already proved himself an inspiring leader in battle. Only weeks before, he had been rapturously received in London and unofficially crowned. However, as Edward's army approached the windswept plateau, he could see he was outnumbered. The additional troops promised by the Duke of Norfolk had not yet appeared, his own men had marched many miles from London and he must have wondered whether his allies had let him down at the critical moment. Facing him were the Lancastrian forces, the supporters of the unstable King Henry VI, Edward's opposite in many ways. He had inherited the throne at the age of nine months, but not the warlike energies of his all-conquering father. Weak, peace-loving and easily swayed by his unpopular favourites, he did not command his armies in person but waited in York to hear the outcome of the day's engagement. Loyal to this long-standing king, the southern-facing archers drew their bows and took aim. The wind was against them. Their arrows fell short.

What followed has been estimated as the slaughter of 28,000 men. They fell during exhausting hours of fighting at close quarters, wielding poleaxes, hatchets and swords;

often they found themselves walking over the bodies of the fallen, which began to pile up as the day passed. Edward remained at the fore, inspiring his men with his courage and energy, until the eventual arrival of the Duke of Norfolk with fresh troops turned the tide of fortune in the Yorkists' favour. Desperate to escape, the Lancastrian armies headed down the steep valley slopes of the Cock Beck, only to drown or be cut down as they tried to use the bodies of the dead as rafts to cross to safety. Many had thrown off their heavy armour and helmets in order to run faster, making themselves more vulnerable to the enemy arrows raining down from above. One bridge collapsed under the weight of the fleeing army and many survivors were swept away in the freezing waters. The Croyland Chronicle describes the blood of the slain mingling with the snow and 'running down the furrows and ditches' while the bodies, piled up for a distance of 10 miles out of the field.[2] Those who fled to nearby York were hunted down and killed, except for Henry VI and his family, exiled in Scotland. At the end of the day, there was only one king left in England. Triumphantly, Edward IV rode south to arrange his formal Coronation.

1

The Rising Star
1466–1469

Is't possible your rash, unlawful act
Should not breed mortal hate betwixt the realms
What may the French King think when he shall hear
That whilst you sent to entreat about his daughter,
Basely you take a subject of your own?[1]

It was time the new king married. Three years had passed since his victory at Towton and the spectacular Coronation in Westminster Abbey, when two archbishops had placed the heavy, jewelled crown of Edward the Confessor on his head. Entering the massive Gothic structure of flying buttresses, ribbed vaulting and pointed arches, he had been following in 400 years of tradition, where every English monarch had been crowned since 1066. The procession must have been a blaze of colour, with the city's aldermen dressed in scarlet and 400 mounted Londoners in green; twenty-eight newly created Knights of the Bath followed, in blue gowns with white silk hoods. Mindful of the recent conflict, Edward had issued a promise to protect his people from oppression and manslaughter; his subjects in turn received him with rapturous acclaim. 'The commons love and adore him as if he were their God',[2] wrote one, which was confirmed by an awestruck Italian diplomat;[3] others presented him as a saviour, comparable to Moses and Joshua. His iconography drew on prophecies and astrological devices, like the 'sun' of York later immortalised by Shakespeare. Physically, he conformed to medieval concepts of kingship and majesty in an era when rulers were recognisable primarily through looking the part. Taller than most of his contemporaries by about a foot, fair-haired and handsome, he was described as 'the handsomest knight in England',[4] 'the handsomest Prince my eyes ever beheld', in possession of a beauty 'it hath pleased Almighty God to send' him.[5] It seemed to many that Edward was God's chosen king, sent to replace the weak-willed and uncharismatic Lancastrian usurper.

By 1464, Edward's councillors were keen to see him advantageously married. Many had 'marvelled' that he had remained single for so long, considering his personal and political situation. The existence of the deposed Henry VI and his son would always provide a figurehead for rebellion, so the tenuous Yorkist position could only be consolidated by a union with a powerful, established foreign dynasty and the birth of a Plantagenet heir. Plus, the young king was gaining something of a reputation; one chronicler described him as 'not over-chaste in living'[6] and according to another, he had already fathered at least one illegitimate child, by one of his many mistresses. His licentious reputation had quickly spread. The Burgundian chronicler, Philip de Commines, wrote that he 'thought nothing but upon women' while the Italian writer, Dominic Mancini, claimed he pursued women of all ranks indiscriminately, 'overcoming all by money and promises'.[7] In early September 1464, Parliament met at Reading Abbey, where the assembled councillors were preparing to conclude what was expected to be a straightforward deal. Richard Neville, Earl of Warwick, Edward's cousin and right-hand man, was about to leave for France after a year of negotiations. His job would be to finalise the arrangements for the king's marriage to Bona of Savoy, teenage sister of the French queen, which would ensure the permanent support of Louis XI against the Lancastrians. The plan had been mooted for a long time, with other potential brides from Castile, Scotland and Burgundy rejected in her favour and Edward himself had raised no objection to Bona's youth, lineage or reputed charms. Portraits from the early 1470s onwards depict a stout, matronly-looking woman who married into the infamous Sforza family; yet if Edward had commissioned her picture, no record of it survives. He had put his trust in his envoy's descriptions of her impressive clothing and appearance and Warwick, in his turn, stood to gain considerably by his role as matchmaker. Discussions had already been underway in Reading for ten days and it seemed Westminster would soon be playing host to a royal wedding. But on 14 September, as the lords assembled in the abbey's impressive refectory and the commons squeezed into the Chapterhouse, their king had an unexpected confession to make. Sheepishly, he halted Warwick's flow of arrangements: there would be no embassy to France after all. Bona would not be coming to England. Edward already had a wife.

The shock in the abbey must have been palpable. For Warwick, it was a personal humiliation that marked the beginning of his eventual estrangement from the king; envoy Lord Wenlock had also been promised a substantial reward by Louis XI once the French match went ahead. Not only did the news come as a complete surprise to all those assembled but Edward's choice had fallen upon a woman they considered completely unsuitable. The king's wife of four months came from an obscure Lancastrian family, many of whom had fought and died for Henry VI, in opposition to many of Edward's loyal supporters. In addition, many of those gathered there that day fiercely resented the rise of what they considered an upstart family at the expense of what could have been a powerful political alliance. Many were uneasy at the king's defiance and duplicity in having presented them with a *fait accompli*, acting without consultation in a most secretive manner, while allowing them to believe in his complicity with Warwick's plan. Parliament did not hold back but expressed surprise and disapproval in no uncertain terms; while the woman's beauty and virtue was not in question, the daughter of a simple knight was 'no match for a Prince'. The Croyland chronicler wrote that the 'immoderate' haste and 'ardour of his youth ... the nobility and chief men of the kingdom took amiss'.[8] Their trump card had thrown itself away.

When Edward's mother, Cecily Neville, heard the news, she was 'sore moved' and chided her son that it was his 'honour, profit and surety also, to marry in a noble progeny out of his realm'.[9] Edward, however, was adamant. While admitting his choice may not 'be to the liking of all', he would have 'no other wife' and there was little now that anyone could do. Into Edward's mouth dramatist Thomas Heywood put the defence that 'all true subjects shall have cause to thank God, to have their king born of a true English woman'. He appeals to a sense of national pride, claiming that 'it was never well since we matched with strangers' which created 'chickens of the half kind' instead of 'birds of the game'.[10] By exercising his personal choice, Edward had managed to alienate almost his entire court and family in one sweep. The woman who had caused so much controversy was a twenty-seven-year-old widow with two small sons. Heywood made Cecily refer to her as a 'foul blemish' and 'stain' on his princely state, 'which yet the child that is unborn shall rue'. That unborn child, their first of nine, would be Elizabeth of York, a future Queen of England.

Edward's marriage to Elizabeth Wydeville divided opinion at the time and has continued to do so over the next five centuries. The circumstances of their meeting have been romanticised by successive historians as the start of an enduring love affair or else cited as an example of a scheming woman's manipulation of a lust-driven youth. Elizabeth may have been the daughter of a mere knight but her mother, Jacquetta of Luxembourg, was a duchess, previously married to a son of Henry IV and the highest-ranking lady at court after Margaret of Anjou. Elizabeth had been married young to Sir John Grey, who died in 1461 at the second Battle of St Albans, six weeks before the Yorkist victory at Towton. At twenty-four, Elizabeth was left with two small sons and a struggle on her hands: Edward had confiscated her father's possessions and her late husband's lands were in legal dispute. It was to resolve these matters that she threw herself on the new king's pity, so the legend goes, placing herself at a strategic point under a great oak in Whittlebury forest, while the king hunted near her Northamptonshire home. They may well have met earlier as the Wydvilles had been prominent at the court of Henry VI, for which they had been pardoned in 1461, when Edward visited nearby Stony Stratford. Later, historian Thomas More described the encounter in romantic terms: 'he not only pitied her but also waxed enamoured on her … whose appetite when she perceived she virtuously denied him'.[11] Edward was used to pursuing women who submitted. Elizabeth's refusal to become his mistress only inflamed his interest. While later detractors used this as evidence for her ruthless ambition, contemporary Italian poet, Antonio Cornazzano, described her as saintlike and described her response to Edward's attempts to seduce her in terms reminiscent of Shakespeare. Offering him a dagger to end her life, she states death was preferable to living in the 'eternal filth and squalor' after his 'vain pleasure were soon over'.[12] Mancini also cited a similar episode, except his Edward is more aggressive and wields the weapon himself. Other chroniclers depict a more romantic courtship, with More suggesting 'much wooing and many great promises' and Weinreich claiming they dined frequently together.[13] The young widow's constant refusal to become his mistress, coupled with her beauty, modesty and awareness of her unsuitability to be his wife, won the young king over. On 1 May 1464, they were married 'in most secret manner' at her home of Grafton.[14]

So why such secrecy? No banns were published, barely anyone was present and Edward explained his absence to his concerned household as a hunting trip. The bride's father may not even have been aware that the king was being smuggled into his daughter's bedroom under his very roof, according to historian Polydore Vergil. Opinion continues to divide over Edward's character and motives and after five centuries it is impossible to ascertain his true intentions. He appears to have only confessed to the match under duress, four months later, when Warwick's plans would have forced him into a bigamous French liaison and possible conflict with his Burgundian alliances. Was the king truly in love with Elizabeth, or was it a case of impetuous lust? Had he gone through some sort of ceremony with her in order to satisfy that lust, which he later hoped to dissolve? Secret marriages were not unknown when the family or circumstances opposed the union; five years later in 1469, Margaret Paston was clandestinely wedded to the family's bailiff, Richard Calle. An extract from one letter he wrote to her that year may echo some of the emotions of the royal couple:

> I recommend myself to you with very sorrowful heart, as one that cannot be merry, nor shall it be ... considering the great bond of matrimony that is made between us, also the great love ... I beseech Almighty God to comfort us as soon as it pleases him, for we ought of very right to be most together are most asunder.

Medieval marriages could be made and unmade on all sorts of grounds. A simple prior arrangement, promise or 'handfasting' could be enough to invalidate later unions, while other matches were dissolved on the basis of age, political expediency or lack of consummation. Edward was clearly aware of the objections his family and nobility would raise to the match and it may not have been the first time he had made promises to a woman to get her into bed. Elizabeth Lucy had already borne him at least one illegitimate child on the pretext of 'kind words', and twenty years later a bishop claimed to have officiated at a previous marriage service between the young king and another supplicating widow, Eleanor Butler, neé Talbot. Perhaps Edward was genuinely in love with Elizabeth. Alternatively, he was driven by lust, acting in haste and thinking of the consequences later; perhaps he had cynically hoped the secrecy would invalidate the marriage once it had been consummated and that he would never have to admit it. If that had been the case, the very date itself may have been significant.

May Day in the fifteenth century could potentially be a riotous time. Customs of misrule and disorder, based on status and gender, were permitted at certain times of the year, deriving from Pagan rituals associated with cultivation of the land and its annual cycles. Marginal figures experienced a brief 'play' at power: servants gained the temporary upper hand over masters, as did women over men and children over adults. Lords of Misrule and Robin Hood figures presided over festivities at ritual moments of the year, holding their own Coronation, ruling courts and dispensing punishments, typically for a period of several days. Women could pursue men, greater sexual liberty was tolerated and temporary unions made. Until the 1520s, at Hocktide, on the Monday and Tuesday after Easter, men were permitted to capture and hold to ransom any woman they found in the street. However, on the following day the privilege was reversed and women were allowed to band together and detain men of their choice.

Some of this was exaggerated in later Puritan propaganda, such as the writing of Philip Stubbes who claimed that the May Day celebrations resulted in the defiling of two-thirds of all maidens.[15] Yet women were also empowered. Contemporary parish records of May ales or games include the crowning of a number of mock-queens, such as in Wistow in the 1460s, where a 'royal' couple, selected from the village youth, presided over an afternoon of entertainment among their 'court' or in Salisbury in 1461, where the king and queen were fined 8*d* each if they refused to 'serve'; about 15 per cent of English parishes at the time recorded similar mock-regal ceremonies.[16]

Edward and Elizabeth's ceremony lacked the most crucial public and theatrical display of such customs. It probably took place at dawn at the manor of Grafton Regis itself or else in the tiny hermitage on the edge of Wydeville land, rather than in the public parish church of St Mary the Virgin; little now survives of the building but excavations in 1964–5 unearthed fifteenth-century chapel floor tiles decorated with the arms of Wydeville and York. This secrecy may have been a gesture designed to honour his bride, or else a possible future opt-out clause, as part of the ritual year's theatrics. Edward never used the occasion to excuse or explain himself yet he may have seen a fitting symmetry in the day's date: by choosing to marry then, he was allowing a commoner an unprecedented degree of licence and exploiting the day's carnivalesque tradition to seize his opportunity. Alternatively, it may have simply been coincidence.

Whatever Edward's intentions on that May morning in 1464, the pair remained married for the next nineteen years. He formally presented his wife to the court on Michaelmas day, 29 September, when she was led into Reading Abbey by none other than Warwick himself. The abbey was an important, impressive twelfth-century bastion of royalty and pilgrimage, the third-largest and wealthiest in the country; carved fragments now in the town museum give an idea of its former splendour. As Elizabeth entered, she must have been aware of the significance of the moment and the hostility of many of those gathered. In some ways, it was a political coup for Edward, a step towards greater autonomy as king but it was also a deeply personal occasion, as Elizabeth was led into the abbey quarters where her honeymoon would be spent. A picture of the scene, painted by Ernest Board in 1923, now hanging in Reading Town Hall,[17] depicts Edward leading his demure-looking wife to the chair of estate in the chancel, while members of the council raise their swords to the roof in a gesture of chivalric support. The reality was probably far more tense, with the observance of strict protocol which had been designed to enhance Elizabeth's status as the first commoner to marry a king since 1066. Her Coronation in May 1465 was lavish, having required a whole year for proper preparation. £400 was allocated for her expenses, while £27 was spent on silk for her chairs and horses, £280 on cloth of gold, £20 in plate for her feast and a further £108 on a cup and basin of gold. The drawbridge of London Bridge was fumigated before she passed and fifty knights of the Bath were created before she reached Westminster Abbey.[18] An illustration of Elizabeth in her Coronation robes, from the *Illuminated Book of the Fraternity of Our Lady's Assumption*, shows a long scarlet gown with bodice of ermine under an ermine-lined blue cloak edged with gold. Her heavy gold crown is surmounted by a cross and her long blonde hair cascades down her shoulders as she looks out serenely but directly at the reader.[19] The subsequent feasting lasted hours and would have employed the finest golden plate, napery and ritual of the era: a comparable menu at the enthronement of George Neville as Archbishop of York that year featured 1,000 sheep, 2,000 pigs, 4,000 swans, 2,000 geese, 4,000 pigeons, 1,200 quail and hundreds of oxen, veal and deer. It was finished off with over 13,000 jellies, tarts and custards and washed down with 300 tonnes of ale. By now, there could be little doubt that Edward was serious about his queen but he may have had another cause to celebrate. It was during these heady days leading up to her Coronation that Elizabeth conceived their first child.

Westminster Palace was to be central in the life of Elizabeth's daughter, whom she would also name Elizabeth. It had been the home of kings for 400 years before her birth and symbolised the power of regal government alongside the cultural and material privileges of status. Extensive rebuilding by Richard II in 1394 had made it one of the most modern and impressive of the king's properties. The royal apartments and famous painted chamber sat alongside the major London thoroughfare of the Thames, with formal gardens to the north, beyond which lay the business end, with its Great Hall and Exchequer. The city lay further downriver to the east, centred on the present Square Mile, so the palace was relatively quieter than its location might suggest; foreign trade from the busy port would have been unloaded a few miles away and a single street led all traffic from Charing Cross to the palace entrance on the site of the present Parliament Square. It was here that Elizabeth went to await the birth of her child in privacy and luxury. From her apartments, she could look out at the open fields surrounding Lambeth Palace and marshes, still underdeveloped in the maps of Wyngaerde (1543) and Hoefnagel (1572) and watch the boats headed for the villages of Greenwich, Richmond and beyond: a ferry crossed regularly to the archbishop's palace from the abbey steps. Her household, separate from that of the king, would have comprised servants assigned to the various departments of kitchen and wardrobe, heralds and jewel-keepers, finances and stables, down to those responsible for building her fires, washing her clothes, rowing her boats and cleaning up after the enormous business of moving between her residences of Ormond Place, Sheen and Eltham. By the time Edward went about revising the royal households along Burgundian lines in 1471, their unnecessary scale had already become apparent. The queen had limited her waiting staff to 100 and cut back in areas where her predecessor had overspent, yet she was still comfortable and well-attended: that year she spent over £1,000 on her wardrobe, as well as £54 on her goldsmith and £14 on sable furs; £10 was spent on three minstrels and more than £18 on medicines from an apothecary.[20]

The London where the little Princess Elizabeth was born was much smaller than the present city. It was also greener, with a higher proportion of private gardens and open spaces. A map of 1300, when population has been estimated at roughly 80,000, shows the main inhabited area lay between the Tower in the east and Bridewell Palace, at the start of Fleet Street, to the west. Little was developed to the north beyond Bishopsgate and Cripplegate, with several large monastic establishments, like St Bartholomew's, St Mary Spital and St Catherine's well outside the walls. Greenwich was barely a village, surrounded by countryside: Wyngaerde's 1554 illustration shows a scattering of small houses either side the waterfront palace with its enclosed gardens; the little princess also stayed at the equally remote Sheen Palace (in Richmond) upstream from Westminster. The Thames was the city's main thoroughfare, wider than it is today and bobbing with vessels of all types, but there was only one bridge and the South Bank was barely developed. Generally, roads were difficult to pass in bad weather, dirty, rutted and choked with waste. Close living and poor hygiene made the population prone to fire and illness. The 1348–9 plague epidemic had decimated between a third and a quarter of the population, which took almost two centuries to recover, so it is unsurprising that Elizabethan maps show a similar-sized city. Still bounded by the Tower to the east, the settlement was by then creeping west towards Whitehall and north towards Shoreditch, where the first theatres were being established. In the 1460s though, London's walled interior was dominated by monastic buildings and the estates of the wealthy, whose grand stone town houses were built around courtyards backing onto the river, with their own gardens and orchards. Increasingly, however, these were being encroached on by the homes of wealthy merchants, while more modern dwellings spread upwards rather than outwards, several storeys high, made from painted mortar and timber. One such, Crosby Place in Bishopsgate, was described by Elizabethan antiquarian, John Stow, as a 'great house of stone and timber', with extensive gardens, courtyard, great chamber, chapel, solar, great hall with marble floors and an oriel window.[21] Beyond such establishments, smaller lanes teemed with dark, overhanging dwellings, whose cellars and garrets housed the poor.

In spite of the crowding, clear social and physical boundaries existed. Medieval people knew their place, although the traditional social division of the three estates (those who prayed, fought or worked) was being complicated by rise of the middle classes. London merchants had got wealthy trading in wool and the city was a major international port, with ships arriving from the Continent and beyond, bringing and exporting luxury goods. Extremes of poverty and affluence sat side by side. Roads were named after trades, with signs for the illiterate. Mancini described three principal streets: Thames Street with cranes and warehouses for the loading and unloading of ships, Candlewick Street with its cloth merchants and Cheapside, where luxury goods such as tapestries, gold and silver, jewellery and silks were on sale. Yet these irregularly paved streets still saw the disposal of waste and the slaughter of animals at the many open-air markets. A study of over 4,000 London wills made between 1374 and 1486 found that the most common occupations were victuallers (inn keepers, vintners, bakers, butchers, food suppliers, etc.) employing 22 per cent of Londoners. After that, merchants and grocers comprised 14 per cent, 12 per cent were making or retailing clothing, 11 per cent worked with leather, 6 per cent were in construction and 2 per cent made a living through transport.[22]

Edward's court rolls are full of the business of the London citizens on whom he frequently relied: men like William Asser, cutler; William Chariar, bladesmith; Everard Newchurch, pewterer; John Hill, draper; Henry Dumpstede, mercer; John Kemp, fishmonger; John Hobbes, doctor; Thomas Crowherst, haberdasher; Thomas Russell, butcher; William Danyell, stockfishmonger; Robert Abraham, salter; Thomas Dalston, glover; William Grey, mason; John Girlyng, goldsmith and William Payne, skinner, who appear in the 1468–9 records alongside the knights, gentlemen, justices, chaplains, citizens and others.[23] In general, though, most people lived outside the cities. England still had a largely rural population despite the urbanisation of the previous century; most people lived on the land but urban numbers would swell greatly on key days in the calendar, with non-residents travelling in for business and trade. At times of seasonal employment and the occurrences of markets and fairs, daily population figures could soar, before non-residents hurried home before the city gates were locked at night. Little of this would have impinged on Elizabeth in the royal nursery, where mercantile interactions and provisions were handled by members of the household. It was common for Londoners, especially poorer ones, to bring the family gifts in hope of recompense, such as fruit in season, eggs, butter, bread or whatever they could produce. In November 1502, Elizabeth would reward different citizens who had presented her with a wild boar, tripe, pork, puddings, a buck and pheasants; in December she received apples and pomegranates![24]

Although it was a prosperous and pious city, the era was dominated by superstition. London's medieval patron was Saint Erkenwald, its bishop in the seventh century. He had been the subject of an alliterative poem of 1386, perhaps by the 'Gawain' poet,[25] in which he baptised the resurrected corpse of a pagan judge. Over 100 churches stood within the walls and citizens can never have escaped the regulating peals of their bells. Omens and predictions were taken seriously as indicators of God's will: the Croyland Chronicle in the 1460s records wondrous signs, all pertinent to the national disorder, from Edward IV's famous parhelion (three suns in the sky) to a shower of blood that stained the grass. Horsemen were seen rushing through the sky, while a pregnant woman in Huntingdon, near her time, reported she had felt the child weeping in her womb. All these were taken seriously enough to be investigated by Archbishop of Canterbury, Thomas Bourchier, as indicators of impending national calamities and the approach of divine vengeance for the nation's sins. Elizabeth Wydeville was deeply pious and typical of her era in taking her faith seriously, endowing abbeys, founding chapels, petitioning the pope, undertaking pilgrimages, sheltering and promoting religious figures and making regular offerings on saints' days. She may have chosen the gillyflower (the pink, or carnation) as her personal device, as it appears in several depictions of her in stained glass and illuminated manuscripts. This flower associates her closely with the Virgin Mary and ideals of devoted motherhood, as it supposedly bloomed where Mary's tears of grief fell.[26] This is reinforced by its inclusion in a contemporary song, describing it as gentle and familiar to the queen: 'the gillyflower gent, that she well knew'. Her eldest daughter would follow in her example.

The Scottish poet William Dunbar, who visited the 'sovereign' City of London in 1501–2, compared it with the city of Troy, gems and flowers, including the rose (a

would have been present as well as her midwife Margery Cobbe. Their collective experience of childbirth would have been more valuable at the time than the theoretical knowledge of men who had never witnessed a live birth. The light would be blocked out, as it was thought to be harmful for newborns, except for one window to allow Elizabeth a view outside; the fire stoked up and candles burned continually as the women passed the long hours of waiting. Servants brought food, drink, clean linen and wood to the door, where they were handed over for the little community inside. It was customary for an expectant royal mother to retire a month before her due date but predicting this was by no means an exact science. When her labour pains began, Elizabeth would have attended mass, as its blessing would extend to her unborn child, as birth was a period of great danger. It was literally a matter of life and death for both mother and baby and during the process both were considered tainted by the sin that had resulted in conception. They were in physical and religious peril until the child had been safely delivered and baptised and the mother churched.

With no pain relief, Elizabeth would have relied on herbal remedies and the power of prayer: as a Catholic queen, she may have used relics such as the girdle of the Virgin Mary, from Westminster Abbey, as well as holy water, icons and the blessed wax cakes called Agnus Dei, in order to appeal to the saints to help her through. This was her third child though and by now, after bearing Sir John Grey two sons, she knew what to expect. All the court, in fact all the country awaited her news. As a queen, the intensely personal, physical experience of birth she would undergo was also of national significance. London chronicler Robert Fabyan recorded how one Master Domenico (de Serigo) had predicted the arrival of a prince and waited in the inner chamber to spread the news. When he heard the child's first cry, he called out for news but the women dismissed him.[29] Luckily all went to plan and the queen was delivered of a daughter on 11 February. The baby was cleaned and swaddled and laid in the ceremonial cradle; it was not the hoped-for boy but the little girl was healthy enough. She was the first important heir to Edward's Yorkist regime, a sign that God had blessed the marriage and dynasty: the king rewarded his wife with the gift of a jewelled ornament worth £125. A few days later, the baby was christened in Westminster Abbey 'with great solemnity' and named Elizabeth. It was to be the beginning of her long association with the building, which would witness all the key rites of passage of her life.

At the end of March, Queen Elizabeth's churching was recorded by Gabriel Tetzel, who was travelling in the retinue of the Queen of Bohemia's brother. Churching was an important ritual of purification, during which the veiled mother was received back into the church and community, offering thanks for having survived the ordeal. Until this time, she was considered unclean and supposed not to leave her confinement or interact with the world. Elizabeth was followed by a huge procession of lords and sixty ladies, 'priests bearing relics and by many scholars singing and carrying lights' with musicians and heralds.[30] With her eyes cast down, Elizabeth walked under a canopy into the church, where she sat in a special pew, accompanied by her midwife, did her penance and received a blessing. After that, a huge feast was held in the palace, where 400 guests were seated, although Elizabeth ate alone in an 'unbelievably costly apartment', seated on a golden chair, attended by her relatives and noble women on bended knee. 'Courtly reverence' was paid to the queen, even during the dancing that followed, which she watched from her chair of state before the celebrations ended in the reading of the mass. Such ritual was designed to underline how the birth had significantly improved her status, a customary feature of protocol, rather than the evidence of her aloofness that some later historians have claimed.

The baby Elizabeth would have been unaware of the festivities, being cared for by her wet-nurse and rockers far from the noise. Most babies were kept swaddled in their cradles for the first years of life, partly as a protective measure away from open fires, doors, water and other dangers, although the royal princess would be carefully watched at all times. Contemporary court rolls prove just how common fatal accidents were among those children in the city who had just started to toddle about. Soon Elizabeth would be established in her own considerable household under Margaret, Lady Berners, at the old palace of Placentia in Greenwich, while her mother resumed her duties as a royal wife. Queens did not breastfeed or tie themselves down to the duties of the nursery, allowing them to recommence sexual relations, and therefore conception, more quickly. Only nine months would pass before the royal couple's second daughter would be conceived; after Mary's birth in August 1467, a further nine months would elapse before the queen fell pregnant again with Cecily. Soon there were three little princesses in the quiet, countryside nursery.

One memorable event of Princess Elizabeth's early years was the betrothal of her aunt Margaret of York to Charles the Bold of Burgundy, called, by some, the marriage of the century.[31] While Warwick still favoured a French alliance in some form, Edward had been drawing closer to the influence of the Burgundian Netherlands, in a cultural, political and mercantile sense. As the heart of Northern European trade, the English economy depended on the export of cloth to this market and the accession of Charles the Bold in 1467 sped up the final negotiations. Chronicler Edward Hall wrote that Charles had sent his fiancée a ring via his envoy and half-brother, the Bastard of Burgundy, who visited England in 1467. Edward paid the first section of his twenty-one-year-old sister's dowry the following April and a return ring, valued at twenty pounds, was sent back from Margaret to Charles. Preparations then began in earnest. While Margaret would travel to Burgundy for the wedding, which the Plantagenet princesses would not attend, the city would have been abuzz with the necessary arrangements for such an elaborate and important occasion. Writing to the Duke of Milan, Giovanni Panicharolla stated in June that Edward was 'a poor man' and could only raise large sums through imposing 'another tax on the lords, barons and towns of the kingdom'.[32] It was the wealthy merchants of London to whom the king actually turned for funds and, with their assistance, was able to equip his sister splendidly. The bride's trousseau comprised £1,000 worth of silk, £160 of gold and silver dishes and £100 of soft furnishings; her golden coronet was trimmed with pearls, gems and wrought enamelled white roses, which spelled out her name in red, white and green. Margaret set out from London on 18 June, stopping to pray at the Canterbury shrine of St Thomas before boarding ship at Margate. While this was only the first stage of her journey and the magnificent wedding that followed, it marked the end of any involvement that may have affected Elizabeth, although her family's connection with the Burgundian court would continue. Later, her aunt would be significant in her life for other, less pleasant, reasons. The nuptial excitement soon died down, only to make way for a new sort of disquiet which would have a dramatic impact on the early years of the princess.

Although Edward had retained the throne for almost five years, the recent civil unrest had not gone away and 'the storms of this tempest were gathering apace'.[33] In July 1465, the royal couple had been at Canterbury, when they heard of the capture of the fugitive Lancastrian, Henry VI. Edward ordered the news to be proclaimed publicly and a service of thanksgiving held in the cathedral. Henry was imprisoned in the Tower but his continued existence was still a thorn in the newer king's side. Queen Margaret and her son had fled the country but their continual plots to reinstate the old regime appealed in different measure to the dissatisfied Warwick and Edward's second brother, the ambitious George, Duke of Clarence. The promotion of Wydeville relations has been cited by some chroniclers, notably Croyland, as a reason for increasing dissatisfaction among the nobility but in reality, the situation was more complex. The euphoria of Edward's accession had faded, along with his promises to increase prosperity and restore order, which he had been trying to achieve by raising taxes; additionally the Burgundian alliance was unpopular among the pro-French faction, headed by Warwick. Croyland also cited an ancient Welsh prophecy, supposedly from the time of Cadwallader, that the English would be driven out by the ancient Britons, which was seen as pertinent to the moment. In Scotland too, Queen Margaret was also stirring up dissent. A number of minor rebellions in 1468 had been ruthlessly suppressed by Edward and the ringleaders executed in an attempt to curtail further revolts. Yet these were just the precursor to a far more serious attack on his power. In the spring of 1469, two uprisings had broken out in Yorkshire, under the anonymous 'Robin of Redesdale', alias 'Robin-Mend-All', and Robin of Holderness. Both had been suppressed by Warwick's brother, the Earl of Northumberland, but while Holderness had been beheaded, Redesdale, probably a member of the Yorkshire Conyers family, had escaped.

The following summer, the king undertook a progress through East Anglia, accompanied by his brother Richard, Duke of Gloucester, stopping to visit key towns and give thanks at the shrines along the route. Further indication of the family's piety is suggested, as that part of the country was the centre of the Marian cult and contained the highest concentration of her dedicated holy sites. Edward's privy seal was in use at Bury on 15 and 16 June, at Norwich on

19 and 21 and at Walsingham on 21 and 22.[34] This visit
had been planned for months. The prominent Norfolk
family, the Pastons, were aware of it as early as the start of
April. By June, John Paston was worried about acquiring
the appropriate clothing necessary to attend the king:
equipping himself and his retainers could be very expensive
but might yield diplomatic results. A suitable livery of
'blue and tawny' may help ensure 'hys gode lordeschype in
tyme to kome'. On his arrival Edward was 'worchepfully
recyvyed', with 'right good cher' and 'gret gyftys'; two of
the queen's brothers, Anthony and John were among a
party who dined with John Paston 'with good cher' at his
mother's house.[35] Yet the nature of the royal visit was soon
to change significantly, due to the increased activity of the
northern rebels. In the meantime, Robin of Redesdale had
travelled into Lancashire and raised more troops. Reports
of unrest reached Edward in Norfolk that June and it was
at Norwich that he gave orders for the royal wardrobe to
equip 2,000 men with armour, jackets, banners and the
royal standard. Further orders were given for the artillery
to be mobilised and the Earls of Pembroke and Devon
to muster their troops in the Midlands, before Edward
went to offer his prayers at the shrine of Our Lady of
Walsingham. He was anticipating a fight.

Elizabeth did not initially accompany him on his
journey, having delivered her third child late in March and
remaining in London to recover. By early June, though, she
travelled north from London with her two elder daughters,
intending to meet Edward at the Neville family home at
Fotheringhay Castle, Northampton. Travel across land
was not easy for a royal retinue with small children, even
in the summer months when the roads were usually dry.
Worse still, rain could cause lengthy delay when most of
England's main routes were simple mud tracks, turning
them into rutted, impassable swamps. Significant areas
of the country were still covered in woodland, which

might harbour thieves ready to prey on a party of helpless women, so they would require a sizeable escort. Their retinue would have necessitated a significant amount of baggage, which would have slowed them down further, taking the cavalcade of horses and carts, with all their attendant goods and provisions, a few days to travel the 86 miles north from London. Between 10 and 15 miles per day was considered the norm at the time, while 20 was fast. Lone messengers on horseback, delivering urgent news, probably travelled the fastest.[36] As royalty and as females, Elizabeth and her daughters would have either occupied litters supported between two horses or sat in larger coaches equipped with seats, beds, tapestries and cushions but no suspension, so the ride would not have been that comfortable. Some women rode side-saddle but this necessitated special clothing and was not quite decorous for a queen. For a three-year-old princess, the tedium of the journey must have been offset by the opportunity to see a little of the world outside her usual routine inside the Westminster walls. The family was briefly reunited at their favourite Fotheringhay for a week before Edward set off north to deal with the rebels.

Elizabeth must have been anxious as Edward departed, for his own safety and that of herself and her family. Yet she was probably unaware of the full scale of the potential danger and, as queen, went on with her daughters to fulfil a royal promise to visit Norwich. On 9 July, Mayor John Aubrey wrote to Sir Henry Spelman, recorder of the city, that the queen would arrive 'up on Tuysday cometh sevenyght suyrly' and that he was writing to London to be advised how 'she woll desire to be resseyved and attended as wurshepfully as evir was Quene'.[37] It is most likely that they travelled through the main towns and cities along the route, allowing for more comfortable overnight stops, via Peterborough, Wisbech, Lynn (which became King's Lynn in 1537), Dereham and on to Norwich, arriving on

18 July. Second only to London, the city was a sizeable and important centre of medieval religion and trade. By the mid-fifteenth century, it was defined by its prominent castle, cathedral, over fifty churches and over twenty religious establishments. Its walls stretched for almost 2½ miles, enclosing a larger area than those of London, while the River Wensum provided a vital artery for the wool trade.

As the queen and princesses discovered soon after arriving at the Westwick gate, the city had prepared an impressive welcoming display. Mayor Aubrey led them to watch the first of several pageants, similar to the contemporary morality and miracle plays: near the gate a stage had been constructed and covered in red-and-green worsted, adorned with the figures of angels and the royal coats of arms. Abstract and symbolic figures welcomed and entertained them; angels, apostles and virgins as well as giants made of wood and leather, stuffed with hay, as settings for the pageant of the Salutation of Mary and Elizabeth. From there, they were led to the gates of the Friars Preachers, where the great chair of St Luke's guild was provided for the queen and a choir of small boys under a Mr Fakke sang until a heavy downfall of rain interrupted the proceedings. The women hurried into their lodgings, to recover from their journey, while the performers hastily dismantled their tableau. Elizabeth would have found the Friars Preachers an impressive new building, occupied for less than twenty years, as part of the rebuilding of the city following the terrible fire that decimated the previous house in 1413: the years between 1440 and 1470 saw lavish and magnificent restoration through the gifts of its wealthiest citizens.[38] By the time of the family's arrival, it was truly a lodging fit for a queen. No doubt Elizabeth and her daughters would have also, at some point, visited the eleventh-century cathedral in order to give thanks for their safe arrival and pray for Edward's safety. He was in need of their prayers. Elizabeth could not have anticipated the string of events that would play out in the coming weeks and completely overturn the direction of their lives and the governance of the country. While they were in Norwich, terrible news reached them. The old lawlessness had broken out again. Relatives had been murdered, friends had become traitors and the Lancastrians were on their way back. The three-year-old princess was about to see her life turned upside down.

2

Reversal of Fortune
1469–1471

Now Warwick, wilt thou open the city gates
Speak gentle words and humbly bend thy knee
Call Edward King and at his hands beg mercy?
And he shall pardon thee these outrages.[1]

Resentment was brewing at court. The ever-ambitious Earl of Warwick had watched the preferment of the Wydeville clan with increasing annoyance since the king's marriage. As Edward's cousin, he disliked the power and influence of this large family of what he considered to be upstarts. Nor was he alone. In the late fifteenth century, it was never more true that 'manners maketh man'. English manuals of the time, such as *The Book of Nurture*, *The Book of Courtesy*, *The Babees Book* and *The Young Scholar's Paradise* gave detailed advice on behaviour and conduct for those wishing to rise through the ranks by aping their social superiors. This was particularly concentrated in the Westminster court and the prosperous City of London, where protocol was strictly observed. It mattered what you wore and where you stood in line. The urban merchant classes were becoming increasingly wealthy through trade and their lifestyles reflected it. This brought obvious benefits for the city but it threatened the cultural superiority of an older elite, reduced in number by recent wars, who attempted to curtail their rivals' behaviour. One way was through appearance, that contemporary way of advertising social standing. Seven sumptuary laws were passed between the mid-fourteenth and sixteenth centuries, designed to limit the ability of the upwardly mobile to express their new-found wealth through clothing. Certain colours and fabrics, long-tailed shoes and garments slashed to reveal other material beneath, were banned for most. The most recent had been in 1463, just a year before Edward's own secret wedding.[2] The large and unpopular clan of Wydevilles received increasing patronage from the crown, although Edward did try to balance this by distributing favour to established families, like Warwick's own. His brother George was made Archbishop of York in 1465 and celebrated in style. However, it was not enough.

Warwick was still smarting over the secrecy of the royal match. By encouraging him to negotiate a union with the French, Edward had made him look foolish when forced to finally reveal his marriage. The king's choice not to take the earl into his confidence publicly demonstrated that Warwick was not as influential as he had thought and realigned the close relationship they had previously enjoyed, making it more on Edward's terms. Nor did this appear to be a one-off. Increasingly, Edward was moving towards an alliance with Burgundy, which compromised Warwick's Francophile objectives. And Warwick, later to be known as the kingmaker, did not like to be made to look a fool. He had been instrumental in helping Edward gain the throne in 1461, fighting beside him in battle; now he felt his influence slipping away. Ironically, it was through his own marriage to Anne de Beauchamp in 1449 that he had inherited the vast swathes of land which now made him one of the most powerful nobles in the land. Perhaps this exacerbated his dislike of the Wydevilles, who had risen by the same method: if he could do it, so could they. He now moved to ensure his own future.

Just as Elizabeth's clandestine wedding had shaped the Yorkist fortunes early in the decade, Warwick planned to use similar methods to assert his own claim, although by the late 1460s it was becoming clear that he had one major disadvantage. His wife Anne had only borne him two daughters and the couple were now in their forties. The all-important son and heir had never materialised. However, both girls had reached their teens and were of marriageable age. To preserve his inheritance, Warwick was in need of a son-in-law, the more high-connected the better.

Who better to marry Warwick's eldest daughter Isabel than Edward's second brother, George, Duke of Clarence? The Burgundian chronicler Jean de Waurin claims this match was mooted as early as 1464, although it is unlikely that it was officially proposed until later.[3] With Queen Elizabeth still to bear a son, Clarence was next in line to the throne and the question of his marriage was likely to prove controversial. Rumours even circulated that Clarence was actually the true King of England. His mother Cecily Neville had supposedly enjoyed an adulterous liaison with a Rouen archer named Blancborgne, who fathered Edward IV. This damaging accusation would later resurface but was unlikely to have been true. Edward's foreign birth contributed to speculation but the complete separation of his parents during the window of conception cannot be proved: Richard of York may well have visited his wife at the salient moment and babies notoriously arrive late or early. His birth date of 28 April is forty-one weeks before his father's departure on 13 July, making him only a week or so overdue. It is unlikely, too, that Cecily would have risked such an affair given the importance of legitimacy and inheritance that a woman of her class would have understood; still, it suited Warwick to employ these rumours. Mancini claimed they originated with Cecily herself in 1464 as an attempt to disinherit her eldest son on learning of his marriage, but this seems a fairly drastic step of self-destruction. According to Tudor historian Polydore Vergil, Cecily herself later complained of these slanders, 'afterwards in sundry places to right many noble men' and tried to get them silenced. Nor is Mancini's view supported by contemporary sources, many of which place the origins of the rumours firmly with Warwick in 1469, as clear attempts to discredit the king and promote Clarence's supposedly more legitimate claim along with his own interests. In addition, there was a strong family resemblance between Clarence and his elder brother: the young George certainly shared Edward's attractive, kingly qualities. John Rows' *English History* described him as 'witty' or intelligent, 'seemly of person and well-visaged'.[4] Undoubtedly with his credentials and wealth, he was a good match for the eighteen-year-old Isabel. The king's mother, Cecily, certainly thought so, in contrast to her dislike of the marriage of Edward to his unsuitable widow, five years before.

Edward himself, however, was less keen. The marriage would give the already ambitious Warwick considerable power and pose a potential threat to his own heirs if Isabel was delivered of a son. His other main objection lay in the couple's kinship: as first cousins they required a papal dispensation, although this was relatively normal among the aristocracy of the period, who tended to marry within a small, interrelated gene pool. While Edward initially blocked their application, Warwick's persistence produced the results, with the necessary paperwork being dated to 14 March 1469. To defy the king in this respect was not illegal or treasonous in the fifteenth century; Elizabeth Wydeville's own parents, Richard and Jacquetta, had wed in the face of regal disapproval and been forgiven after the payment of a hefty fine. However, it was not politic to commit such an open act of defiance when it came to the line of succession and was intended as a deliberate statement of opposition. The ceremony took place on 11 July in Calais, where Warwick was captain. It was not to be a secret affair like the king's. The earl deliberately made it a public and indisputable occasion, fitting of a future king and queen. Five days of festivities followed the service, which was attended by Warwick and his wife, five knights of the garter, various lord and ladies and possibly Cecily Neville herself, who had certainly been with them at the port of Sandwich in Kent, where they had embarked for France. If she was present, Cecily was probably unaware just how far one brother was prepared to act against the other. The ceremony marked a declaration of war. Warwick and Clarence knew they had crossed the line and used it as an opportunity to throw in their lot with the northern rebels. The following day, they issued a manifesto in support of Robin of Redesdale, denouncing Edward's government. Then they set sail for England to raise an army.

Meanwhile, Edward had travelled north to Newark, arriving around the date of the marriage. Reports reached him of the size of Redesdale's army, which was much larger than the forces he had mustered, so he turned back to Nottingham, to await the arrival of reinforcements led by the Earls of Pembroke and Devon. While waiting, rumours reached him of the activities of Warwick and Clarence, which he received in disbelief. He summoned them to appear before him and prove their loyalty, trusting 'ye wole dispose you according to our pleser and commaundement'.[5] They did not reply. The die was already cast. By this time, they had landed in Kent and were marching towards London, gathering troops as they went. This confirmation of their treachery left the king stunned; for a while he waited at Nottingham, uncertain of how to proceed. Delay, coupled with bad luck, turned the tide against him. The two rebel armies were able to bypass Edward altogether and unite in one large force, which met with the approaching men of Pembroke and Devon at the Battle of Edgecote on 26

July. It was to prove a disaster. From before it began, the encounter was dogged with confusion and bad decisions. The night before, Pembroke and Devon had disagreed and divided their forces, leaving one half of the army without the essential support of archers. Even when the Yorkists gained the upper hand, the arrival of Warwick's advance troops caused them to panic and flee the field, with the loss of several thousand men; Croyland claims that 4,000 were slain, while Milanese envoy Luchino Dallaghiexia put the figure closer to 7,000. The news then spread to the approaching king's army, who panicked and deserted. Among those captured and executed by Warwick the following day were Pembroke and Devon, as well as Earl Rivers and John Wydeville, Elizabeth's father and brother. Condemned in a hasty and illegal trial, they were sentenced to death and beheaded at Kenilworth Castle, although the charge of treason can hardly have applied to men fighting in the name of their anointed king. Such acts therefore, would have constituted murder in many eyes. However, it was a personal triumph for Warwick, having removed two members of the queen's unpopular family, whom he saw as his enemies and rivals.

The news must have been devastating for Elizabeth, waiting in Norwich. The deaths marked a turning point for her, clarifying the depth of hatred her enemies felt and the lengths to which they were prepared to go. It is unlikely that the young princesses understood much of the threat their uncle posed; the summer days probably passed more smoothly for them, attended by a retinue of ladies and benefiting from the rich variety of hospitality the city could offer as a centre of international trade. Perhaps they sensed their mother's helplessness as she awaited further developments and prayed with her at the cathedral's Lady Chapel that better times lay ahead. However, worse was to follow. Warwick's public intention had always been to remove Edward's 'evil' Wydeville councillors and help him 'reassess' his policies. This was a long-established strategy that should help him avoid charges of treason, such as had been used in the reign of Henry VI. Yet after Edgecote, what were Warwick's private feelings? With such a formidable victory to his name, he was in an unprecedented position with Edward in his power and his aspirations may have widened to include the replacement of Edward with Clarence, making him father-in-law to a new, more pliable king, over whom his influence would not be in doubt. Yet Warwick hesitated. It would prove a crucial break for Elizabeth and her family.

The earl knew he was on very dangerous ground. Edward was still king despite his defeat and his signature was still required on legal documents for government to run. Warwick had acted independently and there was no guarantee that London or its council would support him, particularly when his intentions were unclear. The rebels' manifesto he and Clarence had supported from Calais had likened Edward to his predecessors Edward II and Richard II, two previously usurped and murdered kings. To depose the anointed monarch meant fully embracing treason, with all its deadly connotations, and he may have reconsidered before taking this final, decisive step. Edward and Warwick had worked together to depose a monarch in 1461, but the circumstances had been very different. Despite his many good qualities, Henry VI had proved himself an ineffectual, impressionable and reluctant monarch whose bouts of mental instability had plunged the country into chaos: the same could not be said for the competent and powerful figure of Edward IV. More significantly, Henry was still alive. Would Warwick follow the precedent of imprisoning his predecessor or send him into exile, meaning the rule of his candidate Clarence would never be secure from challenges? The alternative was Edward's death.

In an uncharacteristic act of uncertainty, Warwick delayed any irrevocable action, preferring, in the interim, to take Edward into custody. Croyland claims this was to prevent his rescue by loyal subjects from the south and chroniclers Hall and Vergil describe the earl sneaking up to the king's camp, killing his guards and taking him by surprise. Edward was kept first in Warwick Castle, then further north at Middleham, the Neville stronghold. It was a formidable place to be a prisoner, a typical defensive bastion of its time, with a huge curtain wall, moat and drawbridge. The twelfth-century stone keep had walls 12 feet thick, although the accommodation inside would have been luxurious. Hearing of this development, Elizabeth must have feared for her husband's life and those of her remaining immediate family, following the murder of her father and brother. Additionally, there were the personal attacks contained within Warwick and Clarence's declaration, naming her as a 'widow of quite low birth' who had always 'exerted herself to aggrandise her relations' and that the king 'did not have good ministers about him'.[6] It was time to flee to safety. Gathering her daughters together, she began the journey south, arriving in London some time before 16 August, when Dallaghexia was able to write that the queen had arrived and was keeping 'very scant state'.[7] Together with her newly widowed mother, Jacquetta of Luxembourg, Duchess of Bedford, she may have stayed at Westminster or in one of her London town houses while waiting to see what would follow. The next attack turned out to be more difficult to fight and potentially much more dangerous.

The nature of the allegations levelled against Duchess Jacquetta in the summer of 1469 cut to the heart of gender differences in fifteenth-century warfare. A man of rank might be openly challenged in battle, attainted or arrested on many genuine or dubious charges, as Richard III would later prove. The removal of a female enemy, though, was a more complex matter. Women were more likely to be attacked on moral, superstitious and cultural grounds, sometimes as a means of indirectly targeting their unassailable menfolk or removing their influence. Witchcraft was a serious accusation which could be stretched to purpose and cover an infinite range of behaviours and outcomes. Fifteenth-century men and women genuinely believed in the existence of witches and the deadly extent of their powers. Fears of witchcraft and its effects ran deep in a society that frequently relied on superstition to help make some sense out of the inexplicable; the 1484 *Malleus Maleficarum* or *Hammer of the Witches* would argue for their existence, their predominantly female identity and describe the appropriate methods of discovery and conviction. Equally, it was an emotive and easy charge to level against an enemy who was immune from, or innocent of, other potential slurs. That Jacquetta was targeted with such charges at this time shows the deep unpopularity of her family and a willingness to exploit their weakened state in the aftermath of the battle; it also allowed some of Edward's less popular decisions to be attributed to the influence of magic, scapegoating the duchess while excusing his involvement. Philippa Gregory suggests a formal trial took place,[8] with Jacquetta arrested at Grafton by Warwick and although the exact details are unclear, it must have been a terrifying moment.

The accusations would also have resurrected bad memories. Five years earlier, popular rumour had placed the responsibility for Edward's marriage to Elizabeth firmly at the feet of his mother-in-law's sorcery and, although the king's support for his wife's family had kept these in check, it was too powerful a weapon to be easily relinquished. A generation before, Jacquetta's first husband had given the order for the burning of Joan of Arc, with all the associated rumours of her sorcery and visions contributing to her condemnation for heresy. Similar allegations had been used successfully before against important royal women, when Henry V had charged his stepmother Joan of

Navarre of attempting to kill him using magic. There was also another family precedent. In the 1430s, Jacquetta's sister-in-law Eleanor, Duchess of Gloucester, had sought the assistance of the then-infamous witch of Eye, Margery Jourdemayne, in order to conceive a child. Margery had furnished her with various potions, while some astrologers she consulted had predicted that a serious illness would afflict the young Henry VI. As the wife of the heir to the throne, such speculations had a serious political dimension for Eleanor. Summoned before a council of bishops and clerics, she admitted the use of various images of wax and metal, which had been intended to boost her fertility. The duchess and her associates were convicted; her public penance involved walking barefoot through the London streets on market day, as well as forcibly divorcing her husband and spending the remainder of her life in prison. One of her astrologers died the horrific traitors' death of hanging, drawing and quartering, while the witch of Eye was burned at the stake. Elizabeth Wydeville had been four at the time and, growing up at Grafton Regis, she probably did not witness Eleanor's shame, although undoubtedly the events had entered family legend. Now her own three-year-old daughter must have felt the tension in the household at this new source of terror.

The allegations originated with one Thomas Wake, a follower of Warwick. He produced a leaden effigy in the shape of a man, which had been broken in the middle and bound together with wire. Such images, used in folk magic, were associated with the casting of spells upon the unfortunate individuals they represented. How it came into Wake's hands is unclear, as is who the figure was supposed to depict, although it was presumably the earl himself. Wake also claimed the existence of two other images representing Edward and Elizabeth, although the suggestion that the duchess's own daughter was her intended victim was stretching credibility to the limit. It seems illogical to accuse Jacquetta of plotting against Elizabeth given the evidence of their closeness. If this really had been the case, perhaps the intention was not to harm. Superstitious effigies could also, theoretically, be used to increase an individual's prosperity and power, but Wake did not claim this, asserting instead that Jacquetta was plotting against the leading Yorkists, including Elizabeth. While such allegations were by no means as common as they were to become a century later, they were not unknown in London. In the 1470s, the home of one Alice Huntley in Kent Street, Southwark was searched and 'mamettes for wychecraftes' were found.[9] The duchess's response was to appeal to the mayor and aldermen of London to investigate the claims and an enquiry was opened. The present mayor was one William Taillour, a wealthy London grocer and alderman whose term of official business was recorded on 29 July, 21 and 29 September. However, on 13 October, a grocer named Richard Lee was elected and sworn in two weeks later at the Guildhall to serve his second term.[10] Presumably both these men were involved in investigating the allegations and would have proceeded with caution, given the current political climate. There was little the women could do but wait in the absence of any proof. On his examination, Wake claimed the original broken effigy had been exhibited at the nunnery of Sewardsley.[11] However, Wake was relying on the evidence of a single witness, a parish clerk named John Daunger, from Northampton, who suddenly proved unwilling to comply.

Luckily for the queen and her mother, the tide was about to turn again. Quite unexpectedly, Edward was released from captivity in a 'manner almost miraculous and beyond all expectation'. Warwick may have had little choice. Having achieved his advantage and taken the king into custody, he was unwilling to embrace full treachery: he now either had to declare against the king or set him free. At the crucial moment, the earl found he was less popular than he had hoped. Attempting to raise troops, he met with little success. People were reluctant to commit themselves to him and incur the severe penalties if he were to fail. Then, outbreaks of lawlessness erupted across the country, with malcontents taking advantage of the political uncertainty. The situation threatened to spiral out of control and Warwick lacked the resources to contain it. He freed Edward in the knowledge that his visible presence would be a local and national act of popular reassurance. Other chroniclers, though, suggest this was less by design than accident. Vergil claimed the king was able to convince his guards to set him free with 'plentyfull and large promises' although the word was later put about that it was done with the earl's consent. Hall says he was able to go hunting and managed to meet a number of his allies who had rallied under Stanley, vastly outnumbering his captors and facilitating his escape.

Whatever the truth behind the incident, Edward was able to raise troops in York and march on London, arriving in October. Writing home to his wife Margaret that month, John Paston reported that the king had entered the city, where Mayor Richard Lee, his aldermen and 200 craftsmen turned out in all their finery to see and support him. The people had chosen Edward over Warwick. If reprisals were expected, they did not come. It appeared that for now, the king was prepared to forgive and reconcile himself with both Warwick and his brother Clarence, although their treachery would not be forgotten. Paston wrote that Edward had had 'good language of the lords of Clarance of Warwyk ... seyng they be hys best frendys' but conceded that 'his household men have other language'.[12] The second Croyland chronicler wrote of Edward's 'outraged majesty' and Warwick's 'guilty mind, conscious of an over-daring deed'[13] while Vergil claimed he and Clarence 'ragyd fretyd and fumyd extremely' that they had been thwarted.[14] Queen Elizabeth probably received word of her husband's release before his arrival and the family would have been reunited at Westminster or the more private Baynard's Castle. While it was a relief to have him back safely, as well as an uncomfortable truce with their recent enemies, Elizabeth can hardly have forgotten the losses she had suffered at Warwick's hands. The earl himself was well aware of this and kept away. That December, a public reconciliation ceremony took place in Westminster between the brothers. Although a temporary calm descended over the capital for the coming winter, recent events were never far from the royal couple's minds.

They celebrated Christmas 1469 at Westminster. For the young Princess Elizabeth and her two sisters, the festivities must have represented a period of welcome peace and normality. Approaching her fourth birthday, she may already have developed the taste she later displayed for revelry and disguisings. Later accounts of entertainments planned for this time of year include dancing, singing, carolling and card playing, Christmas day rewards to the children in the king's chapel and in the privy kitchens, as well as for supplies of Rhenish wine and offerings to saints. No doubt that year it was particularly important for the family to re-establish their position through the usual methods of ceremony and spending. In the great hall at Westminster, where the fires burned and splendid feasts were served, the reunited royal couple and their small daughters dressed in their velvets and cloths of gold to dance and be entertained in the latest styles. The Dukes of Burgundy set the fashion for courtly disguisings and pageants like the nine-day L'Arbre d'Or celebrations for Margaret's wedding at Bruges the previous year; it was based on the legend of a lady confined in a mysterious isle and the various labours which had to be undertaken to free her. Eyewitness John Paston wrote home that he had seen nothing like it outside of King Arthur's legendary court, an analogy that would have pleased Edward.

The nature of early English drama was undergoing a transition following the Burgundian influence and the royal family were keen patrons of the new-style performances. Impressive pageant carts set with elaborate scenes, costumed figures, music, special effects and choreographed battles or dances would have made such entertainments exciting for the young princesses. At such a time, Elizabeth may also have encountered Alexander Mason, a minstrel also known as a geyster or jester, who she was to come to know well, in service to Edward IV, Richard III and Henry VII. The first account of a performance by a 'disour' comes from the year 1469: a man named Woodhouse was known in Edward's court as a sage dyzour or clever sayer; a storyteller, joker or precursor of the jester. According to the London chronicler, Woodhouse was in good favour for his 'mannerly raylyng and honest dysportys which he offtyn exercysid in the court', even if he did make some jokes about the Wydevilles which were a little close to the bone. Edward also had a dwarf in his service from Constantinople; such figures were traditionally musicians and poets. Fools and innocents played their part in seasonal revelry like that of John Howard, Duke of Norfolk, named Tom Fole (perhaps the origin of 'tomfoolery').[15] It is clear from his records a decade later that Edward kept thirteen minstrels and a 'wait', a group of pipers featuring crumhorns, lutes, fiddles, citterns, shawms and other instruments.[16] For Queen Elizabeth, the season must have afforded great contrast with the privations and 'scant state' of the recent months of uncertainty. No doubt there were great banquets and memorable entertainments, lasting the full festive period until Twelfth Night.

Edward's return also meant a positive change for his other female relatives. In January, Parliament formally cleared Jacquetta of the alleged charges of witchcraft. Edward had ordered the examination of the claims made by Wake, resulting in the restitution of his mother-in-law's reputation. What happened to Wake is unclear, although his actions must be seen within the framework of Warwick's animosity and the probable outcome, therefore, as a function of the fragile pardon the earl received. Also that month, Princess Elizabeth found herself to be a key player in negotiations designed to keep the national peace. Approaching four, she was an important person in her own right. Until a son was born to her parents, her position as the house of York's eldest daughter made her a powerful bargaining tool. Although she could inherit her father's claim, public opinion was against the sole rule of a female monarch, so any potential husband would become king at her side. Another eighty years would pass before a woman would ascend the throne in her own right. That January, little Princess Elizabeth was betrothed to the three-year-old George Neville, son of the Earl of Northumberland, Warwick's brother. It was a reward for Northumberland's support in the face of his brother's increasing hostility as well as a conciliatory gesture for the Neville family, considering Warwick's lack of sons to inherit the throne. This was the next-best thing. The boy was made Duke of Bedford in anticipation of this union but what Elizabeth thought of it was not recorded, nor would it have been considered particularly relevant at the time.

Dynastic betrothals were often made between aristocratic families to cement alliances but few came to fruition. Elizabeth's own younger brother, Richard of York, would be married at the age of four to the five-year-old heiress Anne de Mowbray. Of course, such young couples were not expected to live together or even consider themselves permanently bound. In the event of parental death, one might be raised in the household of the other but usually, they met infrequently, if at all. When they came of age, at twelve for girls and fourteen for boys, the vows would need to be reaffirmed with the potential brides' and grooms' consents, otherwise the match could be dissolved without prejudicing any future unions. Elizabeth's union was not a particularly prestigious match for the heir to the throne and strongly suggestive that Edward anticipated the birth of a son and made the offer out of political expediency without expecting to honour it. It is likely that the princess went through some sort of formal betrothal ceremony with George Neville or a proxy but the event would hold as little reality for her as the possibility of its future consummation. Is it not clear what her mother thought of this alliance with the family who murdered her relatives.

The Christmas peace was short-lived. The New Year arrived and the traitors were soon to show their true colours again. Unrest in Lincolnshire over a local dispute that spring escalated, bringing fears of reprisals from the king. Amid a mood of mistrust and uncertainty, Edward marched north swiftly, calling to Warwick and Clarence to support him against the unruly forces headed by Sir Robert Welles. As a gesture of trust, he issued commissions authorising Warwick to raise forces in his name. In reply, the pair sent messages of loyalty while gathering their own opposition troops and liaising with Welles to depose Edward and replace him with Clarence. There can be little doubt that after their failure of the previous year, the intention was to kill Edward; they could hardly expect him to be so forgiving a second time. John Paston wrote to his eldest son that March that it was 'supposed' that Warwick would join the king although this had divided opinion: 'some men seye that hys goyng shall doo goods and some seye that it dothe harme'. News reached Edward that Welles had headed for Leicester to rendezvous with Warwick's waiting troops, which finally forced him to accept the earl's desertion. Paston's cousin described the king's forces: 'itt was seid that wer never seyn in Inglond so many goodly men and so arreiyed in a feld' in comparison with his enemies who had 'litill favour'.[17] The conflict would be decisive for all.

The armies met at Empingham in Rutland, 5 miles from Stamford on 12 March 1470. It was all over in a relatively short space of time, with almost 30,000 rebels being easily defeated by the royal forces. Morale had already broken under the weight of rumours that Edward was going to make an example of the Edgecote rebels, who fled at the sight of the king's army. Their attempts to flee were hampered by their heavy clothing and as they ran, they threw off their jackets, earning the site the name of Losecoat field; this may also have been an attempt to discard the incriminating evidence of Clarence and Warwicks' livery. By now Edward was in no doubt of the ringleaders' identities and scarcely needed the confirmation that the *Chronicle of the Rebellion of Lincolnshire* describes, of letters found in a helmet on the field outlining the extent of the treachery. It has been suggested by later historians that this chronicle, written by Edward's clerks, deliberately maligned his enemies but other factors, including the subsequent behaviour of Warwick and Clarence, makes such evidence superfluous. The letters in the helmet were not needed to incriminate the rebel leaders. Their captured troops readily confessed the plan's intentions to replace Edward and after Warwick's requests for a pardon were denied, he and Clarence took flight with the king in pursuit. Their disappearance sealed their fates. Edward had pardoned them much in recent years; now his patience had run out. Nowhere in the kingdom was safe, so they set sail from the south coast, prompting Edward to issue a proclamation denouncing them as traitors with a price on their heads. Denied entry to Calais, they finally landed at Honfleur and were received by Louis XI and later, the exiled queen and wife of Henry VI, Margaret of Anjou. Although they were no longer on English soil, this could prove a very dangerous alliance against Edward.

Warwick did not give up. He had not improved his position in the last year, as all his planning and attempted assaults on the throne had placed him in a worse position than before. In some ways though, as a pronounced traitor, he had nothing to lose and he still had another daughter. That summer, Anne Neville was fourteen. She had witnessed her elder sister's marriage to Clarence and her father's changing fortunes. As they had waited impatiently on board their ship to enter Calais, she had been present when Isabel went into labour and lost her first child. Now she was to form the pivot of her father's new schemes to displace Edward IV. Warwick abandoned the claim of his son-in-law Clarence in favour of an alliance with the house of Lancaster. On 25 July 1470, Anne was formally betrothed to Prince Edward, the son of Henry VI and Margaret of Anjou. By all accounts, he was a bloodthirsty and ambitious sixteen-year-old, who had been present at the beheadings of his enemies since an early age. The ceremony took place at the magnificent Chateau d'Amboise, recent favourite palace of the French kings, although certain dispensations were required and they would not be properly wed until that December. It was a masterful blow for Warwick, who had turned the tide of Margaret's hatred and had, apparently, guaranteed the future of his heirs whichever side finally emerged triumphant. In the meantime, he began to plan his return to England.

Back in Westminster, Queen Elizabeth was expecting her fourth child. Having conceived in early February, she must have felt the baby quicken around the time of Anne Neville's betrothal. That summer she made preparations for her lying-in at the Tower, ordering sumptuous furnishings and provisions for the autumn, when she expected the new arrival. With Warwick and Clarence out of the country, Edward having returned in triumph and her mother cleared of all charges, it may have seemed that she was to deliver her next child in a period of relative peace. However, that peace was not to materialise yet. In July, discontent flared again and Edward was forced to quell another insurrection. Warwick's brother-in-law, Lord Fitzhugh, had roused the rebels in Yorkshire, causing sporadic outbursts and compelling the king to ride north to deal with them. He was unaware, however, that this was a planned diversion, stirred up to draw him away from the capital and leave it vulnerable. Warwick had also been liaising with discontented Kentish sailors and rebels; the county was traditionally a hotbed of dissension. Now he had troops waiting to sail for England, only delayed by bad weather and a blockade by the Burgundian fleet. While Edward was absent, the storms dispelled the enemy ships and Warwick was able to embark, landing at Plymouth on 13 September. Gathering troops, he marched to London and freed the deposed Henry VI from his imprisonment in the Tower. Word reached Edward that his own capture was imminent and he took flight at once, crossing the Wash in terrible conditions and sailing for exile in Holland. London was no longer safe. The inviolable bastion of the Tower now housed the readepted King Henry VI, making his Yorkist enemies traitors once more. That night, the heavily pregnant Queen Elizabeth and her children left the Tower and rowed upriver in the darkness to seek sanctuary in Westminster Abbey. Henry VI was moved into the very apartments Elizabeth had so carefully prepared for herself and her baby.

The night must have been a memorable one for the little princesses, travelling down the Thames in darkness as lights burned in the city to their right, with a few possessions swiftly bundled up in the boat beside them, fearful of being spotted and captured. Most vessels were moored up at night and the motion of a boat across the waves could attract attention. To what extent did they understand what was happening? Sleepy and afraid, the three little girls huddled together as they approached the Westminster steps, in sight of the royal apartments where they had recently spent happier times. They disembarked and hurried the short distance through the Palace Yard towards the area known as Broad Sanctuary, now a street of the same name. From early times, religious asylum had been offered to political, financial and social outcasts within the confines of a holy space, whose boundaries were generally respected by those in pursuit. The massive, two-storied building at Westminster, with its single entrance, could potentially harbour a spectrum of criminals as well as those whose positions had been compromised by the changing climate of warfare. It encompassed a massive keep of ragstone, only demolished with some difficulty in 1750. Within its grounds stood around fifty dark, crowded tenements with shared latrines, populated by murderers, debtors and common criminals and bounded by Thieving Lane and unhealthy marshlands.[18] These buildings were let for a profit by local businessmen, often with an outlet used as a shop; otherwise their 10- by 20-foot area comprised a cellar and kitchen. Here, in the darkness, Elizabeth arrived 'in great penury and forsaken of all friends', according to Holinshed[19] and was received by Abbot Thomas Milling. Some sources suggest he offered her the use of three of the best rooms in his own house in the precincts, while others place her within the sanctuary's tower although theories that she lived in 'royal comfort' are probably less accurate. Holinshed describes how she lacked even 'such things as mean men's wives had in superfluity'.

But Elizabeth had not fled a moment too soon; Warwick's men entered the city unopposed and two days later, the Constable of the Tower surrendered and the capital was in rebel hands. Yet she was not as friendless as she had feared. Regardless of his political unsuitability, Henry VI was a compassionate and generous man, sending Lady Scrope to attend on Elizabeth during her confinement and even Warwick gave instructions that her refuge was to be protected. A London butcher, William Gould, provided her with weekly supplies of mutton and beef and she had the support and company of her mother, her midwife Margery Cobbe and possibly the doctor, Domenic0 de Serigo. The coming weeks would have been difficult and uncertain for the queen and her daughters, largely confined indoors, awaiting Elizabeth's labour and the news from London and abroad.

Giving birth was always a risky business, even for those of high status provided with all necessary luxuries. Maternal and infant mortality was affected by lack of gynaecological understanding and poor hygiene. Now Queen Elizabeth was facing the process in cramped, unhealthy and difficult circumstances, dictated by events beyond her control. Isabel Neville had lost her first child when she went into labour on board the ship that summer after Warwick was denied entry to Calais. Although they were usually exempt from the executions and battles that decimated their menfolk, women and children's health and survival were dictated by a broader political climate that frequently placed them in danger. Early in November, Elizabeth went into labour. If her eldest daughter, almost five, had previously been protected from the realities of birth, she could not now escape the bustle and activity that overtook their lodgings. Normally, children were excluded from the birth chamber, with the exception of suckling babies brought along by a woman's gossips or assistants. The princess would have seen her mother retire and emerge weeks later, triumphant and recovered: now with her mother and grandmother busy, she would have seen and heard the frantic preparation of bed linen and water boiling as well as the prolonged cries of pain that accompanied the queen's labour. Childbirth would have suddenly become a very real and terrifying event. However, on this occasion, mother and baby came through the ordeal. On 2 November, Elizabeth gave birth to a son, the heir to the Yorkist dynasty. He was christened in the abbey and named Edward.

Meanwhile, in London, chaos had broken out. Elizabeth had sent word to the newly elected mayor, then a John Stockton, asking him to take command of the Tower and secure the city against attack, but none of them had estimated the extent of the unrest. Stirred by Warwick, rebels in Kent had marched up from the east, attacking the residences and businesses of Dutch and Flemish weavers. Vergil described the situation as 'most myserable' with 'churches and houses ... every wher spoyled, swoord and fyre ragyd all over, the realme was wholy replenyssed with harnesse and weapon and slaughter, bloode and lamentation; the feildes wer wastyd, towne and cytie stervyd for hunger and many other mischiefes happenyd'.[20] Fabyan says they grew wild and 'assembled themselves in great companies', releasing prisoners along their way to join them.[21] They marched up to Southwark and crossed the Thames at St Catherine's, 'robbing and spoiling' all the beer houses, which lay just beyond the eastern side of the Tower. It turned the tide in favour of the royal family. The city had always welcomed Edward IV, with his promotion and protection of the valuable Burgundian trade, even if he had drawn heavily on its merchants for loans. The mayor had come to terms with Warwick upon his arrival in order to protect the city from pillaging, but with this wanton destruction, it was little wonder that Warwick's brief surge in popularity began to wane. With so many changes of allegiance, ordinary citizens were wary of whom to back and fearful of accusations of treason. Elizabeth's Wydeville relations were again the target of attacks, with a warrant issued on 19 October for the arrest of her brother Anthony, Lord Scales, although he was now beyond reach in exile in Burgundy with the king.[22]

In London, there was a new king. Or rather, an old one, 'readepted'. To introduce a note of stability and justify his invasion, Warwick had Henry VI dressed in robes of state and paraded through the streets. Symbolically, the earl carried his train, almost as if he were visibly pulling the strings of his restored puppet. Henry was re-crowned in St Paul's abbey, 'mute as a crowned calf' according to Commines.[23] The bewildered king was moved from the Tower into the royal apartments in Westminster Palace recently occupied by Edward's family and presided over Parliament late in November. Warwick also began planning an invasion of Burgundy, with French support. However, Parliament would not agree to this and he further alienated the London merchants whose trade would be affected. News of this reached Edward in exile, where he was gathering troops to return, with the help of his brother-in-law, Charles the Bold. Warwick responded by posting his agents along the east coast and the Channel was patrolled by his nephew, the Bastard of Fauconberg. Now there were two fleets waiting to sail to England: those of Edward IV and of Margaret of Anjou and her son, both hoping to return and re-establish their rule. Who would arrive first?

The weather decided in favour of Edward. The storms that prevented Margaret's fleet from leaving the mouth of the Seine delayed the king by only nine days, allowing him to depart on 11 March and drop anchor off Cromer, Norfolk, the following day. The county, however, proved hostile: the duke and other Yorkist allies had been taken into custody and the Earl of Oxford was in charge instead, raising local troops to repel Edward's landing. On 17 March, Oxford wrote that 'the kyngs gret enemys and rebellis, accompanyd with enemys estraungers, be now aryved ... to the utter destruction of his roiall persone and subversion of all his realm'.[24] Edward's fleet sailed north and landed at Ravenspur in Yorkshire. Here he received no warmer a welcome than he had in Norfolk but, in explaining that he had returned only to claim his Dukedom of York, he gained access to that city and tried to gather a few troops. Support for his cause seemed very thin on the ground. Finally, the arrival of Norris and

Stanley at the head of 3,000 men began to swell his ranks and more men flocked to join him, so that by the time he reached Coventry, where Warwick currently was, he was in a position to challenge the earl to come out and fight. Warwick refused. Feeling betrayed by his father-in-law over the Lancastrian restoration and urged on by his mother and sister, Clarence now raised a troop of 4,000 men and was reconciled with his brother. The later recorder of these events in *Historie of the Arivall of Edward IV* describes how a miracle spurred Edward onwards to victory; on Palm Sunday he prayed in a church in Daventry to an alabaster statue of St Anne, which was closed over with boards, according to tradition, until Easter day. Then, 'even sodanly … the bords compassynge the ymage about gave a great crak and a little openyd … the Kynge … takynge it for a good signe, and token of good and prosperous aventure that God would send him'.[25]

Edward marched south, recruiting more supporters as he went. He was welcomed back into the capital on 11 April and briefly re-crowned. Henry VI was captured and sent back to the Tower and Edward then gave thanks for his victory before hurrying to reunite with his family and see his young son for the first time. The relief for Elizabeth and her daughters at his return and their freedom from sanctuary must have been immense. She had spent months hoping for this moment, with no guarantee of their fortunes improving, 'in right great trowble, sorrow and hevines'. She presented her husband 'to the Kyngs greatyst joy, a fayre son … to his herts synguler comforte and gladnes'[26] and the family went to stay for the night with his mother Duchess Cecily at Baynard's Castle. Rebuilt on the water's edge following a fire in 1428, its huge river frontage was set with narrow turrets flanked by hexagonal towers at each end, enclosing a private courtyard; improvements in the 1440s had created four wings in a trapezoid shape and by the early 1500s it was considered 'beautiful and commodious' as well as strong. It was a deliberate move to relocate to such a building, showing that the royal family no longer needed to hide away and were established again in their capital. In the morning, though, the king rose early and set off to meet his enemies.

The remaining threat to Edward's reign was speedily dealt with. In thick fog on the morning of 14 April, his troops approached the Lancastrian army who had gathered near Barnet; in the 'crewell and mortal' confusion, his enemies fired upon each other and fled in confusion. Among those killed in the retreat was Warwick himself. The significance of this for Edward can hardly be underestimated: years of treason and uncertainty were almost at an end with the removal of his main adversary. By the time Queen Margaret and her son finally arrived in England, the great kingmaker was no more and the Lancastrian claim was in chaos. The armies clashed at Tewkesbury on 4 May and Prince Edward, Henry VI's son and heir, was killed. Legend has it that Edward sent Elizabeth his gauntlet to indicate his victory in the battle. It seemed that peace was finally within sight for the king and queen, yet there would be one final flare of danger. Ten days later, the Bastard of Fauconberg attacked London and burned Southwark with an estimated army of almost 20,000 Kentish men assisted by the mayor of Canterbury, Nicholas Faunt. This time, the capital fought back: a surviving letter from Fauconberg, dated that May and addressed to the 'Commonality of the city', desired permission for him and his army to pass through the city 'in order to seek out and oppose the usurper of the throne' and stating he had no intention to 'despoil' as he went. The official response denied him access, explaining that they were keeping the peace for Edward IV and could 'suffer no disturbance therein' and informing him of Warwick's death.[27] Fauconberg did not accept no for an answer. The mayor and aldermen fortified a stretch of the Thames from Baynard's Castle along to the Tower 'against a large fleet' which appeared and attacked London Bridge on 12 May: 5,000 rebels attacked local brewhouses and tenements but were repelled by Londoners defending the walls. Mayor Stockton and his predecessor Richard Lee, among others, were later knighted by Edward for their efforts. A contemporary French manuscript illustration, possibly by Jean Spifame, depicts the siege: rebels hold flaming torches mounting the city walls with ladders, while black-armoured guards ride out to meet them. The facts are misleading, as the troops are supposedly headed by Edward IV, but the atmosphere of violence and impending threat is real.

Fearful of Fauconberg's intentions, Queen Elizabeth had again fled briefly into the Tower with her children and brother Anthony, Earl Rivers; chronicler Fabyan describes what they must have heard outside the walls as the 'riotous and evil-disposed company ... shot guns and arrows and fired at the gates with cruel malice'.[28] The alliterative poet, Thomas Malory, a Lancastrian imprisoned at the time in Newgate, bore witness to these events and later used descriptions evocative of those days, setting the fabled court of King Arthur in London and the Tower. Placing Queen Guinevere in sanctuary there, he painted the fictional attack in familiar terms as Sir Modred 'went and laid a mighty siege about the Tower of London and made many great assaults thereat and ... shot great guns'.[29] The rebels also plundered a supply of oxen in the Tower's meadow, brought again by the obliging London butcher, William Gould, in order to feed the queen and her family. But Elizabeth's ordeal was not to last long this time. The news of Edward's approach caused Fauconberg to retreat, with Rivers' troops in pursuit. The king headed him off at Sandwich, where his waiting fleet was taken; Fauconberg was captured by Richard, Duke of Gloucester and executed. His head was set on London Bridge as a deterrent and sign of the city's success; Faunt was beheaded in Canterbury.

On 21 May, Edward returned triumphant, to the sound of trumpets as his banners fluttered in the breeze. That night, the unfortunate Henry VI was murdered in the Tower, probably on Edward's orders and his body carried through the streets, where it bled on the pavement. Officially, he was described as having died of 'melancholy'. The death of his heir at Tewkesbury removed the safeguard to his life and the decision was taken in order to prevent further uprisings: Edward could not risk a repeat of that spring's events. The threats to the house of York had been quelled. Edward and Elizabeth undertook a pilgrimage to Canterbury to give thanks at the shrine of Thomas Becket. Finally, something like a relatively peaceful childhood could emerge for Princess Elizabeth and her siblings.

3

The Life of a Princess
1471–1483

The most splendid court ... in all Christendom.[1]

For many reasons, it is difficult to reconstruct the life of a medieval child, even a privileged one like Elizabeth of York. Traces of their lives survive in fragments and apart from the frequent death records of a society with high infant mortality, their lives have gone unrecorded. Even more so than those of women, the medieval child's voice has been lost. This is partly because of a later sea-change in attitudes towards childrearing and pedagogy. The concept of childhood as we understand it in the twenty-first century is a modern invention, as previously there was little value placed on the experiences or significance of the early years. Most children in all classes and professions simply fitted around adult routines, apparently just sitting out their infancy until they could become useful members of society. Often they were contributing to a household at an early age by undertaking work or assisting parents; archaeological investigations have discovered the bones of children as young as six or seven displaying the effects of hard labour.[2] However, it is a common misconception that they were treated as miniature adults.[3] Medieval parents did understand that developmental differences meant their offspring could not be treated as adults and a proliferation of parenting manuals of the period indicate that the early years were considered a period of training. Certain key developmental stages were observed. Seven was a significant age of reason ending the period of effeminacy for boys, necessitating a change of dress and routine. It was the age of work and separation from the family: apprenticeships began at seven, while other children were sent to lodge with other local aristocratic families, sometimes after a marriage had been arranged. Fourteen marked the age of majority for boys, with an end to whatever formal schooling they may have received and the consummation of marriage; for girls, maturity came earlier.

Predictably, a gulf existed between the lives of boys and girls, just as it did for men and women. Princess Elizabeth's status was altered significantly by the arrival of a brother, taking her a step further away from the throne. Although there was no law in England preventing female inheritance, males automatically took precedence, relegating women's importance to their marital potential and the qualities they could bring to their roles as mothers and wives. Even as a king's daughter, there was no guarantee in which degree Elizabeth would marry, let alone that she might be a queen; only hindsight informs us of her future royal status. From an early age, however, the princess would have been aware of the possibility that she may hold high status and follow the model of queenship and maternity set by her mother. Her parents' marriage was unusual, though. The medieval wife and queen was supposed to enter an arranged match as diplomatic intercessor and counter her husband's warlike masculinity by promoting charity, religion, culture and mercy. In an age that equated beauty with moral goodness, she was also to be an ornament capable of upholding the appearance and ceremonies of majesty. Given the turbulent years of her early life, the princess would have understood the importance of projecting and maintaining the royal image in the public eye as well as the speed with which regimes could be overturned. She had had her taste of penury and although her choices as a woman would be limited, she understood the precarious nature of fortune.

Initially, the princess's life would have been a simple one, based in the old palace of Placentia at Greenwich. Nothing remains now of the buildings Elizabeth would have known there as a child, which would be demolished and rebuilt by her future husband, Henry VII. It started life as a manor house in 1447 and was extended by Edward IV, probably to improve and extend the royal apartments as he had done by building a new great hall at Eltham Palace and additional chambers, latrines, turrets and kitchens at Fotheringhay. It would have been a modern, convenient and peaceful place for his son and daughters to be raised, with occasional visits downriver to wherever the court was in residence. The children would celebrate feast days and key social and political events at Windsor, Westminster, Eltham and the Tower of London but were most often in their own establishment at Greenwich. Edward and Elizabeth's increasing brood was presided over by Margery, Lady Berners, a long-standing Wydeville ally, although evidence suggests their parents were a constant and close presence. Convention dictated that royal children were separated early from their parents and established with their own household, brought up by carefully appointed nurses and servants under a carefully planned regime. This would have determined everything from the structure of their days, who served them at meals and how, to their domestic and travel arrangements. Among the surviving provisions made for the family of the Earl of Northumberland is a menu for a nursery breakfast, comprising a manchet (bread roll), one quart of beer, a dysche of butter, a pece of saltfish, a dysche of sproittes or mutton bonys.[4]

Typically, the arrangements for boys were afforded greater priority and significance, especially those that may be destined to rule. Prince Edward's nursery of 1471 was overseen by Elizabeth Darcy as Lady Mistress and Avice Welles as nurse, who may have previously been part of the princess's household. While his sisters remained at Greenwich, comparatively close to their parents, Edward was given a permanent establishment at Ludlow at the age of three. In September 1473, a set of ordinances was drawn up regarding his routine and upbringing. He was to rise at an hour 'convenient' to his age, attend mass and matins, then take breakfast. His morning was spent receiving instruction, including 'such noble stories as behoveth a prince to understand and know' and after lunch, partaking in physical activity such as horsemanship, archery, swordsmanship, followed by vespers and supper. His meals, 'with meat', were served by 'worshipful folks and squires' in livery accompanied by noble stories that 'encouraged virtue, honour and wisdom'. All this when he was only three years old; only at the end of a long day did the toddler have time to play! According to Mancini, the prince 'devoted himself to horses and dogs and other useful exercises to invigorate his body'. He was sent to bed at eight until he was twelve years old and a watch kept over him as he slept. As a five-year-old boy in 1475, he was appointed the nominal guardian of the realm while his father was in France between July and September: the queen was granted £2,200 yearly for her son's maintenance while he stayed at court.

His father's court had little difficulty in indulging its magnificence in the 1470s. During this decade, the crown received huge increases in customs duties, boosted by the economic benefits of national stability; luxury goods arrived on merchants' ships and after 1475, the king received a substantial French pension. The Lancastrian Sir John Fortescue had drawn up *De Laudibus Legum Anglae* or *The Governance of England* to guide the ascetic Henry VI in maintaining a lifestyle appropriate to his status but its advice was far more suitable to the Yorkist court of Edward. Including information on the understanding, creation and application of laws and the machinery of government, it also exhorted a king to present himself in accordance with his state: 'buy him rich clothes and rich furs ... rich stones and other jewels and ornaments ... rich hangings and other apparel for horses ... and do other such noble and great costs ...'[5] Clothing and jewels were certainly something that Elizabeth's parents took seriously as symbols of status and success. In the year of their daughter's birth, the queen's personal allowance of £919 was less than her wardrobe expenses of £1,200 which did not include an additional £14 spent on furs and the £54 her goldsmith received in payment.[6] To celebrate their eldest princess's birth, Edward paid £125 for a jewelled ornament 'against the time of the birth of our most dear daughter' and two years later, he spent £2,450 on his sister Margaret's trousseau and entourage.[7] Nor did Edward neglect his own person; in 1480, he ordered twenty-six gowns, doublets and jackets in the Burgundian style. One goldsmith's bill of 1478 included a £6 golden flower set with a diamond, another set with a sapphire for 40s and an £8 gold toothpick set with diamonds, rubies and pearls. His keepers of the Royal Wardrobe, Sir John Say and Thomas Vaughan, also his Keeper of Jewels, must have been busy in the building that housed their work off Carter Street, close by Baynard's Castle. The whole court had to be provided for and entries in the court rolls like those of 1466, when the yeomen tailors were ordered to provide 'livery of raiment winter and summer' for servants William Hall and John Woode are typical. However, sumptuary laws restricting the use of fabrics and colours according to rank allowed the aristocracy and royalty to look the part and became increasingly critical in a developing climate of sensitivity to etiquette. Only women of the royal family were permitted to wear cloth of gold or the colour purple;

veils, silk and furs were also subject to restriction. Princess Elizabeth was one of the few to be decked out in such finery. Looking at the little girl's appearance, no one could be in any doubt about her status. However, self-importance and opulence were not always seen to be compatible with the values of a deeply religious society and could encourage arrogance and pride. A princess's education must counter her wealth and advantages with humility and charity.

Written in 1405, the Venetian Christine de Pisan's *The Book of the City of Ladies* was an influential manual which challenged female stereotypes and presented models of behaviour for women at all levels of society. A copy was owned by Princess Elizabeth's grandmother, Jacquetta of Luxembourg. In the absence of a formal programme of education beyond the expected courtly manners, needlework, music and dancing, it can provide a useful overview of the theories of female identity that probably shaped the little girl's upbringing. Pisan initially presents the luxury with which those in power find themselves living: 'When the princess … wakes up in the morning … lying luxuriously in her bed between soft sheets, surrounded by rich accoutrements and everything for bodily comfort and ladies in waiting around her focusing all their attention on her and seeing that she lacks for nothing … ready to run to her if she gives the least sigh … to obey all her commands.' She shows how easy it must be to fall into fleshly temptation – 'all you have to worry about is pleasing yourself … You cannot lack for wines and foods … and every other pleasure' – in terms that must have resounded with the wealthy Yorkist court of the 1470s. 'You must have such gowns, such ornaments, such jewels and such clothing made in a particular way and of a particular cut.'[8] Pisan's commentary on such wealth seems particularly appropriate for the queen and her daughters, given their recent experiences: 'you who are a simple little woman who has no strength, power or authority unless it is conferred on you by someone else'. The author advised that temptation must be resisted through religious good works and devotion, as even the wealthy were still poor and weak and subject to infirmity. Pisan's model of the 'Good Princess' was a woman well informed by good and wise people, who avoided mortal sin and strove to be honourable, patient, charitable and humble. Suffering was to be expected: 'she will take all adversity willingly for the love of Our Lord'. This also translated into behaviour and gestures; 'she will behave respectably and speak softly, her conduct will be kindly and her expression gentle and pleasant, greeting everyone with lowered eyes'. The role of women in everyday life was as mediators and promoters of peace, as it was for queens. These tenets would have founded the basis of Elizabeth's upbringing and appear to have guided her during her adult life.

Good manners were becoming increasingly important among those rising up the social scale, like the Wydevilles and their followers. Elizabeth and her sisters would have been taught to personify stately codes of conduct, in order to maintain the family's position. They set the tone for those below. The proliferation of behavioural and parenting manuals in the late fifteenth century indicates the rise of the middle classes, offering advice for their children's potential social elevation, including eating, appearance, hygiene and behaviour. In 1460, John Russell, marshal to Humphrey Duke of Gloucester, produced a *Book of Nurture* containing job descriptions and rules for the buttery, butler, carver and other servers at table: 'do not claw your head or your back as if you were after a flea', 'do not wipe your nose or let it drop clear pearls' and 'do not pick your teeth or grind or gnash them'. The implication was that young people, unused to the protocol of the court, could rise to positions of domestic, household and financial service if they conformed to a certain set of manners. According to Russell, a chamberlain must be 'neatly clad, his clothes not torn, hands and face well washed and head well kempt' and he outlined instructions for the care of a master's wardrobe and the preparation of his bath.[9] The anonymous medieval poem 'What the Goodwife Taught her Daughter' prepares a young lady for marriage in a similar vein to Pisan. She must go to church regularly, even in the rain and pay her tithes and offerings to the poor and bedridden; she should not gossip or laugh at people's appearances, be 'fair of speech ... glad and of mild mood', keep from sin, villainy and blame, 'laugh thou not too loud nor yawn thy not too wide'. She should dwell at home and love her work, without drinking in taverns, talking to men in the streets or visiting wrestling or cock fighting, nor spend or borrow too much to make her husband poor.[10] The 1475 *Babees' Book* specifically addresses noble and royal children: they are to be respectful, diligent and observant, standing 'still as a stone' until spoken to, not jangle (chatter) but speak 'things fructuous'. Distinctions of class delineated their behaviour by negative example; they were to share meat, not possess it like churls or cut it like field-men.[11] Likewise the poem 'Urbanitatis' reinforced the centrality of protocol to social advancement with phrases like 'good nurture will save your state' and 'good manners always make good men'.[12]

The major household manual of the period was Edward's reorganisation of his court along Burgundian lines in the 1471/2 *The Black Book of the Household* and *Ordinances* of 1478. Compiled by a household official, it gives an insight into the running of the court above and below stairs and was designed to clarify the roles and needs of the royal establishment and tighten spending. Duties outlined in the *Domus Regie Magnificencie* include those of the treasury, coffers, counting house and steward, whose primary function was to maintain the splendid appearance of the court. Behind the scenes, the provisioning of bakehouse, pantry, spicery, butlery, confectionary and wafery are outlined in the *Domus Providencie*, with the wages and duties of those involved. The process of dining and serving was rewritten along more modern, formal lines. These reforms were inspired by Edward's recent sojourn at the sophisticated Burgundian court. His chamberlain and fellow exile, Lord Hastings, had requested information about household management from the Burgundian Master of Ceremonies, Olivier de la Marche, about questions of court etiquette and ceremony. This may have prompted Marche to compose his own *L'Etat de la Maison de Duc Charles de Bourgogne dict le Hardy* of 1473–4. Also, there was *La Toison d'Or*, a work of 1470 by Guillaume Fillastre, Chancellor of the Burgundian Order of the Golden Fleece, who wrote that a prince's chief virtue was magnificence demonstrated through lavish display. What Edward had seen in exile influenced his court in a number of ways and this dialogue was to continue over the years. The details of such works remind us of the daily experiences of court life that Elizabeth would have encountered – the need for candles, clean rushes, wood, straw, the arrangements for dining and the cleaning and preparation of bed linen and clothes – that kept the magnificent establishment running. Edward was also a significant builder in the Burgundian tradition, making his court a centre of patronage for world-class craftsmen. In 1475, he built new kitchens at Eltham at right angles to the great hall with a new buttery and pantry. Princess Elizabeth, along with her siblings, would have joined her parents there for the festivities one Christmas where 2,000 people were fed.

We catch a glimpse of the growing princess in the autumn of 1472, at the age of six and a half. At Windsor that September, she was present when her parents welcomed Louis de Gruthuyse, who had sheltered Edward during his Burgundian exile. The account of one Bluemantle Pursuivant, a junior officer of arms, shows the family relaxing in one of their favourite castles: the queen played *morteaulx* (a game like bowls) with her ladies, while others played nine pins and danced and Edward partnered Princess Elizabeth. As the eldest child, she was also seated at the high table with her parents for the great feast of the following evening, after which she danced with the Duke of Buckingham. With the presentation and preparation of royal dishes developing commensurately with the formal household reforms, it would have been an occasion to remember. No doubt they would have worn the new, Burgundian-influenced fashions, which saw the male tunic evolve into the doublet, shoes lengthen into points according to status, women's hemlines and sleeves grow longer and their headdresses become more pointed and tall. Probably Princess Elizabeth was dressed in a smaller version of these elaborate costumes, in the royal colours and fabrics. Gruthuyse was lodged in splendid, carpeted chambers hung with white silk and linen, with a bed covered in gold counterpane and canopy of gold cloth. He also had access to a bath covered in tents of white cloth and a couch of feather beds inside a tent of netting.[13] That month he was created Earl of Winchester in gratitude for his assistance the previous year. A few years later, Edward followed the same style again at Windsor by installing a bay window in the queen's great chamber, developing the Perpendicular Gothic St George's Chapel and making alterations in the king's apartments as well as a fashionable new garden which featured low railings. Queen Elizabeth may have taken an active role in these alterations, witnessed by her daughter; the princess herself would later help design new gardens for her favourite retreat of Greenwich.

It had been the library of Louis de Gruthuyse in Bruges that inspired Edward's taste for collecting manuscripts. He would amass over twenty-five lavishly bound illuminated books from Bruges and Ghent, most of which were historical romances following the Burgundian style of decoration and preference for French over Latin. Four manuscripts bore the name of his wife at the time of her death, an *Hours of the Guardian Angel*, the *Histories of Troy*, a collection of French Arthurian legends and *Jason and the Golden Fleece*; perhaps some of these stories were told to her children in their nursery or on occasions when they visited the court. It was under the nose of the court that the most important literary innovations took place. The Kentish merchant, William Caxton, had been travelling to Bruges for twenty years, eventually becoming a member of the household of Margaret, Duchess of York, where he had set up his first printing press in 1473; three years later he did the same within the precincts of Westminster Palace. He would produce over 100 books there before his death in 1491. The first presses, invented in Germany, had been developed from those used to press grapes and involved metal letters held in a wooden frame, over which a sheet of paper was held in place; this process revolutionised the previously laborious hand-copying of documents. Ink continued to be made from gall (the insect or fungal growths on oak trees), copper and gum. Caxton's first printed page was an indulgence, a papal pardon which exists in the National Archives, issued for a Henry and Catherine Langley in 1476. Other early publications included a copy of Chaucer's *Canterbury Tales* as well as the moral proverbs of Christine de Pisan, translated by Princess Elizabeth's uncle, Anthony Wydeville, in 1478. At the age of twelve, it is highly likely that the young girl had access to a copy of this work. Fluent in French, she also wrote her name into the front of a manuscript copy of the *Romance of the Saint Graal* and the exotic *Testament de Amyra Sultan Nichhemedy, Empereur des Turcs*. Her developing womanhood was set against a backdrop of cultural innovation and opulence that emphasised the privileges and formalities that came with a royal existence. She may have read Pisan's advice carefully, conscious that she would one day be responsible for setting a queenly example in her own court; after all, she was now betrothed to a prince, with every likelihood of inheriting a throne for herself.

Edward's 1475 campaign against the French had been settled peacefully. As part of the settlement of the Treaty of Picquigny, which had granted him a welcome pension, the nine-year-old Elizabeth had been betrothed to King Louis's son, the Dauphin Charles, then aged five. The young pair never met; it was probably a lucky escape for the princess, for although Charles was known as 'the affable', he was sickly and not considered to possess suitable leadership qualities; he would also conveniently put aside his next fiancée when a more wealthy heiress appeared. For the next seven years, though, Elizabeth was potentially the next Queen of France and referred to as My Lady the Dauphine; she was also made a Lady of the Garter in 1477. Hers was not the only marriage arranged for the royal children during these years. Edward was keen to ensure important dynastic alliances for his increasing brood; many matches were planned with leading European families but were curtailed by his early death: had they come off, he would have established an immensely impressive network of relations. Elizabeth's closest sister was Mary, born eighteen months after her, with whom she must have shared many early experiences. Negotiations were made for a match between her and Hans of Denmark, Norway and Sweden, but it came to nothing; perhaps Mary had always been weak and ill; Hans married elsewhere in 1478 and the princess died at the age of fourteen, in 1482, at Greenwich. It must have been difficult for the sixteen-year-old Elizabeth to lose her closest sibling in age. For the remainder of her life she would be close to her remaining family members and promote their marriages and interests herself. Next in line was Cecily, born in 1469 and betrothed at the age of five to the son of James III of Scotland, the future James IV;

for a while, she was styled Princess of Scots and Edward continued to pay her dowry until 1482, when the Treaty of Fotheringhay betrothed her instead to the Duke of Albany. Ironically, James would marry Princess Elizabeth's own daughter almost thirty years later. A match was proposed for the new Yorkist heir too. Prince Edward was betrothed at the age of ten to Anne of Brittany, then aged three; she would inherit her father's fortunes to become the richest woman in Europe and eventually marry Elizabeth's erstwhile fiancée, Charles the Affable. These occasions would have been marked by court ceremonies, feasting and dancing, at which the young princess would have featured prominently, dressed in her finery.

Nor was the royal family yet complete. Following Edward's return, six more children were born at various locations around the country, giving an indication of the court's itinerary as well as the continuing closeness of their parents' marriage. By the time the reunited king and queen paid their visit to Canterbury in September 1471, to give thanks at the shrine of Thomas Becket, Elizabeth was already pregnant again. The following April, she was at the solid old castle at Winchester, grieving for the loss of her mother Jacquetta, where a daughter was born and christened Margaret. The queen had already conceived again when the little girl died that December at the age of eight months. In August 1473, she was at Shrewsbury to give birth to her second son by Edward, whom they named Richard. At the age of four, he was married to the Norfolk heiress, Anne de Mowbray, although the little girl died at the age of nine, bringing her husband a wealth of lands and properties. Another daughter, Anne, was born to the royal couple in November 1475 at Westminster; she was betrothed to Philip the Handsome, son of Maximilian of Austria, at the age of four. A third brother to Elizabeth, named George, arrived at Windsor in March 1477 but died at the age of two, reputedly of the plague. The queen was at the newly refurbished favourite residence of Eltham in August 1479 for the birth of Princess Catherine, who was promised to John of Asturias, eldest son of Ferdinand and Isabella of Spain at the age of two weeks, while no match was considered for the youngest child, Bridget, born in November 1480, also at Eltham and destined for the church. In all, Elizabeth bore Edward ten children, over a period of seventeen years. Given the potentially high rates of infant mortality during the period, they were fortunate to lose only two in infancy and one in adolescence: however, future events would ensure that more would not live to adulthood.

It is hard to know, at this remove, exactly what the queen's feelings were with regard to Edward's many mistresses. It was fairly common for a king to take lovers in addition to his wife, whose role was primarily for dynastic reproduction rather than companionship or pleasure. Most queens turned a blind eye to this, in the appreciation of the advantages their royal status brought and a worldly acceptance of the status quo. It did not imply unhappiness or failure by the standards of the time. Fifteenth-century marriage ceremonies only insisted on the faithfulness of the wife. But Edward and Elizabeth's marriage had been a love match, not subject to the usual rules. Additionally, Edward had earned a reputation for womanising long before his accession, commented on by Commines, More, Mancini and Croyland. More gives Buckingham a speech which does not hold back when it comes to Edward's appetites: 'no woman was there anywhere, young or old, rich or poor ... he would importunately pursue ... and have her, to the great destruction of many a good woman and great dolor of their husbands'. Slander aside, many of his liaisons appear to have been brief encounters with married or recently widowed women, which may have been a safety precaution in the event of fathering an illegitimate child. One of the attendants at the queen's funeral in 1492 would be 'Mistress Grace, a bastard daughter of King Edward'. All England knew of the king's peccadilloes, with the notorious 'Jane Shore' and Elizabeth Wayte or Lucy, mother of his son Arthur, some details of which were later to come back and haunt his family. Edward, his friend Lord Hastings and Thomas Grey, one of Elizabeth's sons by her first marriage, were all lovers of Jane Shore. Jane, christened Elizabeth Lambert, had been the wife of a London merchant although her first marriage was annulled in March 1476, on the grounds that her husband was impotent. Three bishops were instrumental in trying the case before the thirty-year-old became the king's mistress, being mentioned in the court patent rolls that December after his return from France. She was to become his most enduring and favourite mistress; as More wrote, 'many he had but her he loved'. Some chroniclers have echoed Buckingham's words in suggesting Edward had a cavalier attitude towards women, whom he bedded and discarded or passed on to his friends; certainly there was discord between the queen and Hastings, whom she saw as one of his procurers of women.

The young princess was present at the re-internment of Richard, Duke of York, her paternal grandfather, at Fotheringhay Castle in 1476. It was an impressive display, full of pageantry and ceremony, to honour the family's Yorkist roots and reinforce their regal claims. After a long procession, the king and his family took part in the obsequies and ritual offerings that followed; Elizabeth followed her parents in showing reverence to the coffin, probably dressed like her mother in the blue of royal mourning. Afterwards, she would have been present at the huge feast, where guests were accommodated in canvas pavilions and almost 5,000 came to receive alms. The following year, we catch a glimpse of the princess again, at her mother's side for the feast of St George at Windsor Castle. Both she and her mother were dressed in 'murrey' or plum-coloured gowns as they took their places in the great hall for the celebrations. Newly imported Burgundian extravagance and etiquette would have made these impressive occasions. Croyland wrote of the court in later years, that 'you might have seen, in those days, the royal court presenting no other appearance than such as fully befits a most mighty kingdom'. Perhaps the apogee of this was the celebrations held to mark the wedding of the children Prince Richard and Anne Mowbray. For the wedding in January 1475, Elizabeth sat with her parents under a gold canopy in the queen's chapel at Westminster, hung with azure carpets decorated with golden fleur-de-lys. Three days later, a great tournament was held at Westminster, where Elizabeth and her sisters distributed the prizes; the princess gave a golden letter 'E', set with a ruby, to Sir Richard Haute. 1480 marked the visit of Margaret of Burgundy to England. The queen's brother, Sir Edward Wydeville, was sent aboard the *Falcon* to fetch her, when she sailed from Calais to Gravesend then up the Thames. Twelve years had elapsed since she left England; now she stayed mainly at Coldharbour House, where new beds with red and green hangings were prepared for her comfort, along with fine bed linens, curtains, screens and tapestries, one depicting Paris and Helen of Troy. She also visited Greenwich, where a state banquet was held in her honour, and would undoubtedly have met the fourteen-year-old Elizabeth, whom she had last seen at the age of two. In the late 1470s and early 80s, Edward's court was still peripatetic, moving between Windsor, Westminster, Sheen, Eltham and Greenwich, while retreating for hunting at Woodstock. Improvements were made to the queen's apartments at Westminster, where a great chamber made 'unto our dearest wife the queen in her lodging and for a privy kitchen to be made new', but the royal family stayed increasingly close to London and rarely ventured north. The king was winding down.

Elizabeth's teenage years also saw their fair share of tragedy and disappointment. In 1477, the Duke of Clarence pushed his luck too far. Having been forgiven by his brother for his frequent treasonable activities of the past, he sought the hand of Mary of Burgundy in marriage following the death of his wife, Isabel Neville. Cautioned by rumours of Clarence's intention to invade England using Burgundian resources, Edward forbade the match and the brothers were again estranged. Clarence's behaviour became increasingly aggressive; he refused food at court, hinted the king wanted him dead, spread rumours that Edward was a magician and murderer, burst into council meetings and defended two members of his household indicted for using black magic to imagine the deaths of Edward and his sons. He was condemned to death in February 1478. The following year brought a terrible outbreak of plague to the capital. The king avoided it by staying at Eltham and Sheen, acquiring a papal dispensation to eat meat, eggs and milk products during Lent, as fish was injurious to his health! However, his youngest son, George, succumbed to the disease at the age of two and was buried that March in the newly decorated chapel of St George at Windsor Castle. Another child was lost soon after, in May 1482. Princess Elizabeth's closest sibling, Mary, died at the age of fourteen while the family were at Greenwich. She was laid to rest with her brother at Windsor.

A personal disappointment for Elizabeth occurred in 1480, when her engagement to the dauphin was broken. As part of the negotiations, King Louis had agreed to pay a dowry of £60,000 when she reached marriageable age. When Edward tried to claim this in 1477, Louis demurred and tried to betrothe his son elsewhere, which angered the king, but the arrangement limped on. By 1480, when Elizabeth turned fourteen, Louis made offers that fell short of the previous agreement and finally, in December

1482, married his son Charles to Margaret, daughter of the Emperor Maximilian. Princess Elizabeth was no longer Madame la Dauphine and her marital future was again uncertain. One contemporary song claims the 'lily-white rose' did rue or regret the 'fleur-de-lis', a reference to her loss of the French throne. She had no idea, however, just how insecure her position would soon become.

4

Uncle Richard
1483–1485

And he wold have put away his Quene
for to have lyen by my bodye![1]

Events of early 1483 moved rapidly. Once again, sudden changes precipitated a complete revolution in Elizabeth's personal life and status, as well as in the wider arena of national politics. The recent years of stability and prosperity were to be swept aside in a series of unprecedented moves that have posed some of the most controversial questions in early modern history. First, Elizabeth's father died. No one could have predicted the early demise of Edward IV at the age of forty-one; the vigorous youth who had shone on many battlefields had overindulged to excess but in the end, his demise was swift and surprising. By Easter he realised he was dying and added a codicil to his will naming his brother Richard as Protector of his twelve-year-old son and heir, Edward V. This was a crucial role. The last-minute alteration may have been intended to ensure family unity but it denied the queen and her relations the role they had anticipated and provided Richard with the opening for his subsequent actions. This could not have been further from Edward's intentions. Ten days later the king was dead. Almost at once, things began to fall apart at Westminster. As the London chronicler Fabyan wrote, 'grudge and unkindness began to take place between the kings and the quenes allye'. Ultimately, Edward himself had been the crucial element suppressing the warring factions during his reign. His deathbed attempts to reconcile the unpopular Wydevilles with their enemies failed and the resulting power struggle would create some terrible casualties.

That February, Princess Elizabeth had turned seventeen. The *Ballad of Lady Bessie* describes her as 'faire on mold', her face as white as silk, and hands white as milk; all predictable contemporary stereotypes of beauty and status. Later portraits and descriptions paint her as having inherited her parents' good looks, with her long, golden hair and regular features. Her face was apparently the model for the original Queen of Hearts in a standard pack of playing cards, with its hooded lids and rounded chin, surrounded by ripples of hair. This image certainly bears a likeness to the surviving contemporary wax effigy of Elizabeth in the museum at Westminster Abbey. She was portrayed in the ballad as literate as well as possessing all the requisite accomplishments and 'well shee cold work by prophesye', which is perhaps an allusion to the allegations made against her grandmother, but certainly indicative of later awareness of her 'destiny'. 'Prophesye' or divination is easily back-dated by hindsight; it could refer to supernatural insights into the future as well as an above-average degree of wisdom. According to the poem, Edward IV left her a book of prophecies stating the inevitability of her queenship but its composition is datable to the early years of Henry VII's reign, after Elizabeth's marriage. By this time, her future was no longer in doubt. Equally, the ballad employs characters as fictional devices, using poetic licence rather than seeking to record the veracity of events. Elizabeth's portrayal is spirited but misleading. At the time when the poem was set, it seemed unlikely she would ever be queen and any future marriage was beyond her divination. Her two previous engagements had already come to nothing and the recent death of her fourteen-year-old sister Mary was a further reminder of mortality, if she needed one. There was no inevitability about the princess's future in the months following her father's death.

On his father's death in 1483, Prince Edward was twelve and a half. From that April, according to their father's will, he was England's uncrowned king. It was considered an age of significant maturity but not yet sufficient for him to rule alone; Henry VI had attained his majority shortly before the age of sixteen but he was not considered particularly fit to govern and had been dominated by unpopular favourites. A minority rule could allow the ascendancy of potentially harmful ministers, who might gain the ear of the young king and plunge the country back into the turbulence that precipitated the civil war. It was imperative that Edward should be crowned as soon as possible and gain a degree of autonomy; then the role of Protector would be rendered unnecessary. In the meantime, the real power in the kingdom lay in the hands of his uncle, Richard, Duke of Gloucester. The subsequent events are easy to narrate but far more difficult to explain.

The boy king was making ready to depart from Ludlow, guarded by his Wydeville relatives and a scaled-down force, so as not to cause alarm. Elizabeth Wydeville had initially wanted a larger escort but had finally agreed to this, believing it to be in her son's best interests. Waiting to receive him at Westminster, his mother and sisters anticipated the ceremony by making the necessary preparations, trusting that he was in safe hands. Royal robes had been commissioned for his Coronation and were being hurriedly sewn and embroidered by the busy fingers of seamstresses. Before he even reached London, though, the child had been intercepted by his uncle Richard, apparently solicitous for his safety. Having sworn an oath of loyalty and appearing friendly, Richard then arrested Rivers,

Elizabeth's uncle, and Vaughan, on grounds of treason. Rumours circulated about the Protector's intentions, the legitimacy of the royal marriage and even the status of the dead Edward IV himself. As soon as this news reached the widowed queen, she knew trouble was brewing. This time, she no longer had the protection of her queenship, so she resorted to what had worked in the past. With her remaining children, she fled again into sanctuary, lodging in the abbot's fourteenth-century manor of Cheneygates in Westminster Close. The original house had a tower, garden and impressive great hall, representing considerably more luxury than the family experienced during their previous confinement, although their situation was in many ways more precarious. More describes the chaos of their sudden arrival, with servants hurrying in carrying chests and coffers, while Elizabeth Wydeville sat alone on the floor in despair. There would be no returning king, triumphant from exile, to rescue them now. The situation showed just how vulnerable a woman, even a queen, could be and her total dependence upon the support and wishes of men.

A week later, Richard sequestered his brother's property, denying his widow and children access to the 'great fortune' they had supposedly been plundering. Later accounts continued to perpetuate the story of the Wydevilles' 'theft' of treasure from the royal coffers, although in reality, Edward had little to leave by 1483. A date for the Coronation was set and delayed. Edward V arrived in the capital but his family did not see him, as he was conducted to the Tower, the traditional lodging of kings before their Coronations. Then, early in June, rumours reached the widowed queen that Richard alleged she was plotting his death; after placing her under considerable pressure, he extricated her younger son, Prince Richard, from sanctuary and sent him to join his brother. Elizabeth Wydeville would never see her sons again. That month, Edward's old friend Hastings, Rivers and Vaughan met with violent deaths and the royal children were declared illegitimate in a sermon given by Dr Shaa or Shaw at St Paul's Cross. This made Richard, Duke of Gloucester, next in line to the throne; he was proclaimed king only days later on 26 June. The Princes in the Tower were seen less and less before their final disappearance that summer and were soon presumed dead. Those few short weeks witnessed an effective and brutal coup d'etat enforced by subterfuge and violence. For Elizabeth, now of an age to be married and until recently referred to as the Dauphine of France, her family's very existence was under threat and her status was again in doubt.

So what really happened and why? It is difficult to disentangle the many myths surrounding Richard III. His identity, actions and motives have been shaped and reshaped by a complex process of historical reportage and propaganda that began during his lifetime and continues until the present day. The many different versions of Richard have incited academic controversy to an unprecedented degree but he is usually viewed in extremes, as the murderous, usurping villain of Shakespeare or the reactive, responsible king who reluctantly assumed the mantle of power. Before 1483, Richard had proved his loyalty and devotion to his brother, accompanying him into exile, fighting at his side and ruling in his stead in the north. His actions in the summer of 1483 appear to be out of character, unless he genuinely believed he was in danger from a Wydeville plot, or that his nephews were not legitimate. Either that or he had previously concealed his true nature and now saw an opportunity to prevent power transferring into the hands of his enemies and a return to the instability of civil war. His contemporaries were swift to make up their minds. The scandalous accusations regarding his accession cannot be explained as the simple, political blackening of later Tudor writers, keen to cast him as a foil to Henry VII. Richard was a complex and compelling figure who has been reduced to a one-dimensional villain in spite of recent attempts to explore his reign and character in a more objective manner. The stereotypes are entrenched in popular culture. Was he the murderer of the Princes in the Tower, Elizabeth's brothers? Did he deliberately set out to usurp the throne from its legitimate claimant? Was he a hunchback with a withered arm? What did Richard's contemporaries think of him? Was he the victim of Tudor propaganda? Elizabeth's relationship with him can only be understood in the context of such questions.

It appears that many of Richard's contemporaries believed he was responsible for the murder of the Princes in the Tower, as early as the summer of 1483. A number of chroniclers recorded various rumours in the capital and across the south, while some made more explicit accusations in ink. While gossip is notoriously unreliable, it can give an indication of popular beliefs and opinions about the king, indicating whether people believed him capable of the act. One crucial commentator on this is the visiting Italian, Domenic Mancini, author of *The Occupation of the Throne by Richard III*. Mancini was in England from 1482 until the summer of 1483 and may have got some of his information from a fellow Italian, Doctor Argentine, who was in attendance on Princes Edward and Richard in the Tower. According to Mancini's account, the elder boy 'like a victim prepared for sacrifice, sought remission of his sins daily, in confession and penance because he believed that death was facing him'.[2] This was also believed by a contemporary London chronicler, who wrote that 'King Richard ... put to death the two children of King Edward, for which cause he lost the hearts of the people',[3] as well as Weinreich's Danzig Chronicle of 1483 and the speech of Guillaume de Rochefort at Tours in January 1484. Later, Croyland would write that 'the people of the south and ... west ... began to murmur greatly, to form assemblies ... many were in secret, some quite open …' about the princes' fates. Fabyan wrote of their 'secret' deaths and More (a child at the time) would speak of people weeping in the streets when they thought of Edward V and his brother. Holinshed (born 1529) described the event in imaginative detail: the murderers came upon them as they slept and 'suddenlie lapping them up among the clothes, so to bewrapped them and intangled them, keeping downe by force the fether bed and pillows hard unto their mouths, that within a while, smothered and stifled, their breath failing, they gave up to God their innocent soules'.[4] There seems to be little doubt that the boys died; the question is how. In 1674, building work to a staircase in the White Tower uncovered a box containing the skeletons of two male children, which corresponded to the ages of the princes; these were re-interred in an urn at Westminster Abbey. They were re-examined in 1933, when contemporary dating evidence of the bones and fabrics suggested they may well have belonged to the princes. The urn has not been opened since.

Apart from the princes' fates, there was widespread general discontent at the ascendancy of Richard. Writing that June, a Simon Stallworthe reflected the mood of 'much trouble and every man doubts other' while Croyland wrote of 'the greatest doubts' regarding his position.[5] There were uprisings in July that year, across the south of England from Kent to Cornwall, aiming to restore Edward V to the throne and rumours of an attempted plot to smuggle Elizabeth and her sisters to safety abroad. Richard took these seriously. His reaction was to order the capture of the rebels and surround Westminster Abbey with troops; other slanderers suffered the traitors' death of hanging and disembowelling. The one thing he did not do to dispel the rumours was put the princes on public display. By the autumn, rebel loyalties had been transferred to Henry Tudor, a clear indicator that the malcontents believed Edward and his brother were dead. This clearly pre-dates

Tudor propaganda, perpetrated by writers such as More, Holinshed, Hall, Bacon and Shakespeare. However, just because the chroniclers reported these rumours, which appear to have been prevalent, it does not mean Richard was guilty; they are insufficient to condemn him on more than a balance of probability. What does matter is that his contemporaries believed he had murdered the boys. In the light of this, what were the private thoughts of Elizabeth and her family?

The widowed queen and her daughters did not have many choices. Elizabeth Wydeville and Margaret Beaufort may have been involved in the many plots to overthrow Richard that autumn which culminated in the failed invasion of the future Henry VII and execution of Buckingham. After their failure, old charges surfaced afresh. The Parliament of January 1484 passed the Act *Titulus Regis*, stating that Edward's and Elizabeth's 'pretend marriage' of twenty years before had been 'of great presumption ... without the knowing and assent of the laws of this land' and 'by sorcery and witchcraft'. This time, the dowager queen herself, not just her deceased mother, stood accused of having employed magic. Further evidence, supposedly deriving from Richard Stillington, Bishop of Bath and Wells, stated that Edward had been pre-contracted, if not actually already married, to Dame Eleanor Butler, now conveniently dead. The result was the legal confirmation that Edward's children could not inherit the throne: 'all the issue and children of the said king ... be bastards and unable ... to claim anything by inheritance'.[6] Elizabeth's bargaining position was considerably weakened if Richard was aware of the attempt she had made to liaise with Henry Tudor and the rebels of the previous autumn. He certainly knew of Margaret Beaufort's involvement and confiscated her lands as punishment. Eventually, on 1 March, Elizabeth Wydeville agreed to leave sanctuary on the condition that Richard swear a public oath to protect her children. This was an unprecedented step for a king. The promise was made before an assembly of nobles, clergymen and Londoners, in which Richard bound himself to defend the five princesses, 'in surety of their lives' and suffer no hurt done to them 'by way of ravishment or defiling contrary their wills'. He would put them 'in honest places of good name and fame ... to have all things requisite and necessary to marry them suitably as his kinswomen'.[7] For Princess Elizabeth it was a fragile but necessary truce with the enemy.

This oath suggests the dowager queen believed in Richard's guilt but was faced with little choice, given her confinement at Westminster and the continual, increasing pressure he put on her to leave it. She may have been aware that no mercy had been shown to sheltering combatants at the Battle of Tewkesbury, who had been forcibly evicted from sanctuary and executed;[8] there must have been little doubt in her mind that he would use violence to expel her if necessary. It may seem hard for a modern reader to believe that she would trust her daughters to the care of their brothers' murderer but the situation was complex and necessity dictated her actions. Her sons were beyond her reach. She could act now only for the benefit of her children still living. In a typically misogynistic response of the sixteenth century, Holinshed repeats Hall's attitude almost word-for-word, blaming her female frailty without understanding her wider motivation:

suerlie the inconstancie of this woman were much to be marvelled at, if all women had been found constant, but let men speake, yet women of the very bonde of nature will follow their own sex. But it was no small allurement that king Richard used to overcome her for we know by experience that women are of a proud disposition and that the waie to win them is by promises of preferment and therefore it is the lesse marvell that he by his wilie wit had made conquest of her wavering will.

Holinshed would have us believe all Elizabeth's maternal scruples were won over with 'glorious promises and flattering words' which made her 'blot out the old committed injurie and late executed tyrannie', as she was but a 'weake woman of timorous spirit'. In contrast, More presents a powerful image of her distress: 'the quene sat alone on the rushes all desolate and dismayed'. 'Woe worth him,' More has her say, 'for it is he that goeth about to destroy me and my blood.'[9] According to Vergil, she 'fell into a swoon and lay lifeless a good while … she wept, she cried out loud and with lamentable shrieks made all the house ring. She struck her breast, tore and cut her hair … prayed also her own death … condemning herself for a madwoman … for (sending her younger son) to be murdered by their enemy.' It seems unlikely, as Gairdner asserted, that the 'queen dowager had been completely won over by Richard'. There seems little reason to doubt the sincerity of the bereaved mother's grief or her lack of choices.[10]

Events of the turbulent fifteenth century illustrate the frequency with which people did ally themselves with even their mortal enemies, such as the union between Warwick and Margaret of Anjou and the marital career of Anne Neville. Medieval survival was characterised by intense pragmatism and lack of choice; for those at the top, it was a constant daily struggle to ride out the political changes and placate those who happened to be holding the reins. It may have been politic for the ex-queen to appear to concede to Richard's wishes in early 1484. There was no way she could have predicted Henry Tudor's successful invasion. As far as she knew, Richard may retain the throne for decades and the fortunes and lives of herself and her daughters depended on his favour; as such, she can hardly be blamed for making a 'deal with the devil', nor does this suggest she did not love her sons, grieve them deeply and burn with hatred and revenge against their killers but realistically, they were now beyond her reach. She had little doubt about Richard's capabilities of making enemies disappear at will. The lives of her remaining daughters still needed to be determined. The *Ballad of Lady Bessie* makes Elizabeth's belief in her uncle's guilt explicit: she asks Stanley to help her defeat Richard because of the murder of her brothers, claiming he killed them in their beds and also that he drowned them with a pipe of wine, which perhaps confuses the issue with the supposed fate of Clarence. She says to her uncle's corpse:

> 'How likest thou the slaying of my brethren twain?'
> She spake these words to him alone ...
> 'Now are we wroken upon thee here
> Welcome, gentle uncle, home.'[11]

The dowager queen bought her daughters' freedom at a price: she was to enter the custody of John Nesfield, where she was dependent on an allowance from Richard of 700 marks; her title was denied her and her dowry was confiscated. However, her eldest daughter, at least, would have a degree of freedom.

While the widowed queen merely exchanged one form of sanctuary for another, Princess Elizabeth entered the court of Richard III at Westminster. Perhaps this was of her own accord or by Richard's command. He was aware of the oath Henry Tudor had sworn to marry her at Rennes Cathedral the previous Christmas and perhaps wished to keep her within his sights. By now Richard was thirty-one, married almost twelve years, with one son, Edward. Thomas More described the new king as 'little of stature, evil featured of limbs, crook-backed' with a 'war-like visage' or what 'common people call a crabbed face', also 'malicious, wrathful and envious'. His history perpetuated the myth of the king's caesarean birth, that he 'could not be delivered of his mother without her being cut', feet-forward, with teeth and long hair. There is little contemporary evidence for this. Almost all the surviving portraits of Richard date from after his reign and feature the familiar enlarged shoulder and miserly expression. One image in the Rous rolls confirms that he took after his father in appearance, yet Rous revised his descriptions early in Henry VII's reign to incorporate the worst of the stereotypes. Where Edward and Clarence had been tall, fair and handsome, Richard was short, slight and dark. In terms of character, More's Richard was a 'deep dissembler', 'outwardly familiar where he inwardly hated'. While the king's character was maligned as early as 1483, all the descriptions and images of physical deformation date from after Bosworth, so none can be trusted.

An alternative view is presented by the visiting Silesian, Nicolas von Popplau, who met Richard that spring and was impressed by his choir, his feasting, ceremony and the welcome afforded the guests. The new court was rapidly becoming a similar cultural centre to that of his brother. The new king added histories, literature, law, medicine and theology to the royal library, including Caxton's 1484 *Order of Chivalry* by Ramon Lull, which featured a dedication to 'my redoubted, naturel and most drade soverayne lord'. Richard also collected works by Chaucer and Lydgate, hagiography and treaties of war, lives of British kings and Monmouth's history of England and commissioned a copy of the Roman handbook for princes, *De Re Militari*. The royal library, kept at Richmond, was considered impressive enough to display to the visiting French Ambassador in 1483. Also at court, Elizabeth would have frequently encountered her aunt Anne, ten years her senior, although her young cousin Edward was frequently ill and resided mainly at Middleham castle. It was while Richard and Anne were on progress through north in April 1484, that they received news of their son's death. Croyland leaves little doubt about the depths of their grief: 'you might have seen his father and mother in a state almost bordering on madness, by reason of their sudden grief'.[12] Some contemporaries saw this as a divine judgement on the king's usurpation.

Without an heir, Richard's regime was less secure. Briefly he considered making Clarence's son, Edward, Earl of Warwick, his heir but the act of attainder passed against his father in 1478 barred his inheritance. There were ways around this, but to remove such an impediment would have given the boy a stronger claim to the throne than Richard himself. Then he turned to his nephew, John de la Pole, Earl of Lincoln and son of his sister Duchess of Suffolk, who was a few years Elizabeth's senior. In 1485 he named him as heir, appointing him head of the influential Council of the North and increasing his revenues. As such, de la Pole would later challenge the legitimacy of Henry VII's reign and be defeated at the Battle of Stoke. However, even while he was making these arrangements, Richard was considering the possibility of fathering another son himself. His marriage to Anne had produced only one child and her delicate health was giving way. Soon it was apparent that she was dying; predictably rumours circulated that he was considering divorcing her or had resorted to poison. The Neville family chronicler John Rous believed he had. Croyland wrote that her decline was exacerbated by marital cruelty and her husband spurning her bed; accounts from the London mercers described 'much simple communication among the people, by evil-disposed persons'[13] to the effect that Anne was murdered. Richard was still a young man, who could easily marry again and have another family. Already at court, right under his nose, was the perfect candidate. Elizabeth of York was now eighteen, healthy, available and beautiful; she also represented a powerful claim to the throne, which was supported by many of his subjects. She was also his niece but Richard had already swept away significantly worse impediments to his ambition: the right clergymen could be found to issue the necessary paperwork. He had already wooed and won a wife in comparably difficult circumstances. Anne had been the daughter of Warwick; her father and first husband were killed fighting the Yorkists, while many believed Richard was directly involved in, if not responsible for the death of her father-in-law Henry VI. Could he now win Elizabeth's hand in marriage in spite of recent events?

The events of 1485 raise the thorny question of Elizabeth's private feelings. Here, the biographer is on dangerous ground, viewing the past through the filter of modern sensibilities and prey to the remnants of evidence that might be coloured by unknown motives. The simple answer is that we do not know for certain how Elizabeth felt. She has long been cast as passive and reactive, largely for her own survival. The image of her as Richard's victim, the sister of the murdered princes and wife of his overthrower, provides a straightforward interpretation of her role. This is the portrait that hindsight has favoured, along with the glorification of her beauty and gentle qualities, creating a degree of ambiguity about her character. Perhaps there is a good reason for it. As the mother of the Tudor monarchs, later accounts have been coloured by the dynasty's dependence on her lineage and the vilification of Richard III. It would hardly be politic to cast her in the role of Richard's lover. Yet even as late as the summer of 1485, there were no guarantees that Henry Tudor's bid for the throne would be successful. Richard was the reigning king and her uncle. Perhaps he was also her suitor. Evidence to suggest that he contemplated marriage with her has recently been explored more seriously by historians, where they have previously been dismissed as impossible. They run contrary to the powerful chroniclers of Tudor history and the enduring characters of Shakespeare. His Elizabeth is one-dimensional, yet the experiences of his Anne Neville, married to the killer of her father-in-law and husband, are memorably self-destructive and bitter.

Yet what was the truth? The possibility that Elizabeth herself was 'in love' with her uncle and prepared to marry him offends modern sensibilities to the point of disbelief. It would be incestuous according to our laws and repulsive given his probable culpability in the infanticide of her brothers. If this was the case, were her motives purely those of survival? Aware of her role as a dynastic pawn, she was prepared to marry Henry Tudor, whom she had probably never met before and can hardly have 'loved' at the time of their wedding. Did she actually entertain romantic feelings towards either him or her uncle? Is it anachronistic to pose such a question? Perhaps these are simply the irrelevant scruples of a modern reader; Elizabeth's motives may be far more complex than originally suspected or, paradoxically, far more straightforward. Perhaps she fell headlong in love with him and committed adultery in anticipation of her aunt's death, as some recent historians have claimed. On the other hand, it may have been a question of placating the enemy for the sake of her and her remaining family's survival. After all, Richard had shown no scruples in the rapid and brutal removal of those Wydevilles who got in his way.

The first apparent piece of evidence for their relationship arises at Christmas 1484, which was kept at Westminster. The Croyland chronicler describes a feast celebrated with great splendour, singing and dancing, including many changes in dress of similar design and colour between Elizabeth and Anne, who were of a similar size despite being a decade apart in age. American author Arlene Okerlund cites sumptuary laws as prohibiting someone of Elizabeth's abased status from wearing the same apparel as the queen; however, it does not preclude the queen from wearing an outfit suitable to Elizabeth's rank, especially if it was a costume, part of a pageant. This has been frequently interpreted as sinister. However, it need not be the case; in fact, the opposite many be true. The co-ordination of clothing could be an act of solidarity and friendship; in pageants and celebrations, the colours and fabrics worn by leading royals were often designed to complement each other, particularly if it was fancy dress or a certain season. In 1477, Elizabeth and her mother had worn matching gowns of 'murrey' velvet at the feast of St George in Windsor Castle.[14] Husband and wife in particular would dress to match on key occasions such as visits, weddings and memorable occasions; it is not necessarily the act of aggression and jealousy that some have seen as Elizabeth's deliberate attempt to outshine the queen. This is a very modern interpretation, when actually, Elizabeth's choice may have been intended to show solidarity with the queen rather than to outdo her. Writing in 1486, Croyland claimed the occasion was criticised by 'magnates and prelates', 'the people' and 'many', which still ascribes motives at a remove. Against a backdrop of constant slander, courtly rumour does not conclusively prove Richard or Elizabeth's intentions. Alternatively, there remains the possibility that this was a subtle act of malice, perpetrated by an arrogant teenager in anticipation of death and sex; if so, the entire character of the 'humble and devout', dependent princess needs to be recast.

Other chroniclers seek to explain contemporary rumours of Richard's desire to marry Elizabeth with a range of reasons. Much imaginative projection by later novelists and historians has blurred the lines of fact and fiction by ascribing motives and emotions that can only be speculative. The truth of Richard's relations with Anne also lie at the heart of the question; theories that he was responsible for her death appear to be part of the sustained contemporary and subsequent attacks upon his character; the only concrete evidence suggests he was genuinely afflicted by her demise. Yet, as a relatively young king, without an heir, the imperative to remarry would have been strong. In the spring of 1485, as Anne declined,

Richard did not know he only had months to live; there was no motive for him to line up a bride in advance of her death, unless a genuine attraction had developed between uncle and niece. Still, there was no rush. It has also been suggested that he contemplated marriage to her in order to eradicate the threat of her union to Henry Tudor, yet he only needed to marry Elizabeth off elsewhere in order to achieve this end. She did not need to become his wife. Additionally, to marry her himself would acknowledge her legitimacy and invalidate his claim to the throne, which had been based on the flaws in her parents' union. What we do know for certain is that Richard issued a public denial to combat the rumours of an intended match with his niece on 30 March 1485 and again in a letter to the City of York on 19 April. The campaign to blacken his character has been conveniently attributed to later Tudor slander, yet there were many voices speaking against the king as early as 1483, in regard to his ascendancy, the Princes in the Tower and discontent at the appointment of northerners to supplant long-established families in positions of power in the south. The tide did not turn against him suddenly after Bosworth, it had already begun during his reign. Contemporary accounts of his marital intentions should be read in this context.

Then there is Buck's letter. Many cases for passion, adultery and incest have rested on this single, dubious source, discovered in the seventeenth century. The letter was supposedly written by Elizabeth of York herself in February 1485 to John Howard, Duke of Norfolk, asking him to assist her marriage to the king and expressing impatience that the queen was taking so long to die! In fact, the original letter says no such thing. There are actually two Bucks and two letters. The first was produced by George Buck, an historian and master of the revels to James I, who was born around 1560. He found a copy of *Titulus Regis* within the Croyland manuscript and produced his own history of Richard III's life and reign. Buck claimed to have seen Elizabeth's letter in 1619, then in the keeping of the Howard family, patrons of his work. He was considered insane at the event of his penurious death three years later. Buck's *History of the Life and Reign of Richard III* was edited and published by his great nephew, a pro-Ricardian also called George Buck, in 1646. Significant editing between the two casts the original letter into doubt. Buck's original version (BL MS Cotton Tiberius E. x. f. 238v) is fire-damaged and has been reconstructed to an extent that suggests liberal degrees of 'interpretation' in the 1640s. The first version's assertion that Elizabeth 'feared the queene would nev ...' has become 'feared the queen would never die'. The second version says Elizabeth belonged to Richard 'in heart and in thoughts, in body and in all' although the suggestive word 'body' is absent from the letter of 1619, turning a conventional phrase into a potential physical affair. However, as his niece, whom he had sworn to protect and suitably marry, Elizabeth was his to dispose of bodily. The earlier letter asks Howard to be 'a mediator for her to the K ... (space) ... ge ...' which Buck junior interpreted as a mediator for her in her marriage to the king himself. According to Gairdner,[15] Howard had been sent to France by Edward IV in 1480, to act as an intermediary for the French marriage, so there is also a chance Elizabeth was writing slightly earlier than previously thought. Dating this letter to February 1485, five years later and shortly before the death of Queen Anne, implies a callousness and impatience in the teenage Elizabeth, an anticipation of her aunt's death in order to become her uncle's wife. Another possibility exists though.

Elizabeth may well have written to Norfolk, asking him to intercede with the king to promote her marriage. However, this was not necessarily a match with Richard himself, as quite another union was being proposed for her early in 1485. Early in 1484, Richard had sworn to protect the former princesses and arrange suitable matches for them; he had already married her sister Cecily to Lord Scrope and was now planning a joint match for himself and Elizabeth. A double Portuguese marriage proposal had been suggested by Sir Edward Brampton, in which Richard was to marry the teenage Joana of Castile while Elizabeth would wed Manuel Duke of Beja, later Manuel I of Portugal, who had been born in 1469. The planned union was referred to by Alvaro Lopez de Chaves, as the Portuguese hoped for English support against Castilian rebels and may well have been the match Elizabeth was referring to early in 1485. Ironically, Manuel would later marry Joana of Castile himself and after her death in childbirth would wed her younger sister, Maria. These were both elder sisters of Catherine of Aragon, later to be Elizabeth's daughter-in-law! He may also have considered marrying her to the Earl of Desmond.

Later chroniclers, writing after Bosworth, made Elizabeth's aversion to the match plain. She is the driving force of the *Ballad of Lady Bessie*, instigating and co-ordinating the invasion of Henry Tudor, the 'lover' she had not actually met in 1483. Holinshed described how 'the maiden hirselfe most of all detested and abhorred this unlawfull and in manner unnaturall copulation'.[16] Writing for James I, in the early seventeenth century, Francis Bacon claims Henry was never loving towards Elizabeth, but always cold and distant because of the dislike he felt for her Yorkist connections. While this could be a veiled reference to her love for Richard, it is not explicit enough and not real evidence of this supposed coolness towards her, while there is plenty of evidence to the contrary.[17] Some modern historians are still convinced by the case for Elizabeth's incestuous affair with her murderous uncle. Alison Weir's portrait of a woman scorned,[18] depicting an Elizabeth passionately in love with her uncle, who decides to take vengeance because she had been jilted, owes more to historical fiction than fact. It rests largely on the 1646 version of Buck's letter and the reported rumours by Croyland as well as a degree of romanticisation. The past two years had provided far more powerful motives for Elizabeth to resist her uncle and support Henry than her fictional sexual rejection. Arlene Okerlund exposes the many weaknesses in the Buck evidence but speculates that, after her recent privations, 'what nineteen-year-old woman would not welcome the attentions of a rich, powerful and charming man?'[19] While the fifteenth century abounded in gender stereotypes and recognised those of the 'woman scorned' and the 'sugar daddy', explaining Elizabeth's actions in this way is reductive and denies her social status and the complexity of her situation. Considering the potential roles of the dowager queen and Margaret Beaufort to facilitate Henry Tudor's invasion and the subsequent marriage, the possibility arises that Elizabeth may have been a willing and dutiful pawn in their plans. This does not diminish her personal autonomy or make her dependently passive; she may have been their spy in Richard's court, whose wishes accorded with theirs. Elizabeth's lifelong family loyalty suggests this was a likely scenario. On balance of evidence, she appears unlikely to have been in love with Richard, even if 'love' was a fairly anachronistic concept for the heir to the throne. Nor does this interpretation deny her humanity or her capacity to love: it acknowledges her as a woman of her times.

In any event, the course of 1485 meant that the unions never came to fruition. Two weeks after Anne's death, Richard was forced to issue declarations that 'it never came into his thoughts or mind to marry in such manner-wise'. Perhaps he was not being strictly truthful; the match may have appealed more to him than his niece. The king's councillors were firmly against the match and Croyland was certain the denials were made 'more because of his advisers' than his own inclination. Croyland states that 'many' in the council knew his repudiation of Elizabeth to have been made under duress: opposition would be offered not only 'by voice' but that the north would rebel. Those newly appointed to positions of power feared reprisals by the Wydevilles, if she were to attain a position of power. Elizabeth, however, was not consulted. She was sent north to Sherriff Hutton, near York. Accompanied by her sisters and Richard's two potential heirs, his nephews Clarence and de la Pole, it may have been a precautionary measure in anticipation of Henry Tudor's invasion. It also conveniently placed the attractive young woman out of Richard's sight but perhaps not out of his mind. This was the setting for the *Ballad of Lady Bessie*, where Elizabeth worked with Stanley to organise Henry's invasion and expressed her revulsion at the prospect of marriage to him; it was supposedly a work of her contemporary Humphrey Brereton, her host's servant, composed retrospectively, early in the sixteenth century. If Elizabeth had taken such an active role in orchestrating her future, which seems unlikely in the first half of 1485, it was a bold move given the relevant chances of the key players. In all probability, it would have seemed likely that Richard, the seasoned campaigner, would return triumphant and soon Elizabeth's marriage to some leading Yorkist nobleman would be concluded. However, the course of the battle would overturn all expectations. She would not see her uncle again.

5

A Royal Wedding
1485–1486

... a Welsh mylkesoppe ...[1]

Late in the afternoon of Sunday 7 August 1485, Henry Tudor landed at Milford Haven in South Wales. Later described by Shakespeare as 'blessed Milford', it formed a natural harbour of mud flats at the mouth of two rivers, used as a port since Viking times. The son of Edmund Tudor (maternal half-brother to Henry VI) and his child bride Margaret Beaufort, the invader had lived in exile in France since the age of fourteen. Before that, his early years were spent in Wales, probably at Raglan Castle, home to the Herberts, who bought his wardship from Edward IV. In England, he was a virtual nobody. Perhaps it was the absence of any other suitable candidates that had placed him at the head of rebel hopes since the deaths of the princes in 1483. For many, anyone was better than the usurping Richard, even a complete unknown. It was Tudor's very anonymity that helped his cause. One abortive attempt to invade that winter had been defeated by bad weather and a failure of co-ordination among Richard's enemies. Having vowed to marry Elizabeth of York back at Christmas 1483, he was, in the words of Thomas More, 'sore amased and troubled' by rumours of Richard's intentions to marry her himself. This romantic interpretation makes the princess central to his motivation but was, in fact, one of a set of factors that prompted his actions, which he was careful to downplay following his victory. Now he was returning with a troop of 4,000 French mercenaries and English exiles: marching inland, he drew more support from Wales and the surrounding areas and appealed to his father-in-law, Thomas Stanley, for assistance, although Richard's precaution of imprisoning Stanley's son effectively tied his hands until the last minute. As he marched towards London, his army gathered more support.

The Battle of Bosworth Field has suffered from centuries of romanticism in popular history, art, fiction and drama. The dramatic account, written by Thomas More, has been repeated by Hall, Holinshed, Shakespeare and Bacon to the extent that its events have become set pieces: Richard's pre-battle nightmares, the lone reckless charge into the midst of his enemies, the loss of his horse, the crown rolling into the ditch, the certainty that right had prevailed. In fact, it was a battle Henry should never have won. Backed by 12,000 men, Richard had the advantage of size and experience; he was a seasoned soldier while Henry had never fought, let alone headed an army, plus Richard was on home territory. The hindsight of later writers has made much of the supposed terrible night the king passed before engaging in the field. In a deeply superstitious age, prophecies and omens were interpreted as signs of divine favour or displeasure and acted on accordingly. Throughout the night, Richard apparently 'saw divers images like terrible deviles which pulled and haled him ... it sodeinly strake his heart with a sodeyne fear'.[2] The interpretations follow moral lines. More saw these as 'the sharpe stynge of his mischevous offences' and Hall, drawing on More as his source, added, 'but I thynke this was no dreame' but the pricking of his 'synfull conscience'. Predictably, Croyland described his face the following morning as 'more livid and ghastly than usual'. Shakespeare was perhaps the most eloquent and explicit:

after a night of terrible ghostly visitations repeating that he would 'despair and die', Richard himself recognises the significance: the sun 'disdained' to shine; it would be 'a black day for somebody' and does not doubt why, while Henry's dreams contrast sharply with his: 'methought their soules, whose bodies Richard murther'd, came to my tent and cried on victory'.

On 22 August 1485, in a Leicestershire field, the decisive battle was fought. According to More, the armies engaged in a great morass when neither sword nor bill was spared; the air was filled with the sounds of trumpets and soldiers shouted, men buckled on their armour and arrows flew. It was all over relatively quickly, though. Estimates put the fighting at around an hour and a half, with around 1,000 casualties. Richard saw Henry with only a small group of men about him and approached, 'inflamed with ire and vexed with outrageous malice' spurred on his horse 'like a hungery lion'. He got close enough to slay Sir William Brandon, Henry's standard bearer, and the two leaders locked swords. Hall says this was the point that Sir William Stanley's troops turned in support of Tudor, causing Richard's men to flee and leaving him to his death: the king, 'fighting alone in the middest of al his enemies was overthrown and slain'. There is a chance, though, that Richard took this decisive but fatal act precisely because he saw that many of his supporters were hanging back, reluctant to commit. Some accounts have him shouting 'treason' as he ran ahead to meet his death.

Richard's body was defiled and paraded back through the streets to Leicester, where he lay in state for two days before being buried in the choir of the Grey Friars' church. The rediscovery of his bones in 2013 answered many questions about the nature of his injuries but the exact circumstances of his death are still disputed. Popular culture claims he called for a horse and that his crown rolled under a bush where Stanley or Tudor found it; whatever the truth of this, his sudden act of bravery or overconfidence cost him his

throne and life. Many interpreted the battle's outcome in the
same way as his disturbed night; an act of divine retribution
for the various crimes of his reign. Fabyan was typical in
writing, 'thus with miserie ended this prince, whiche ruled
moste what by rigour and tyranny ... in great trouble and
agonie'. However, one place his death was recorded with
sympathy was in the York rolls: 'king Richard was ...
thrugh great treason ... piteously slane and murdred to the
grete hevynesse of this citye'[3] and in the coming years, his
supporters would continue to assail the throne. Opinion
would divide for centuries. For Richard, though, it was all
over, while for Henry Tudor, it was just beginning. One of
his first acts would be to send an escort to Sheriff Hutton
and bring Elizabeth of York back to London. Hall describes
her as the 'virtuous and immaculate virgin' whom God
had protected and defended, among a great number of
honourable and noble matrons. Soon she would meet the
man who was about to become her husband.

England's new king was a mysterious figure. In Hall's
chronicle, Richard criticises Henry as 'a Welsh mylkesoppe,
a man of small courage and of lesse experience of marcyall
arts and feats of war, brought up by my brothers means
and mine like a captive in a close cage'. The chronicler
himself was more impressed, though; Tudor rode about
giving 'gentle' words of encouragement to his men before
the battle; 'for he was a man of no great stature but so
formed and decorated with all gyftes ... of nature that
he seemed more an angelical creature than a terrestriall
personage'. According to Hall, 'his countenance and aspect
was cheerful and courageous his heare yellow lyke the
burnished golde, his eyes gray shynynge and quicke,
prompt and ready in aunsweryunge, but of suche sobrietie'
he spoke with a 'lowd voice and bolde spirite'. This
contrasts quite sharply with the description of Henry from
the *Ballad of Lady Bessie*, which has him wearing black
velvet as he practised shooting at the butts, with his long,

pale face marred by a red wart. Other sources have him as dark-haired, crisply curled in the European style, with a cast in one of his pale blue eyes that made him look as if he had a squint. Vergil described him as 'remarkably attractive' but with a sallow complexion and bad teeth, although by the time of his writing, Henry's hair had turned thin and white.[4] Later portraits stress his supposed miserly qualities, but in 1485 he was twenty-eight, tall, slender and reserved, dressed in subdued, elegant foreign fashions, having spent the last fourteen years at the court of Francis II, Duke of Brittany. Bacon, who never saw him, painted him as 'revered and a little like a churchman'. Several different contradictory Henries might emerge from these portraits. We cannot know what Elizabeth thought when she first met him, sometime that autumn, either at the home of the dowager queen, or at Coldharbour House, where his mother, Margaret Beaufort, was living. The 'lovers' of the ballad had probably never met before, or had been small children at the time; now events beyond their control had brought them together.

In theory, it was a perfect match. Henry claimed the throne by right of conquest and had overthrown a regime that had been unpopular in many places, tainted by the controversy of Richard's accession and the disappearance of Edward V. His Lancastrian roots gave him the requisite degree of authority but he had not been heavily embroiled in the bloody events of recent decades, making him a new face on the political scene. However he was still sufficiently British, having been born at Pembroke Castle and spending many of his early years as a ward of the Herbert family in their impressive Raglan Castle home; there had been the possibility of a marriage to their daughter Maud before the events of 1485 unfolded. Elizabeth's popularity was legendary. The common sympathy for her sufferings also assimilated much of the outrage and grief surrounding the deaths of her brothers and the majority of England recognised her as the rightful heir of the house of York. However, there was no expectation that she could rule alone. A woman's subordinate position to her husband extended even to those through whom the inheritance travelled. She was of marriageable age, tall, beautiful and had been brought up in anticipation of queenship. The union had been proposed by their mothers through the long days of suffering under Richard, liaising in secret through the offices of a mutual doctor and astrologer while the dowager queen remained in sanctuary. The prospect of success must initially have seemed remote. Equally, if Henry had married either daughter of the protectors of his youth, Anne of Brittany or Maud Herbert, Elizabeth would have been free to marry and take her royal inheritance elsewhere. Providing she chose carefully, she and her husband would then have been rival claimants to the English throne and perpetual thorns in Henry's side. So, to what extent did Henry and Elizabeth choose each other? The union was practically decided by the time they eventually met, probably in early September 1485. More expressed his certainty that in comparison with the prospect of her match with Richard, the union was heaven-blessed: 'God otherwise ordeind for hir and preserved hir from that unlawfull copulation and incestuous bed.' It was the best possible political arrangement for both of them, designed to heal national divides, but it could hardly have been a love match.

Henry's splendid Coronation took place on 30 October 1485. The key buildings to figure in the celebrations, the Tower, Westminster Abbey and Hall, were draped in almost 500 yards of fine scarlet, while the streets between them were cleared and prepared. Henry himself had two new gowns made, one of purple cloth of tissue of gold and another of crimson cloth of gold. This was his first real opportunity to impress his majesty upon the people of London, for whom displays of wealth were a vital indicator of power; if he looked like a king, he was considered a king indeed. The procession through the city streets was crucial. A long cavalcade set out from the Tower, including heralds, trumpeters, sergeants, squires, attendants, members of the court, the mayor and aldermen and the country's nobility, before the king himself, bareheaded, appeared under a canopy of gold. Here, he wore regal purple furred with the exclusive ermine and his horse was trimmed with more of the same. Blue silk banners fluttered from the trumpets before a long train of followers, bearing the arms and badges of the new dynasty. Among other expenses for the occasion were listed yards of white cloth of gold bordered with red roses, crimson velvet for dragons and the cross of St George, dangling silver and gold fringes and spangles, gilt nails for the stage and more velvet to cover saddles. London embroiderers were paid for producing images of falcons and the arms of St Edward and the Welsh hero Cadwallader.[5] More wrote how people already 'exceedinglie rejoised at his presence, as by their voices and gestures it well appeared'; if so, his reception in London that day must have been encouraging. Henry was crowned in the abbey by Thomas Bourchier, Archbishop of Canterbury, and Elizabeth may have been among the assembled nobility gathered in Westminster Abbey to mark the event. If so, she was also present at the sumptuous feast that followed and would have had ample opportunities to observe the man she expected would soon become her husband.

The wedding did not take place, though, for another three months. This is not to suggest Henry was not keen for the match, as some historians have concluded: there was his first Parliament to sit, repeals of the law to ensure that Elizabeth's illegitimacy was rescinded and dispensations to secure, as well as a terrible outbreak of plague in the capital that autumn. It has been estimated that almost 30,000 citizens died of it, including two mayors of London and six aldermen,[6] considering which, delay was a sensible precaution. In addition, the *Titulus Regis* was repealed and the dowager queen's reputation restored: it was ruled that all copies of the act be 'cancelled, destroyed ... burnt and utterly destroyed' by the following Easter. Only one known copy survived, in the Croyland Chronicle, to be discovered by George Buck junior in the seventeenth century. Henry also wanted to ensure his kingship was established and independent of Elizabeth's claim before the ceremony took place. The couple probably met on a number of occasions, both at court and at Margaret Beaufort's home, Coldharbour House, an ancient building originally named La Tour, comprising two linked fortified town houses, with a number of chambers or suites of rooms within its tower and a Great Hall on the riverside. Perhaps Henry was taking the time to get to know his bride; more cynically, it has been suggested he was ensuring she was not carrying the child of his predecessor. Elizabeth was not pregnant. But she may have finally yielded to Henry's advances once the union appeared a certainty. The couple's first child would arrive the following September, exactly eight months after the wedding, a time-frame which has given rise to much subsequent historical speculation. Assuming the baby was full-term, conception must have occurred in mid-December 1485. Parliament approved the match on 10 December 1485, suggesting consummation around that time, almost exactly nine months before the birth. The ordering of Elizabeth's wedding ring that December, which arrived at court at New Year, seems to support that for all involved, the marriage was now a certainty. A verbal promise of marriage or 'handfasting' could be enough to license physical relations and Henry's eagerness to secure his bride and father an heir may have led them to share a bed before the ceremony. Within the privacy of his mother's home, this may have been easily achieved. Alternatively, the child may have been born prematurely, making for almost immediate conception. Given the rapidity with which this took place, it seems unlikely that Elizabeth had been engaged in any sort of physical affair with her uncle, unless some degree of contraception had been employed!

Predictably, early Tudor chroniclers were full of blessings for the match. The fourth Croyland continuer wrote that the marriage, 'which from the first had been hoped for', was lauded for the sake of Elizabeth's title as well as her virtues: 'in whose person it appeared that every requisite might be supplied, which was wanting to make good the title of king himself'. He cites a poem included by the previous Croyland writer that 'since God had now united them and made but one of these two factions, let us be content'. Other writers celebrated that 'harmony was thought to discend out of hevene into England' from this 'long desired' match. Shakespeare presents them as the 'true succeeders of each royal house, by God's fair ordinance conjoin together'. Their heirs would bring 'smooth-fac'd peace, with smiling plenty and prosperous days'. Hall claimed the match 'rejoiced and comforted the hartes of the noble and gentlemen of the realme' and 'gained the favour and good minds of all the common people'. On 10 December, the Speaker of the Houses of Parliament stated that Henry wished to take Elizabeth as his wife 'from whence, through the grace of God, it is hoped by many the continuation of offspring by a race of kings, as consolation to the entire nation'.[7] Henry also sought to obtain a second papal dispensation for the match, as the pair were related within the fourth degree: he already had one dating to March 1484 and could not allow any possibility of the marriage being invalid. This involved religious and legal specialists giving depositions about their respective lineages before witnesses, which was confirmed by the current papal legate to England, James, Bishop of Imola. He was successful on 16 January. Two days later, Elizabeth and Henry were married.

No actual descriptions of the wedding survive. The ceremony was conducted by Archbishop Bourchier, who placed the gold ring on Elizabeth's finger and heard the couple repeat their vows. Certainly there would have been much pomp and ceremony, which, as the astute Henry Tudor had swiftly grasped, was the key to impressing his majesty upon witnesses. In a similar style to his Coronation, the abbey would have been decked out in the exclusive colours and fabrics of royalty: purple and gold, silk, ermine and delicate cloths of tissue. Elizabeth would have been splendidly dressed and adorned with jewels, lace, brocade and ribbons; the choice of white for wedding dresses was not yet an established tradition so she may have worn one of the rich purple, blue or tawny gowns that appear among her wardrobe records that year. The portraits in which she was depicted can give an idea of the magnificence of her dress, as these would also be opportunities to display wealth and status. An anonymous work in the early Tudor style shows her dressed in ermine cuffs, with embroidered borders studded with pearls and heavy, symbolic jewellery. It is clear from Henry's later accounts that in spite of his historical reputation as a miser, he did not stint when buying jewels and adornments for his family: it has been estimated that between 1492 and 1507, more than £10,000 was spent from the royal budget on such symbols. As the couple repeated their vows, lit by burning tapers, they stood before a host of the decimated English nobility, summoned by Henry in order to witness the union which, hopefully, would bring peace. Elizabeth's private feelings on this occasion must have encompassed pride and relief as well as a degree of uncertainty. Although it was a moment of intense personal triumph, she had witnessed her mother's own tumultuous journey as queen and understood that the ceremony brought no guarantees. She was about to experience an irrevocable change in status, not merely as queen but as a woman becoming a wife. It must have been a bitter-sweet moment, aware as she was that her triumph had come about as a result of her family's losses and suffering. But this moment was symptomatic of her life to date. Only recently, she had been enclosed within the restricted walls of Westminster sanctuary; here she was now in its abbey, becoming the wife of the king. Through the course of the extravagant feast that followed in Westminster Hall, she must have been aware of the approach of that symbolic event; the public ritual of the bedchamber.

Henry and Elizabeth's wedding night was probably spent in Westminster's painted chamber, the palace's most luxurious apartment, containing bed, fireplace and chapel, richly decorated as its name suggests. It was habitually Henry's chamber, dominated by a four-poster bed that required preparation by ten attendants who would search the straw mattress with daggers to discover any potential dangers, before the ritual laying down of sheets, blankets and coverlets. Accounts paid to Elizabeth's bedmakers in 1502 give an indication of the kind of luxury available to the king and his new wife. In October, London mercer Thomas Goodriche received payment for the delivery of 60 yards of blue velvet for the queen's use. The following month, John Warreyne was paid for the 'making of a trussing bedde seler testere and counterpoint of crymsyn velvet and blew paned'. The bed also had a matching curtain of 'dammaske crymsym' with blue panels, sewn with red thread and hung on green rings. He also supplied linen cloth and fine white thread for sheets and curtain linings with a white fringe.[8] As they prepared for their first official night together, the couple were still enacting a vital part of the wedding ceremony. In 1501, Elizabeth would help organise the wedding of her eldest son, Prince Arthur, and Catherine of Aragon, which may have been shaped in part by her own experiences. It was usual for the royal bride to be escorted to her chamber by her ladies, undressed and put to bed. Such rituals took place in many towns and villages, in all walks of life, as the culmination of a day's celebrations. The partially undressed bridegroom followed, accompanied by his gentlemen and musicians, who would mark the occasion with bawdy jokes and 'rough music' or charivari. For a king and his wife though, the event would be less raucous and more religious: priests and bishops would pronounce their blessings and sprinkle the bed with holy water before wine and spices were served. Sometimes, before they left, onlookers required the naked legs of a couple to touch or to witness a kiss in order to leave satisfied, as in the case of Princess Mary Rose, whose marriage to Louis XII of France in 1514 was considered consummated when her bare leg touched that of his proxy. One such scene occurs Marie de France's twelfth-century *Lais le Fresne* when the heroine prepares the marital bedchamber by adorning it with the distinctive brocade that leads to her discovery. Similarly, Henry and Elizabeth's chamber may have been decorated with suitable silks, ribbons and hangings. Finally though, the newlyweds were left alone. The consummation of a marriage was a vital stage of its validity; without it, all the church's ceremonial and ritual could be dissolved and the legitimacy of subsequent heirs and inheritance drawn into question. Even among people of lesser rank, unions could be broken through non-consummation; Edward IV's mistress, Jane Shore, gained her freedom in this way, while for Elizabeth's future daughter-in-law, events of her wedding night would later contribute to her undoing. However, history was to prove that the wedding of January 1486 was successfully consummated, if it had not already been so.

The famous iconography of the Tudor rose, combining the red and white flowers, has come to represent the dynasty in the popular imagination. Walter Scott's novels and Henry Payne's 1908 painting *The Choosing of the Red and White Roses*, the depiction of a Shakespearean scene, are typical of the romantic response to the symbol and the blend of later sources. However, this may be something of a misnomer. The civil wars that took place from the 1450s to the 1480s were not referred to at the time as the 'Wars of the Roses'; this is a name which history conferred on those events as a result of the proliferation of the symbol. It is more likely that they were called 'The Cousins' Wars' during their duration. Henry certainly was very conscious of heraldry, legend and the well-placed use of imagery, as is evident from the dragon and dun cow banners he brought to London from Bosworth Field. These were part of a range of heraldic devices to support his lineage, including the Beaufort portcullis and the ostrich feathers from John of Gaunt; Lancastrians also sometimes employed the French fleur-de-lys. Henry used the colour red to emphasise his Welsh descent and help fulfil the Arthurian myth of the union of the white queen and red king. The greyhound and crown resting on a hawthorn bush were also incorporated into his later arms, as depicted on several illuminated manuscripts held in the British Library. It is unclear when exactly the image of the combined Tudor rose entered common usage. One decorated royal indenture made 'the twenty day of novembre the twenty yere of his mooste noble reigne' (1505) only features the red rose, portcullis, dragon and greyhound.[9] By 1485, the white rose was a long-established icon of the Yorkist dynasty but it was less well used than Edward IV's sunburst or sun in splendour. For Elizabeth, the white rose became a powerful early personal symbol, appearing in 1487 alongside the sunbursts embroidered on her Coronation clothing. By the early sixteenth century, the union rose was already well established and featured in ballads, art works, manuscripts and carvings. The tomb of their son Arthur in Worcester Cathedral would depict the *rose-en-soleil*, a rose surrounded by the sun's rays as well as the standard union rose and the portcullis.[10] Whatever the true history of their iconography, when the wedded pair were united in reality early in 1486, the marriage's symbolism had lasting effects.

For women of all social classes in the late fifteenth century, becoming a wife marked a significant change in status. While running her own household brought a woman a degree of autonomy, it also brought her into a new state of dependence, making her virtually a child in legal terms, subject to the control of her husband, for better or worse. Marriage and motherhood were the ultimate social goal, contracted for mutual benefit as well as the advancement of an entire family. Negotiations might be protracted and involve significant clauses dealing with the transfer of land and property and provision for both parties in the event of early death. As the wife of the king, although not yet crowned in her own right, Elizabeth was the highest-ranking female in the land but still subject to her husband's rule. Unlike many married women, she was able to own property and land, from which she received most of her income, and probably played a less 'hands-on' role in the running of her household than many of her contemporaries, who would be expected to engage in and not just oversee the daily practicalities of life. Even for women of high status, there were certain behavioural expectations of a medieval wife. Apart from being supposedly unable to refuse her husband the sexual 'debt', her reputation and conduct could determine her success or failure in all aspects of her life and that of her husband; in this sense, the medieval wife can be acknowledged as holding a considerable degree of power. So, what constituted her duties? Was the uxorial role interpreted in the same way, through the respective eyes of men and women? And just how far could her influence extend?

Wives of the period tend to appear in legal records when financial arrangements are being made for their futures or when some legal dispute arises; often the latter cases are determined on the basis of good 'fame' or character. This

Above left: 1. Elizabeth of York. The first-born daughter of Edward IV and his controversial wife Elizabeth Wydeville, after whom she was named. Contemporary sources agree that she took after both her exceptionally good-looking parents.

Above right: 2. Elizabeth Wydeville, Elizabeth of York's mother. A legendary blonde beauty, already widowed with two small sons when she became queen.

3. Church of St Mary the Virgin, Grafton Regis, Northamptonshire. Elizabeth Wydeville grew up at the nearby manor house and the tomb of her great-grandfather John Wydeville can be found inside.

Above: 4. Edward IV, Elizabeth of York's father. Tall, handsome and athletic, Edward was the ideal of a medieval king.

Right: 5. Richard, Duke of York, father of Edward IV, Richard III and Margaret of York. It was through him that Elizabeth inherited her claim to the throne.

6. Site of the Battle of Wakefield, West Yorkshire, fought on 30 December 1460, resulting in the death of Richard, Duke of York, father of Edward IV.

7. Ruins of Middleham Castle, North Yorkshire, home to the Neville family including the Earl of Warwick. After his death, Edward IV's younger brothers George and Richard lived here; it became Richard III's main residence in the 1470s.

Above: 8. Remains of Fotheringhay Castle, Northamptonshire, favourite residence of the Yorkist kings. Richard III was born here and Edward IV and Elizabeth were frequent visitors.

Right: 9. Edward V, Elizabeth's younger brother. Born in sanctuary during the civil upheaval of 1470, Edward inherited the throne from his father at the age of twelve in 1483. The disappearance of him and his brother meant the line of succession passed to Elizabeth.

10. Warwick Castle, stronghold of the Neville family. Edward IV was held prisoner here briefly in 1469.

Above: 11. The White Tower, Tower of London. The eleventh-century keep, where the bones of two children assumed to be the Princes in the Tower were discovered in 1674, buried under a staircase in a now-demolished building. Was this where the bodies of Elizabeth's brothers were hidden?

Right: 12. Margaret of York, Elizabeth's aunt. Elizabeth would have known Margaret in her early years at Westminster, before she left to be married to Charles the Bold, of Burgundy. Later, Margaret supported the pretender Perkin Warbeck in his attempts to claim the English throne and displace Henry VII and Elizabeth's children.

13. The Tower of London, a key royal palace of Elizabeth's childhood. Elizabeth Wydeville planned to deliver Edward V here and fled here for sanctuary during the instability of 1470–1. It was also the last known place where Elizabeth's brothers, Edward and Richard (the Princes in the Tower), were seen alive in the summer of 1483.

Above left: 14. Canterbury Cathedral, where Edward and Elizabeth went to give thanks in 1471 after their restoration to power. It was a popular destination for pilgrims; their daughter would later make offerings at the shrine of St Thomas.

Above right: 15. Modern sculpture of Edward IV from the exterior of Canterbury Cathedral.

16. Site of the Battle of Bosworth Field, 22 August 1485, where Richard III was slain by Henry Tudor and Elizabeth's future dramatically changed direction.

Above left: 17. Richard's well, where the king supposedly paused to drink on the day of the battle at Bosworth, 1485. The stone cairn was erected in 1813 and is maintained by the Fellowship of the White Boar.

Above right: 18. A modern reconstruction of the banner of Richard III flying at Bosworth Field.

Top: 19. Richard III with his queen, Anne Neville. Richard was Elizabeth's uncle, who became Protector on the death of Edward IV and then king. Elizabeth was present at his court during 1483–5 and as the health of his queen, Anne, visibly failed, rumours of a flirtation arose between uncle and niece.

Above: 20. Statue commemorating Richard III in Leicester Park.

Right: 21. Tudor stained-glass depiction of Elizabeth of York in St Nicholas church, Stanford-on-Avon, Northamptonshire. The panels were found in an old chest in Stanford Hall in the 1930s, having possibly been removed from the church and hidden during the Civil War.

22. Pembroke Castle, South Wales, birthplace of Henry Tudor in January 1457.

Above left: 23. Modern statue of Henry VI from the exterior of Canterbury Cathedral.

Above right: 24. Modern statue of Henry VII from the exterior of Canterbury Cathedral.

Above: 25. Henry Tudor, later Henry VIII. Elizabeth's second son, the robust and energetic child who delighted his parents at the age of ten by casting off his jacket and dancing. He impressed the visiting Erasmus with his learning and it is likely that Elizabeth herself was responsible for teaching him to read.

Right: 26. Raglan Castle, Monmouthshire, where the young Henry Tudor lived for a while as a ward of the Herbert family.

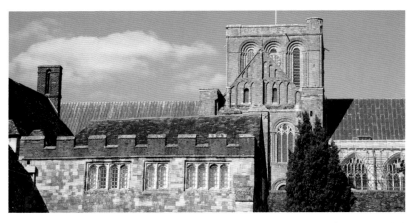

27. Winchester Deanery, Hampshire, formerly the prior's lodgings, standing before the cathedral itself. It was here, in September 1486, that Elizabeth gave birth to her first child, Arthur.

28. Winchester Cathedral, where Prince Arthur was baptised and Elizabeth was churched in 1486.

Left: 29. Margaret Tudor, later Queen of Scotland. Elizabeth's second child and eldest daughter, with whom she did not wish to part too soon, delaying her marriage for what turned out to be the final year of Elizabeth's life.

Above: 30. The Great Hall, Winchester Castle, which still houses the thirteenth-century 'Arthurian' round table. It was probably created for Edward I in around 1290.

31. The coat of arms of Lady Margaret Beaufort, featuring the red rose of Lancaster and the Beaufort portcullis and two yales, above the door of St John's College, Cambridge.

Above left: 32. Henry VII, Elizabeth's husband. Henry invaded England in 1485 and defeated Richard III in battle. He and Elizabeth were married in January 1486 and the question of their marital happiness has been long debated, although he genuinely mourned her death in 1503.

Above right: 33. Margaret Beaufort, Elizabeth's mother-in-law. An intelligent and resourceful woman with a strong claim to the throne herself, Margaret worked tirelessly to promote her only child's interests. She was a constant presence at court and in Elizabeth's life, perhaps dominating the younger woman.

34. Windsor Castle, Berkshire, a favoured palace of Elizabeth of York; she enjoyed designing and developing the gardens here.

Above: 35. The gardens at Eltham Palace, which had been renovated by Edward IV, which Elizabeth chose as the location for her royal nursery.

Right: 36. The gatehouse at Richmond, with royal coat of arms above the arch; all that remains of Henry VII's splendid new palace in the Burgundian style.

37. Remains of the Chapel to Our Lady at Walsingham, Norfolk, centre of the East Anglian Marian cult and location of pilgrimages made by Elizabeth of York.

Above: 38. The combined red and white roses of Lancaster and York in a ceiling boss at Canterbury Cathedral.

Left: 39. A red Welsh Tudor dragon from a window at St Nicholas' church, Stanford-on-Avon.

Right: 40. Tudor coat of arms from St Nicholas' church, Stanford-on-Avon.

Above: 41. Ludlow Castle, Shropshire, location of Prince Arthur's household and scene of his death in April 1502.

Left: 42. Arthur Tudor, Elizabeth's eldest son. Born eight months after his parents' wedding, Arthur symbolised the new union of Lancaster and York. He had the potential to be an impressive young king in the mould of his father but his premature death in 1502 prevented him from ever claiming the throne. Elizabeth and Henry were devastated at his loss.

Below: 43. Christ Church Cathedral, Dublin, where Lambert Simnel was crowned as Edward VI in 1487.

Bottom: 44. Modern statue of Henry VII on the side of a building at Hay-on-Wye.

45. Lady Chapel, Westminster, built between 1503 and 1509, final resting place of Elizabeth of York and Henry VII.

Above left: 46. Tudor roses, Beaufort portcullises and fleur-de-lys on the exterior of Westminster Abbey.

Above right: 47. The Queen of Hearts, which is reputed to use Elizabeth's image.

Above left: 48. Modern statue of Humanist scholar Desiderius Erasmus from the exterior of Canterbury Cathedral.

Above right: 49. The young Mary I (b.1516) granddaughter of Elizabeth of York, eldest surviving child of Henry VIII. She was the first woman to rule in her own right.

Above left: 50. The young Catherine of Aragon, Elizabeth of York's daughter-in-law.

Above right: 51. Perkin Warbeck, a pretender to the throne of England, who attempted to portray himself as Elizabeth's younger brother, Richard, Duke of York. He was received in Burgundy, France and Scotland but had less success in England. After a string of failed invasions, he was kept under careful guard before a final plot led to his execution in 1499.

seems to be crucial to the feminine role, as laid out in Pisan's *The Book of the City of Ladies*. Pisan praises domestic harmony among the rules she considers 'necessary to those who desire to live wisely and wish to have honour': a wife should love her husband and live in peace with him 'or else she will have already discovered the torments of Hell, where there is nothing but violence and tumult'. She should be humble before him in word and deed, obeying without complaint and holding her peace to the best of her ability. 'She will be overjoyed to see him and when she is with him, she will try hard to say everything that ought to please him and she will keep a happy expression on her face.' However, she acknowledges that some husbands are not deserving of this, as they behave so 'distantly' and give 'no signs of love, or very little'. In such cases, it was a woman's lot to endure a man's behaviour and make the best of the situation: 'if the wife cannot remedy the situation, she must put up with all this and dissimulate wisely ... you must live and die with him whatever he is like'. She cites the common female fear of being deserted by a husband, which would incur social shame, as people would 'mock and dishonour' her the more.[11] A woman's personal happiness was of less significance than her reputation and the fulfilment of her duties as a wife. The mid-fourteenth-century poem 'What the Goodwife Taught her Daughter' advises potential wives to be hard-working, devout, generous, serious and charitable but above all, to honour their husband: 'The man that shall thee wed before God with a ring, Love thou him and honour most of earthly thing ...' This was to be accomplished through her attitude and irreproachable lifestyle: 'fair of speech shalt thou be, glad and of mild mood, true in word and in deed and in conscience good, keep thee from sin, from villainy and from blame, and look thou bare thee so that none say of thee shame'. Her role was also one of a peacemaker: 'if any discord happen, night or day, make it no worse, mend it if thou may'.[12] Above all, these instructional texts advocate the 'Patient Griselda' model of wifedom, where the woman endures whatever suffering her husband may inflict upon her, while maintaining a smile and remaining personally above reproach. To the modern reader, such figures may appear almost saintly or martyr-like in their self-abnegation, hardly able to find any correlation with expectations in the twenty-first century.

Elizabeth would not be crowned in her own right until late in 1487. In the meantime, she was fulfilling the role of consort, a unique position as the king's wife. In effect, she was queen in all but name. She had witnessed differing models of queenship in the militant Margaret of Anjou, her own mother and the sickly Anne Neville, yet these were appearing increasingly anachronistic and Elizabeth had to forge her own regal identity, suitable to her circumstances. In 1475, Caxton printed *A Game of Chesse*, written 200 years before by Jacobus de Cessolis, where the emphases of her role were wisdom and discretion: 'a queen ought to be chaste, wyse … well-mannered and not curious', her wisdom ought to appear in her acts and speech, 'she be secrete and telle not suche thynges as ought to be holden secrete', and she should also be 'tymerous and shamefast'.[13] Given the often politically sensitive nature of her situation, this appears to be central to the maintenance of the respect and good reputation all medieval wives were to show their husbands. The 1473 *The III Consideracions Right Necesserye to the Good Governaunce of a Prince* by Geoffroi Langry de Charny also prioritised a queen's discretion; she should have regard to things 'as toucheth the honour and profyte of her lorde' and 'shulde take in hande noo greet maters with oute licence' or permission; Charny even suggested a king should not confide matters of state to his wife.[14] Once again, the female stereotype encompasses silence and obedience. Does this mean all marriages were similar?

Were all women quiet and dutiful in the face of suffering? Of course not; marriages and people in the fifteenth century were as varied as they are today and subject to personal choice and dynamics of relationships. Then and now, every woman's personal circumstances differ. Literature provides us with many exceptions to this ideal, with strong and outspoken women who clearly had the upper hand in their marriages, although these were often caricatured and feared, easy subjects for attack when they broke social or religious codes. Chaucer's works alone encompass the dichotomic nature of the female ideal where women were either revered or derided, although a significant number of clever individuals, such as May, Alisoun and the Wife of Bath, were able to outwit their men and play the marital game to their own advantage. The Wife of Bath's tale tells us that female satisfaction was achieved through control. Historical records furnish us with examples of women who openly or subtly challenged patriarchal authority and expectations; the scale of male disapproval echoed in popular ballads, songs and sayings. Much of the evidence suggests, though, that Elizabeth of York followed the traditional model of wifedom and queenship; her silence and discretion are contributing factors to her enigma, which can make her appear so elusive to modern interpretation. Soon after her wedding, though, it became clear that she had already fulfilled one key aspect of her role. She was pregnant.

6

Motherhood
1486–1487

I love the rose both red and white
Is that your pure perfect appetite?
To hear talk of them is my delight!
Joyed may we be
Our prince to see
And roses three.[1]

Elizabeth must have begun to suspect she had conceived by the early spring of 1486. For the early months of the year, the newly-weds were at Westminster as Henry continued to attend to the business of the new regime. This included orders restoring the reputation and providing for his mother-in-law, the widowed Elizabeth Wydeville. For the young wife, it was a period both of adjustment and continuity. On one hand, she had the security of being restored to the only home she had ever really known, Westminster Palace, whose familiar Great Hall, tilt-yard and royal apartments had witnessed the critical moments of her life. On the other, she was no longer the princess, legitimate or not, dependent and waiting for her moment to come. Her marriage had propelled her into the heart of events as an important figure in her own right, the representative of her husband's rule and possible intercessor on behalf of those seeking his favour. On a personal level, she was adapting to life with a man, virtually a stranger to her, to whose will she was completely subject. In addition, she had to realign her relationship with her new mother-in-law, the formidable Margaret Beaufort, who was beginning to take an increasingly prominent role in their lives. Her own mother and sisters were still close but it must have been a time when the still-fluid hierarchy of the new royal family was being established. Amid the bustle of courtly life, with all its demands, Elizabeth was adjusting to her new role as her body began to change. Perhaps at first, with all the business of the new regime, she merely felt more tired than usual but soon, certain signs would have led her to suspect there was more to her condition.

Pregnancy was not easy to establish in the fifteenth century. There were no reliable testing systems, as are readily available over the counter today. Folklore and superstition had their methods but these were as unreliable as they were unscientific. Only the appearance of certain physical symptoms might lead an expectant mother to conclude she had conceived, yet there were still no guarantees. The proliferation of common infections and untreatable illnesses could lead these symptoms to be mistaken or confused for other diseases. Even a bloated womb could signify something more sinister, while the cessation of menstruation was dependent upon nutrition and body weight. Contemporary herbals are full of remedies to bring on the 'flowers' or 'courses', suggesting that amenorrhoea must have been a common problem. Only with the child's quickening around the fourth month could a pregnancy be diagnosed with any degree of confidence. When it came to her first child, Elizabeth must have relied on the experience of her mother and mother-in-law to help confirm this. There was also a Dr Lemster, recently appointed by Henry as his court physician at a salary of £40 a year,[2] although male knowledge was limited to theory rather than practice, as the birth chamber was at this time an exclusively female zone. The signs they would have looked for were outlined in the medieval tract *Hali Meidenhed*,[3] including increased appetite, full breasts, dull eyes, swollen veins, green tongue, vomiting, strange desires and the end of the menstrual cycle. As her condition advanced, the mother's face may grow thinner or fatter, she may suffer from headaches and dizziness, stitches and backache, constipation and swelling. Women would also be warned against eating certain foods, abstaining from salty or sweet tastes, fruit and vegetables but wine and ale were far safer to drink than milk or water. She should also avoid shocks caused by loud noises, lewd or unsettling thoughts and the ill and infirm, who might transmit their defects to the unborn child. Extremes of temperature and emotion were considered potentially damaging, as was lack of sleep and sudden movement; her clothes should be unlaced and she should rest as much as possible.[4] Given the contemporary lack of medical understanding about the female reproductive system and conditions required for a woman to successfully carry a child to term, it is unsurprising that such a wealth of superstitions and customs were employed to explain a process which must have often resulted in unexplained losses. Evidence suggests that Elizabeth was cautious during these months. While Henry was travelling in the north that summer, in response to threats of rebellion, she retired to Winchester with her retinue to await the birth. It was a deliberate choice.

It seems that Henry Tudor made a conscious, early effort to associate his new regime with ancient myths and stories woven around the legend of the sixth-century King Arthur. The significance of the Arthurian inheritance had been building over the centuries, with the Breton tribes of Wales and Cornwall believing in his return and later works placing him at the centre of a world of chivalry and ritual that appealed to the Tudors. Henry had been born at Pembroke Castle in Wales and spent his early years at Raglan in Monmouthshire. His paternal grandfather, Owen Tudor, claimed descent from Arthur and he had marched under the banner of a red dragon, the Pen Draig, or Pendragon, at Bosworth. Breton minstrels and early Welsh texts such as *Culhwch and Olwen* of 1100 had been drawing on the legend long before the Tudors, spawning a rich tradition of intertextuality and spurious fantasy. The possibility of Arthur's return, or that of his descendant, in times of national trial, was mentioned by William of Malmesbury in the early twelfth century but it was Chretien de Troyes' new genre of chivalric romance which added the courtly veneer and ritual to existing legends of battles and conquests. Romances of the 1200s and 1300s, as well as the Welsh *Black Book of Caernarvon* and *Mabinogion*, sought to connect royal lineage with ancient kings and promote values of chivalry. The association of Arthur with Winchester began simultaneously, with Geoffrey of Monmouth claiming Arthur was crowned nearby at Silchester, which had been occupied since Roman times as 'Calleba' (not too unlike Excalibur). Arthurian legends were a favourite of Edward I who had been present at the supposed opening of the king's Glastonbury tomb and held 'round table' tournaments; the present round table in Winchester's Great Hall has been carbon dated to 1250–90, corresponding with one such event held near Winchester by Edward to celebrate his daughter's betrothal in April 1290. Even Elizabeth's father, Edward IV, had been drawn to Arthurian ideals and produced genealogies to justify his wresting the throne from Henry VI. He commissioned an illustrated genealogy in 1470, tracing his line back through Arthur, the sons of Noah and into the garden of Eden itself![5] In 1483, John Lydgate wrote in his *Fall of Princes* that Arthur shall return 'out of fayrye' and reign, while Caxton's printing of Malory's *Morte d'Arthur* placed 'the city of Camelot that is in English, Winchester'. However, Malory had also set the fabled court of Arthur in the Tower during Fauconberg's revolt and Excalibur drawn out of a stone outside St Paul's; such associations were convenient conventions, with significant locations such as Jerusalem often moved about in literature, art and maps, in order to serve artistic or patronage purposes. In 1485–6, it suited Henry to exploit this myth.

Elizabeth's preparations were in safe hands. Although Henry himself was away, he had left his mother, Margaret Beaufort, in charge of making the necessary practical arrangements, on which she had been working since Easter. As soon as the child had quickened, she began to draw up a set of ordinances, outlining the protocol and detail of the lying-in chamber, from location to the number of cushions required. As one of the richest monasteries in the land, St Swithin's Priory, Winchester, would have had no problem catering for royal guests. Elizabeth was to lie-in at the Prior's House, now the deanery, a three-storey stone building within the Close walls, with an arched entrance portico. The new prior, Thomas Silkested, put his great hall at her disposal, which was rapidly transformed into a bedroom. The chamber was hung with heavy tapestries, covering the walls, ceiling and windows, chosen carefully for their subject matter. Provoking or disturbing scenes, including hunts and wild or mythological beasts, were rejected for fear of their startling effects, in favour of scenes of love and romance. A mother looking upon violent scenes might transmit some of her emotional response to her unborn child, irrevocably shaping its features or character. One window alone was left uncovered, so that she may have light and look outside. A huge temporary bed was prepared, where Elizabeth would labour. A giant, 8 foot by 10, it lay in the middle of the room, stuffed with wool and down, covered with crimson satin and cloth of gold panes. Later she would move to the feather bed embroidered with gold crowns and the royal arms. A round mantle, or shawl, of crimson velvet lined with ermine was made to keep

Elizabeth warm during her coming ordeal.[6] As her family gathered round, her circumstances cannot have been more in contrast to those in which her mother gave birth, in sanctuary, sixteen years before. Much has been made of Margaret Beaufort's dominant role over her young daughter-in-law but the inexperienced expectant mother may well have been grateful for the time and care taken to provide for her. Beside the luxury, Elizabeth's lying-in was marked by court ceremony. She would have made a formal retreat, with prayers and blessings, attended by a crowd of her ladies about a month before the expected date of her delivery. After that, no men would be admitted as she waited for her child to arrive. On the night of 19 September, her labour pains began.

Without pain relief, there was little Elizabeth's ladies could do to alleviate her sufferings beyond herbal remedies, superstition and prayer. The properties of certain plants were passed down through the female oral tradition, from mothers to daughters, regarding all aspects of health, especially at such critical times as birth and recovery. During her weeks of waiting, Elizabeth would have had access to the best remedies available, designed to ease and soothe her aching body, some of which may have had significant effects. One treatment for an expectant mother was to bathe for half an hour in the morning, then lie in bed and be anointed with salves of mallow, motherwell, lily, camomile, linseed, fenugreek and hen's fat; she should drink white wine and almond oil, bound by an egg. For the last-minute pains and practice contractions, she may have chewed fennel, aniseed or cinnamon; to relax her bowels and prepare for the birth, sorrel, spinach and beetroot were added to the existing list of herbs. As labour began, her abdomen might be rubbed with creams made from a mixture of brandy, distilled marjoram and saffron to aid contractions. Of those herbs and flowers used to help lessen the intensity of contractions, including the oils of lilies, almonds and roses, cyclamen, columbine, aquilegia, wild thyme and musk, some must have really helped, such as meadowsweet, which would later be synthesised and called aspirin. Other potions included the more bizarre ants' eggs, powdered eel liver, virgin's hair, ale and red cow's milk.

Religion and superstition also had comforts to offer the labouring mother. As a devout Catholic, Elizabeth would have offered her prayers to the Virgin Mary and a number of saints who may be willing to intercede on her behalf. A crowded reliquary in the birth chamber would display a range of artefacts such as holy bones and girdles, phials of blood, tears or milk and shards of the true cross: she may well have held the famous Westminster girdle, supposedly made and used by the Virgin Mary, but these were accessible only to the elite. Agnus Dei were also popular religious tokens for those who could get hold of them; they were wax discs stamped with the image of a lamb and flag, blessed by the Pope and supposedly offering protection from sudden death and the malice of demons. Simpler, folkloric methods were also available. It was customary for mothers to remove all fastenings: rings, buckles, bracelets and laces were thought to mimic a state of strangulation in the body which could be transmitted to the child. Likewise, no one in the chamber would cross their legs, arms or fingers. Tied around a woman's belly, magic girdles and pieces of paper inscribed with 'charms' offered protection and belts hung with cowrie shells. In her hand, a mother might clasp an 'eagle stone' or aetites, a larger stone which contained a smaller stone within its hollow centre, rattling when shaken, worn on the arm during pregnancy and transferred to the abdomen when labour began. In some places, the skin of a wild ox was tied about a woman's thigh and snakeskin or hartskin belts were worn, the placebo effects of which can only be imagined, in the absence of modern forms of pain relief.

With rates of maternal and infant mortality high, giving birth was a dangerous and terrifying experience for a young woman of any class. Varied modern estimates[7] cite the likelihood of maternal mortality at between 1–2 per cent per pregnancy and between 6 and 7 per cent across a woman's childbearing years so long as the delivery was relatively straightforward. However, breech and unusual foetal positions could almost guarantee long-term maternal damage, if not death, and the possibilities of fatal post-partum bleeding and infection decreased the chances of survival. Young, inexperienced women, whose limbs were supposedly stiff and inflexible, were thought to be particularly in danger. No record is made of the midwives in attendance on Elizabeth, although at least one would undoubtedly have been present. They were indispensable as the only females allowed to physically intervene during the process and may have brought their own 'groaning chair' and tourniquets to expel the foetus, beside their own expertise. It is possible that Elizabeth was attended by her mother's favourite midwife, Marjory Cobbe, who had attended Elizabeth Wydeville's final confinement only six years before. Finally, on the morning of 20 September, Elizabeth's child was successfully delivered. It was a boy. His name was already chosen: they called him Arthur.

Elizabeth was still lying in while her son was christened. It was the custom for women to spend about a month in recovery, with their 'good sisters' or 'gossips', while godparents organised the baptism. Arthur's first few days passed in his mother's chamber, where he was washed down with oil, wine or butter to close his pores, fed a spoonful of sugared water to aid his speech and had his belly anointed with aloe or frankincense. Then he would have been swaddled and laid down to sleep in one of the two impressive cradles in the room, carved and decorated with gold paint and the royal arms. He would be attended by rockers and wet-nurses as Elizabeth recovered. Outside, bonfires burned and *Te Deums* were sung in the cathedral. The children of the priory and Hyde Abbey were paid to perform the '*Christi Descendus ad Infernos*' to celebrate the occasion.[8] News quickly spread through the city and beyond, that a male heir had been born and preparations were made at once, along lines laid out by Margaret Beaufort, for his reception in Winchester Cathedral. Like the bedchamber, the walls and floors were spread with tapestry or carpet and the silver font from Canterbury Cathedral was set on a raised platform and lined with Rennes linen. The city turned out to see the solemn procession, which was captured in an engraving by an unknown artist, showing no less than five people carrying the baby's train under a fringed canopy. He was wrapped in crimson cloth of gold furred with ermine. Elizabeth's family played prominent roles in her absence, with her mother being one of the named godparents. Following the baptism, singing, gifts and offerings at the shrine of St Swithin, Elizabeth's sister Cecily returned the child to his mother to the sound of trumpets and minstrels playing. Equal ritual was employed for Elizabeth's own churching, a ritual that cleansed her from the process of birth and signalled her return to society. It was delayed a little as she suffered from some sort of 'ague' or fever in the following weeks but she was soon strong enough to attend the abbey and recite the relevant prayers. From there, she went to sit in the great chamber under the cloth of Estate, as a mark of her status. By the end of October, the court had left Winchester and moved to Greenwich, where the couple celebrated their first Christmas.

A further year passed before Elizabeth was crowned in her own right. Her pregnancy, followed by unrest in the realm, postponed the event until the end of November 1487 but when it finally took place, her Coronation was a vindication for her mother and the Wydevilles as well as the long-awaited recognition her popularity demanded. The first piece of ceremony was a procession along the Thames from Greenwich to the Tower, dramatic and exciting in its memorable pageantry. Again the Arthurian theme was deployed, with one barge decorated as a huge red dragon spouting real flames; others were adorned with silk banners and streamers, while the occupants witnessed pageants and listened to musicians play along their route. Elizabeth passed the night with Henry in the Tower, as was traditional, before dressing in white cloth of gold and an ermine mantle, with gold and silk laces and tassels. Her hair was covered in a headdress surmounted by a gold circlet set with jewels. She travelled in the middle of a long procession, in a litter overflowing with more cloth of gold and large, downy pillows; the horses of her guardsmen were embroidered with the Yorkist white rose and sunburst motifs. Her popularity with Londoners was never in doubt and the newly swept streets thronged with well-wishers, while the houses had been decorated with brightly coloured cloths and carpets. The mayor, aldermen and members of guilds wore their finest liveries, in crimson velvets or other rich fabrics, while heralds announced their approach and children dressed as angels sang songs which she paused to hear along the route.

It was a remarkable exercise in public relations. Perhaps the date, St Catherine's Day, 25 November, was deliberately chosen, as according to *Mirk's Festival* of 1486, the saint was a 'kynges doghtyr' of 'so gentyll blod' that she 'sette noght by the pompe of thys world'.[9] But pomp was what London saw in November 1487. The day's personal success for Elizabeth was all the sweeter for the privations of her youth and the knowledge it brought of her enduring position in the hearts of her subjects. Hers was very much a London-based story, with its citizens witnessing the rise and fall of her fortunes, often in conjunction with their own; her Coronation was a reminder of the relationship that had bound her father to the capital as well as the grief and confusion surrounding the loss of her brothers. While maintaining his own right to rule through conquest,

Henry understood the enduring power of his wife's claim and the affection in which she was held. This close personal contact with the people, coupled with the visual trappings of wealth and majesty, drawn out over three days of celebrations, was an astute method of restating the success of their union. Hall claims Henry organised the occasion out of the 'perfect love and sincere affection' in which he held his wife. Such was her popularity that the crowd needed to be restrained around Westminster Abbey, as Elizabeth approached, the following day. There, she was anointed twice before the huge assembly of nobles, once on the chest and once on the head before receiving a ring for the fourth finger of her right hand, a gold crown, sceptre and rod of gold. From there, the procession passed back into Westminster's Great Hall, where a magnificent feast was served in the Burgundian courtly style.

An observing herald recorded the arrangements and menu of the occasion. First, onlookers were cleared away by horseback riders, to make way for the guests: lords, bishops and abbots; barons, knights and nobles, beside London's mayor, aldermen, merchants and distinguished citizens, were seated either side of the dais on which Elizabeth would be served, flanked by the Archbishop of Canterbury, her aunt the Duchess of Bedford and paternal grandmother Cecily Neville. Another two noblewomen sat under the table at her feet the whole time to assist her discreetly. Henry and Margaret Beaufort watched the event from a concealed balcony, where a lattice and arras gave them a degree of privacy from the carefully 'selected strangers' who were gathered on an erected stage in order to watch. Trumpeters and minstrels announced the arrival of each course, which was brought in on the shoulders of servants, in solemn procession. Both courses were preceded by a 'warner', not too dissimilar to the 'subtleties' that were served at the end; the latter were elaborate decorations of pastry, spun sugar or marchpane (marzipan) carved into heraldic devices, buildings or religious, historical and literary allegories. The expensive ingredients and ambitious presentation of the meal was an important extension by which the monarchy could further delineate its status. Elizabeth's first course, which was typically a mixture of sweet and savoury tastes, included boar, venison, pheasant, swan, rooster, lamprey, crane, kid, carp, perch, rabbit, tarts, custard and fruits. While the diners paused, music was played and ballads composed. The second course was just as impressive, if not more, with meat decorated in lozenges of gold leaf, castles made of jelly and a peacock re-dressed in its full plumage. After fruit, wafers, wine and spices, the guest of honour finally retired. The following day would involve attending mass, sitting in state in Parliament, more sumptuous feasting and dancing, before Elizabeth and her retinue retired to Greenwich and normal court business was resumed. One person had missed the celebrations though: her mother, Elizabeth Wydeville, was not present, having retired to Bermondsey Abbey earlier in the year.

The dowager queen's absence has caused much speculation among historians. She was present at the birth of Arthur and would be again when Elizabeth had her second child in 1489 but her removal to a life of religious seclusion has been interpreted as a punishment for a range of possible imagined 'crimes'. Some have seen this as Henry's delayed revenge on her for having come to terms with Richard III four years previously, while others implicate her in the uprisings of that year. Bacon was at a loss to explain what he saw as her 'arrest', being so 'severely handled' upon a 'sudden disclosure or mutability of the king's mind' unless she was involved. The reason he gives is that the widow felt the recent marriage had 'not advanced but depressed' her daughter. It would seem to stretch plausibility to suggest that at the moment of her family's triumph, Elizabeth Wydeville would back the claim of a pretender against that of her own 'dearest daughter' and infant grandson.

Far more likely was that this very devout woman willingly embraced religious retirement after a lifetime of suffering and turmoil. In 1486 she had leased Cheneygates House, within the Close of Westminster Palace, and her removal a year later to Bermondsey, just across the river, hardly put her out of touch with her family. Given that she only had five years left to live, she may equally have been suffering from ill health. However, it is true that her surviving son by her first marriage, the Marquis of Dorset, was arrested during the revolt for reasons that remain unclear; he was released, though, in time to attend his half-sister's Coronation and went on to live until 1501. It is unsurprising, then, that later historians have sought to associate Elizabeth Wydeville with the 1487 rebels: their declarations must have been difficult for her to hear, considering that their leader claimed to be one of her dead sons.

Henry VIII's court historian, Polydore Vergil, describes how Elizabeth forfeited all her lands and properties in 1487, which were reassigned to her daughter. This has been widely interpreted as a punishment in the light of her perceived character but no evidence at all supports this theory. Having leased Cheneygates and with intentions to retire to Bermondsey, it may well have been with her co-operation, or even at her suggestion, that certain revenues were withdrawn from her and given to her daughter, in order to reflect their new roles. Henry continued to be respectful to the dowager queen and referred to her as his 'dear mother in law' and she was free to visit court and be visited by her daughters. In 1487 Henry even considered marrying her to James III of Scotland, although this was halted by that king's death the following year. He would hardly have considered putting her in such a position of power if he distrusted her, assuming he was serious; Scottish queenship would have provided her with the distance, funds and support to prove a real threat to the new regime were she so minded. A life at Bermondsey Abbey was hardly a punishment. In such beautiful peaceful surroundings, the ageing widow could escape from the tumultuous life and string of bereavements she had suffered; by late fifteenth-century standards, she was old at fifty and no longer at the centre of events. It seems quite logical that she would wish for peace and quiet while still remaining within the compass of her family's life. In 1490, Henry increased her pension to £400 a year and she was given various grants and payments to aid her expenses. Recently, Alison Weir asserted that Elizabeth Wydeville 'was deprived of estates leaving her no choice but to retire to a nunnery' but the question of choice cannot be substantiated; perhaps she agreed or even offered to hand them over because of her plans to retire. This would be entirely in keeping with her piety and the previous sacrifices she had made for her children. It doesn't accord at all with the possibility that she would act against her eldest daughter and grandson; ambitious as they may be, the Wydevilles were a very close family and her actions during the reign of Richard III showed that the welfare of her children came first.

The dowager queen's reputation has suffered since the day her clandestine marriage was uncovered in 1464. Contemporaries disliked her large, ambitious family who benefited from the patronage of Edward IV at the expense of more established nobles resentful of social upstarts. This was the key to the quarrels that underpinned the previous harmonious relationship between the cousins Edward and the Earl of Warwick. There is no doubt that Elizabeth promoted her kinfolk, yet this was true of all people of the time; family connections, especially through marriage, were a desirable method of self-advancement. Other contemporary families, like the Nevilles, were no less ambitious, but the Wydevilles were more disliked at the time for having no close royal connection through blood, although her mother Jacquetta had been first married to a son of Henry IV and was a descendant of King John. The dowager queen can hardly be blamed for having a large family or being in a prominent position to be able to help them. Nor can she be blamed for entering into a marriage that elevated her and her existing children so far above the status of penurious widowhood. No doubt, her ambitious siblings and cousins annoyed the established court; as the rash of behavioural manuals of the era testify, the acquisition of correct manners could prove a gateway to new worlds for those who were ambitiously minded. Hatred of the Wydevilles tapped into a larger mistrust of the rising middle classes that had been snowballing since the fourteenth century. The responsibility lay with Edward IV to manage the family's rise and the hostility it engendered.

As an individual, Elizabeth Wydeville's reputation still evokes extreme responses. She has suffered from the negativity of later accounts that built unquestioningly on contemporary jealousy, yet modern historians still make emotive, subjective assertions about her character. No doubt she had enemies; there may be truth in some of their claims but these must be balanced against the very powerful instruments of slander that had been employed against her for political and personal motives. While More's Elizabeth is sympathetic, Hall had her as the typical weak woman, 'blinded by avaricious affection', her 'mutable mind ... seduced by flattering words', and Bacon more sinisterly claimed 'no one could hold the book so well to prompt and instruct the stage play as she could'. Both detractors were born after the queen's death. Recorded and interpreted exclusively by men, her character has been determined by the gender politics of her day, in terms of female stereotypes and expectations; as Christine de Pisan pointed out before the queen's birth,

> A clarkes custume is when he enditeth
> Of women, be it prose, rhyme or verse
> Seyn they be wicked, all honour be the reverse.[10]

The twentieth century has judged Elizabeth no less harshly: to G. R. Elton she is 'meddlesome and interfering',[11] Paul Murray Kendall sees her as 'arrogant and vain',[12] Henry VII's recent biographer Thomas Penn pictures a 'cold lynx-eyed beauty' whose 'arriviste' family rushed to court 'scrabbling'[13] for favour, while J. R. Lander summarises her as an 'unworthy', 'arrogant and avaricious' queen.[14] Yet her family was no more grasping than the Nevilles; perhaps their worse reputation arises from their unforgivable sin of being headed by a woman. Her behaviour has been judged by modern standards: her relatives' ambition is indecent and immoral, while her supposed aloofness has not been set in the context of her need to forge an identity as queen and distance herself from her Lancastrian past. Likewise, the hours she spent feasting at her Coronation banquet, while waited on at bended knee, has incited accusations of pride and arrogance rather than being considered within the ritual tradition of ceremonial, so favoured at the time. The new queen would have had little choice about such procedures; the late medieval court was not the place for an outsider to introduce an element of modern equality. She had to establish herself from within its strict codes. After such a distance it appears over-simplistic and partisan to draw such vehement conclusions about the character of Elizabeth Wydeville. Her retirement into a life of religious seclusion and the uprisings of 1487 have provided food for erroneous speculation which may have misled historical interpretation away from the true character of this elusive woman.

7

Married Life
1487–1500

England now rejoice, for joyous may thou be
To see thy King so flowering in dignity.[1]

Henry VII has a reputation for austerity. Writing in 1622, Francis Bacon claimed that 'for his pleasures, there is no news of them'.[2] The popular stereotype prevails of the thin-faced, careworn king poring over his account books, looking sidelong out of later portraits with his thin lips, suspicious eyes and grasping hands.[3] This enduring image makes it difficult to imagine him dancing, laughing or jousting like his colourful son, Henry VIII. But Bacon was wrong; plenty of evidence exists to suggest that, although Henry was careful with money, especially at the end of his reign, the life Elizabeth would have known with him was one of pleasure and patronage. She would have known a very different man, more in line with Leland's 'king so flowering in dignity'. Their court was filled with musicians, poets and actors and Henry spent lavishly on a programme of building to create and modernise a number of pleasure palaces and retreats for his family to enjoy. This rumoured austerity has also been extended to his marriage. Bacon again asserts the king was 'no very indulgent husband' due to his aversion to the house of York, while the pro-Ricardian, Horace Walpole, writing in the 1760s, felt able to state with certainty that 'Henry was a tyrannic husband and ungrateful master'.[4] Even some of the king's contemporaries formed this opinion, with the Spanish envoy writing in 1498, that Elizabeth, a 'very noble woman',[5] was kept in subjection by her mother-in-law, while some modern historians assert this was a deliberate policy on Henry's behalf to keep his wife from meddling in politics as her mother supposedly had.

To what extent is this a true reflection of their marriage? Although cultural expectations of marital ideals survive, it is impossible now to disentangle and apply the ingredients of what constituted a 'happy' marriage in the late fifteenth century in any realistic sense. We simply do not know how Elizabeth and Henry felt. Nor can we assume their emotions were constant; no doubt, as with all marriages, they experienced their own version of 'for better or for worse'. Although the *Ballad of Lady Bessie* describes the pair as 'lovers' during the reign of Richard III, this is far from the truth; actually, they had probably not met, or else met years ago as children. Like most fifteenth-century couples, they did not commit their emotions to paper and their actions were open to interpretation from those who saw them only from the outside. Their status created an almost impenetrable distance and obstacle to interpretation, then and now. However, Privy Purse accounts make clear that Elizabeth certainly enjoyed considerable pleasures and benefits from her union. Small pieces of evidence suggest that the couple were far from estranged and while it is anachronistic to expect such a union to be a love match, the royal marriage contained many companionate elements and appears, on balance, to have been mutually beneficial. 'Love', by the varying definitions of any era, was not considered an essential requirement for success. Of course there is more to a 'happy' marriage than material continuity and security; the pursuit of the question as to whether the queen was 'happy' fails to take account of the specific circumstances of her rank and the formation of the union. The expectation and definition of a 'happy' marriage would vary between couples and over the duration of the match. On a personal level, its subjectivity is dependent on the individual, often unspoken, expectations of any man and any woman across time. Even to ask the question of whether Elizabeth of York's marriage was a 'happy' one is misleading, yet the issue must be addressed due to the persistence of claims made to the contrary.

Gradually Elizabeth would have become aware of the character of the man she had married. Little personal glimpses of Henry emerge from the accounts of others: in 1488 the Spanish ambassador noted his habits: 'the king, according to his usual manner, took his bonnet off his head, and said the most flattering things' and later thought the 'speech of the king was like precious jewels'.[6] The ambassadors also observed Elizabeth herself at this time who, once again, did not disappoint in terms of courtly expectation: 'we also went at an unexpected hour to the queen, whom we found with two and thirty companions of angelical appearance, and all we saw there seemed very magnificent, and in splendid style, as was suitable for the occasion'.[7] In 1497, the Milanese envoy was shown into Henry's presence as he stood absolutely still behind a chair of cloth of gold and found him 'wonderful', in a 'most rich' collar of rows of pearls and gems. He judged the king to be 'cautious and reflects deeply all his proceedings', 'hard of credence' and suspicious of unsubstantiated news.[8] The pair were not thrust into close proximity at once; Henry's early absence in the north was essential to consolidate his rule and establish peace in the realm; the new king must see and be seen. The list of his travels that year is exhaustive: March saw him in Ware, Royston, Canterbury, Peterborough, Stamford and Ely, while in April he was at Lincoln, Nottingham, York and Doncaster, allowing for a few days' travel between. From September onwards, though, his presence in Winchester was increasingly noted as he awaited Arthur's birth: he was in the city and presumably with Elizabeth, from the first to the sixth of the month, again for ten days at the end, on 4 October and between the 13th and 24th, coinciding with his son's arrival.

For a while, this busy, energetic man may have seemed distant to his wife. Much of the time they spent together during this early stage would have been in the company of others, or restricted by protocol or the conditions of pregnancy. Kings and queens also had separate establishments within the same palaces; they might be under the same roof but their dining, living and sleeping quarters were individual to them. To come together and share a meal in private or spend the night together required a degree of foresight and planning; their lives were not so closely lived as those of modern couples. The Great Chronicle captures them in 1492, dining at the same stone table decorated with napery (linen) and lights, while being served separate messes or portions.[9] This distance may either have helped or hindered their union but it meant Elizabeth had time to adjust to her role as wife. The question of her happiness or loneliness, the hints of the individual behind the royal front are almost impossible to capture: as a queen, Elizabeth would never have been alone. Surrounded by her ladies, with her devotion to religion and her children, as well as the bustle of court life and petitions from subjects, she was busy enough. This degree of physical distance between man and wife should not necessarily be taken as evidence of coldness or dislike; her increasing pregnancies and his wish to be with her during times of duress indicates that the couple did desire each other's company. Such arrangements were part of the nature of kingship: Elizabeth had witnessed that in her own parents' match.

There may have been a slow start to the marriage, with Elizabeth's early pregnancy coinciding with Henry's absence in the north, but the couple soon found they had much in common. Elizabeth must have felt a degree of cultural continuity in Henry's activities: like her father, he followed the tradition of Burgundian culture in courtly ritual, revelry, building and patronage. There were not unlimited funds; some thrift was required behind the scenes but ample spending was a common feature of the family's routine, establishing a lifestyle that was commensurate with Elizabeth's childhood and status, as well as being settled and secure. Appearances mattered; in May 1491, Henry paid the huge sum of £3,800 for cloth of gold, pearls and precious stones to adorn his family. His queen was the regular recipient of grants and gifts, including robes furred with ermine, velvets, russet cloths and garters with gold letters in 1489. In comparison with the penury and uncertainty of her early years and late teens, Elizabeth had achieved a degree of equilibrium that must have been welcome. Evenings and festivals were enlivened by feasting and performance, while the court maintained its peripatetic existence between a number of royal palaces and properties. Initially, their favoured residences were Westminster, Windsor, Greenwich and Richmond Manor. Elizabeth would have spent most of her time divided between these familiar places, while political business could take her husband further afield; in 1490, he also visited Canterbury, Maidstone, Eltham, Woking, Ewelme and Mortlake, while the following year saw him at Norwich, Colchester, Bury St Edmunds, Northampton, Leicester, Tewkesbury, Gloucester, Bristol, Wells, Marlborough and Shrewsbury. Elizabeth accompanied him on some of his travels, dependent on her stage of pregnancy, but her life was far more London-based. The huge body of the court comprised many hundreds of people of varying ranks, from Elizabeth's personal servants and waiting women, through to those who fulfilled the basic duties of washing, cleaning, cooking and repairs. Their proximity within palaces that offered little privacy or sanitation required constant moving; after a month or so, their huge consumption and the proportionate waste meant an increased danger of disease and degree of squalor. Then, tapestries and carpets were rolled up, soft furnishings loaded into crates and furniture dismantled for the transfer to their next location. Henry VII's Privy Purse expenses record some of the necessary arrangements: *56s 6d* was paid to a Jack Haute for transporting 'diverse necessaries ... as tables, cheese, glasses and other' in January 1492. Elizabeth would have overseen this process indirectly, allowing the machinery of her court to carry out the required hard work while she made her progress separately down the Thames to her next residence.

The revels and disguisings Elizabeth had always enjoyed as a child were to continue under her husband's reign. Celebrating the Christmas season of 1487 at Greenwich, the court enjoyed the antics of jesters, dancers and singers in unusual costumes, while the mysterious disguisers remained silent and intrigued all with their strange movements. Henry also appointed certain figures to oversee the entertainment; regular payments were made throughout Elizabeth's lifetime for those who performed on a single or regular basis. On Christmas Eve 1491, the court records include a payment of £5 to Ringley, Lord of Misrewle, who also received a further £5 the following October. It was not until 31 December 1494, though, that mention was first made of the office of Master of Revels, which was to become a significant position under the later Tudors. By 1501 Jacques Hawte and William Pawne were paid to organise disguisings and morrises or 'morisques', perhaps indicating their Spanish influence, to be performed at the wedding of Catherine of Aragon. Comedy was popular. A 'Spanyard that played the fole' received £2, while £4 was given to the King of France's fole in 1500 but only *6s 8d* to Thomas Blakall the king's fole. In 1501,

6s 8d was given to a fellow for eating coals! Elizabeth had her own fool, named Patch, who receives regular rewards in the Privy Purse expenses in the 1490s. Twelfth Night was kept with more playful relish than 25 December, which saw more religious observance; on 6 January 1494, a feast was held at Westminster, attended by the mayor of London, after which the court witnessed a disguising of twelve ladies and twelve gentlemen. The hall was hung with arras and 'staged round about with timber' so people could see, in a way reminiscent of early theatre in the round. It was followed by a banquet where the king was served forty dishes of diverse confections and the queen an equal number, followed by wine, wafers and spices. The play, as it came to be recognised in the Elizabethan era, had not yet evolved from medieval miracle and mystery cycles, pageants, recited ballads and disguisings, although a payment of over £1 was recorded as having been made in July 1500 for the delivery of a play on 'Sonday night'. The reward given to a Clemence Clark in November 1496 'for the writing of thamitye of Flanders' may have been for an early type of drama.[10]

Musicians could also expect to be appreciated at Henry VII's court. Regular payments were made to singers and players, like the £1 to a child that played on the recorder and £1 to Cecily of York's minstrels; among other recipients were the Northampton and Essex waytes, a piper on the bagpipes, a damsel that daunceth, to one that had his bull baited, to Newark for making a song, to a merchant for delivering a pair of organs, a Welsh rhymer, morris dancers, a woman that sang with a fiddle and to Cornyshe in 1493 for a 'prophecy'. The last reference was probably to the composer, poet and actor who was to become prominent at the courts of Elizabeth and her son. Almost her exact contemporary, William Cornish would later be employed as the third recorded Master of the Children of the Chapel Royal as well as providing various dramatic entertainments for the royal family, in which he acted and sang. He would form part of the newly created 'players of the Chapel Royal' with access to the Great Wardrobe for costumes and would entertain the court with early 'plays'. He probably arrived at Henry's court under the aegis of his father, a composer of the same name, and took a position as a Gentleman of the Chapel. In the Christmas festivities of 1493–4 he played the part of St George in a disguising by Walter Alwyn, riding into Westminster Hall on horseback to deliver a speech and song before slaying a fire-breathing dragon. Following the pageant, twelve couples danced to the drum and fiddle, the ladies elegantly gliding while the men leaped so that gold spangles fell from their costumes. Henry also patronised the first company of English players, led by John English, who performed on special courtly occasions, and created the Prince's Players for his son. The early playwright Henry Medwall was also composing at this time, under the patronage of Cardinal Morton, producing *Fulgens and Lucrece*, the first known secular play in English, performed at Lambeth Palace in around 1497, and *Nature* before 1500.[11] Contrary to the king's reputation for austerity, it appears that regular entertainments and patronage of the performing arts played a significant role at his court. Other leisure expenses included payments for his playing at cards, at dice, tennis, chess or for shooting at the butts, where he lost £13 4s in 1492. In the same year, 7s 4d was paid to a man named Carter 'for writing a book', while in September 1496, £3 6s 8d rewarded a blind poet and a further gift was given in 1497 to 'a Welsh rhymer'. Money was also given to a man who brought the king a lion, another a leopard and one who brought him a box of 'pomand' or scented pomanders.

Henry also undertook ambitious building programmes which reflected his family's interests. Woodstock, the Tower, Windsor, Baynard's Castle and Greenwich all were developed or redesigned by him in the Burgundian style, although little now survives of the changes or relevant documentation. Descriptions of one palace, though, reflect his interests and tastes. Henry enjoyed hunting and hawking, gambling and games; the new palace he built at Richmond, or 'Rich Mount', costing £20,000, included dancing chambers and 'houses of pleasure to disport in, at chess, tables, dice and cards', as well as butts for archers and tennis courts. The smaller Shene manor had stood on the site originally. It had been given to Elizabeth Wydeville by Edward IV and she held it until the reign of Richard, after which it reverted to Henry and became a popular royal residence. In May 1492, a great tournament was held at the manor; Bacon says to 'warm the blood of his nobility and gallants' in preparation for his French war later that year. Such affairs could be elaborate and costly; in 1494, £66 was paid to the challengers and the same amount to the defenders at a similar joust. The manor house was destroyed by fire while the royal family were staying there for Christmas in 1497: Bacon says it started at night near the royal apartments and that most of the building and contents were destroyed. A contemporary account is more specific, describing how it began about nine o'clock at night on St Thomas' Day, 29 December: 'began a great fire within the king's lodging and so continued until twelve of the night and more ... great part of the old building was burned and much harm done in hangings, as in rich beds, curtains and other appertaining to such a noble court'.[12] The Venetian ambassador thought it had started when a beam caught light in the queen's apartments and that it was 'not due to malice'.[13] No one was hurt, although Henry, Elizabeth, several of their children and Margaret Beaufort had been on the scene.

An impressive new rebuilding programme was begun in the Burgundian style: some of the privy lodgings may have survived, with the new building following the old foundations. However, in appearance, it was innovative. In 1500, the village of Sheen or 'Shene' was commanded to change its name to Richmond, as if to signify the transformation, and the new walls began to rise. The palace was built from white stone with octagonal towers topped by pepper-pot domes; it stood three stories tall around a series of inner courts and bays filled with oriel windows. In 1505, a payment was made of £133 6s 8d to Henry Smyth for finishing the new tower at Richmond and paving its galleries and ledges. The accommodation inside was luxurious for the time; separate dining rooms for king and queen allowed them a degree of privacy from the general court and servants' meal times, as did the livery kitchen with its pyramid roof, visible on Wynegaerde's map, which catered only for the masses; the royal family had their own separate kitchen. A bridge over the moat linked the privy lodgings to a central courtyard flanked by the chapel and great hall, while sophisticated plumbing allowed running water to spout from taps on demand. The process of decoration brought together some of the most skilled craftsmen from across Europe and reinforced the iconography of the dynasty. The chapel had a chequered timber ceiling with plasterwork rose and portcullis motifs and was full of saints' relics, jewels and plate. The hall was hung with tapestries of battles and decorated with statues of famous English kings and everything was carved with red roses. A great court of red brick housed the wardrobe and accommodation for courtiers while the decoration extended to the library full of illuminated manuscripts, bound and decorated with roses and other symbols. A contemporary visitor described 'wyndowes full lightsome and commodious', courtyards paved with 'marbill in whoes mydill there is a conducte' (fountain), passages and galleries 'pavyed, glasid and poyntid, besett with bagges of gold' as well as 'pleasaunt dauncyng chambers … most richely enhaunggid'.[14] Outside, the orchards and gardens were encircled by a two-storey walkway, while topiary mythical beasts; 'lyons, dragons and such othir divers kynde ... properly fachyoned and corved'[15] watched over vines and trees bearing exotic fruit. In 1501, the celebrations following Arthur's wedding to Catherine of Aragon took place there and Wynegaerde's sketch of 1562 shows a fantasia of turrets and gardens.

The royal family continued to expand. Henry and Elizabeth spent Christmas 1488 at Sheen, then still a fourteenth-century manor house. Surrounded by friends and family, the old moated royal lodgings allowed them some privacy from the rest of the court and there must have been much feasting and pageantry. By the following Easter, they were resident at Hertford Castle, built on a Norman site by the River Lea, which Henry had conferred on his wife. Here, Elizabeth may have begun to suspect that she was pregnant again. At the end of October 1489, she went into confinement at Westminster after hearing mass and taking a ceremonial meal of spices and sweet wine. The queen's main chamber, with its attendant chapel and views across the river, would have been prepared in advance, with the late summer months seeing a flurry of activity as carpenters, furnishers, painters and fitters of all kinds set to work. Once again, Lady Margaret Beaufort oversaw the arrangements and was present with her in the chamber as well as her own mother, Elizabeth Wydeville, who left Bermondsey Abbey to be with her daughter at this critical time. The witnesses, led by her Chamberlain, prayed for her safe delivery as she and her women entered the inner chamber, hung with blue arras embroidered with gold fleur-de-lys. Her bed and separate birthing pallet were hung with canopy of gold and velvet with many colours, 'garnished' with the symbolic red roses of Lancaster. To one side stood an altar 'well furnished' with relics, on which Elizabeth would rely to assist her labour, while a cupboard 'well and richly garnished' held other necessaries for the

coming weeks. After almost a month in confinement,
Elizabeth was delivered of a daughter at about nine in the
evening of 28 November.

The birth of a girl was not always as welcome as that
of a boy: it went unrecorded by the London Grey Friars
chronicler who did note the arrivals of Princes Arthur and
Henry, yet girls had their dynastic uses, forging foreign
alliances through marriage treaties. There is no reason
to suspect that little princess's arrival was treated with
anything less than delight by her parents, considering the
existence of a healthy heir and the ability of her mother
to go on and bear more sons. The christening was held at
Westminster on 30 November, again using the traditional
silver font from Canterbury Cathedral. The Marchioness
of Berkeley carried the child from the queen's chamber at
the front of a procession bearing 120 torches, followed by
Elizabeth's sister Anne holding the lace christening robe.
She was lowered into the font and baptised Margaret, after
her paternal grandmother. The party partook of spices and
wine, trumpets sounded and the child was carried back to
her mother. The court would remain at Westminster for
Christmas but an outbreak of measles delayed Elizabeth's
churching until 27 December, when it was held in private.
As the illness had claimed several victims among her ladies,
this was a wise decision considering Elizabeth's vulnerable
post-partum condition. By Candlemas, in early February,
she was well enough to celebrate the purification of the
Virgin Mary by watching a play in the White Hall. Seven
months later she was pregnant again.

The future Henry VIII was born at Greenwich, in the old
manor house of Placentia, begun by Humphrey, Duke of
Gloucester and developed by Henry VI and Edward IV. As
such, it was a smaller and less significant royal property,
more of a country retreat than the symbolic locations
chosen for the arrival of Arthur and Margaret. Within a
few years, though, all that remained of Henry's birthplace

would be completely demolished to make way for a grand new programme of building. Elizabeth would have taken to her chamber there early in June, to await the birth at the end of that month. The usual mechanism of preparations would have ensured all was ready for her enclosure in her chamber, from the yards of cloth and hangings about her bed, to the tapestries on the walls, cradles, pallet bed, all in the richest colours and fabrics as well as the indispensable reliquary. It was her first summer confinement; perhaps in the heat she requested that the one uncovered window might be left open, so she could look out down to the river and watch the distant craft sailing past in the long days of waiting. Finally, on 28 June 1491, the ordeal came to an end and she was delivered of a sturdy, golden-haired son. The little prince was washed gently in any of a number of substances; wine, milk, mallow, rue, sweet butter, myrrh, linseed and barley water, or rubbed with oil of acorns, supposedly another preventative measure against the perils of death before baptism, before being swaddled and laid in the cradle. Alternative methods of care included swathing infants in roses ground up with salt to absorb moisture from their limbs and the mouth and gums cleansed with a finger dipped in honey. As she looked on the face of her sleeping newborn baby, Elizabeth cannot have predicted what the future would hold for him. As a second son, Prince Henry was the necessary 'spare heir', significant as a safeguard but not expected to rule. His arrival was celebrated but few records were made of the event. His birth was a comparatively quiet business: it is symbolic that Margaret Beaufort only briefly mentioned his arrival in her Book of Hours, writing over a correction, while his elder brother and sisters' exact time of arrival had been noted. He was baptised in the nearby church of the Friars Observant, which had been decorated for the purpose with tapestries, cypress linen, cloth of gold and damask, around a temporary wooden stage on which stood the Canterbury silver font. Wrapped in a mantle of cloth of gold trimmed with ermine, he was anointed and blessed by Richard Fox, the Bishop of Exeter. Soon, this tiny prince would be sent away to join his sister at her Eltham nursery where he would be brought up among women and quickly learned to 'rule the roost'.

As with all women of her era, Elizabeth was defined by motherhood. As a queen, she had less direct involvement with her children's upbringing than some of her contemporaries, yet evidence suggests she was a caring and involved maternal figure in their lives. Although her eldest son, Arthur, was established at Ludlow Castle in his role of Prince of Wales, the royal nursery at Eltham kept her other children within easy reach, allowing for her influence to be felt. Generous rewards were given to those who ran the children's households. Dame Elizabeth Darcy headed Arthur's first nursery, along with a handful of other women who received regular payments through his early years; their wages for June 1487 totalled £46.[16] Careful specifications were made for the royal children's education and daily regime, extending from curricula of study through to the arrangements and menus for their meals, time for play and bedtime routines. Arthur's education at Ludlow was supervised by a string of leading academics, among them the blind poet Bernard André, and included the study of Latin, Greek and French as well as time for archery and hunting with dogs. Later André would tutor the young Henry VIII along with fellow poet John Skelton, John Rede, John Holt and William Hone. The Fleming Giles d'Ewes taught French at Eltham and their musical education was overseen by one Guillam, an expert in wind instruments. In 1499, the Dutch humanist scholar Erasmus visited Eltham Palace in the company of his friend, Thomas More, and was impressed by the abilities of the young Prince Henry; this led to a formative correspondence that stands testament to the eight-year-old's abilities. Recently,

Dr David Starkey has suggested that it was Elizabeth herself who was her children's first teacher; by comparing examples of the queen's handwriting with that of the boy Henry, he concludes that she was the one to teach him to write.[17] Erasmus had also been impressed that Henry already had 'something of royalty in his demeanour, in which there was a certain dignity combined with singular courtesy'; by many accounts the younger prince took after his maternal grandfather, Edward IV, while Arthur was more like his father. Henry was also an energetic and physical child, with his father paying fourteen shillings in January 1494 for horses 'for my Lord Harry', then all of two and a half!

A constant figure in Elizabeth's life was her mother-in-law, Margaret Beaufort. A close friend of her own mother and a fellow Lancastrian turned Yorkist by marriage, the queen must have known Margaret throughout her childhood; she attended the re-internment of Richard, Duke of York, and carried Elizabeth's youngest sister Bridget to her baptism in 1480. Equally, she had been present during the reign of Richard III, possibly at times when Elizabeth's own mother was absent, carrying the train of Queen Anne at the 1483 Coronation. On Henry's accession she moved into Coldharbour House where she entertained Elizabeth and facilitated her early meetings with her future husband; it was to her home that Elizabeth would first flee with Prince Henry during the Cornish uprising of 1497. Margaret also kept a suite of rooms for Elizabeth at her estate in Collyweston. Devoted to the son she had borne as a thirteen-year-old widow, the energetic countess was in her early forties at the time of his accession and, technically, had a better claim to the throne. The frequent legal conflagration of both women's identities into 'the queen and my lady the king's mother'[18] shows their proximity at many events, where Elizabeth, as crowned queen, only just took precedence over her mother-in-law who would walk ceremoniously a step or so behind. It appears that Henry's political commitments meant Elizabeth often spent more time in Margaret's company than with her husband but the union was also symbolic. In the king's absence they were the public, physical embodiment of united warring factions; York and Lancaster, white and red roses. On key occasions, such as Twelfth Night 1487, Elizabeth and Margaret appeared in 'like mantle and surcoat' as an indicator of their equivalent rank, although Margaret then tended her daughter-in-law's crown as she feasted. Likewise, on St George's Day 1488, the pair wore matching Garter gowns. The two women were often in collaboration when it came to domestic and religious projects. Margaret took in hand the practical arrangements for courtly life and key occasions such as births and christenings, as well as organising suitable marriages for her and Elizabeth's relations, although she was equally keen to support them when they transgressed, providing a home for Cecily of York when she married without permission. Although the Spanish ambassadors might view this relationship as stifling, with Elizabeth 'kept in subjection' by Margaret, whose influence over Henry she apparently 'did not like', no contemporary accounts can verify Elizabeth's displeasure. Tellingly, the ambassador referred to the family dynamic in terms of stereotypes; the queen's dislike was 'as is generally the case'. Margaret may well have been the overbearing, controlling figure they suggest but she was also indefatigable, highly organised and competent; quite likely she was a tower of strength.

Between 1491 and 1501, Elizabeth bore four, possibly five, more children. She conceived again only three months after the birth of Henry and went into confinement shortly before his first birthday. While awaiting the delivery, she was brought news of the death of her own mother, Elizabeth Wydeville, in June 1492, who for the first time had declined to assist her during labour. When a second daughter arrived on 2 July, the queen named her Elizabeth. The little girl was the first of the royal children to die in infancy, taken by an 'atrophy' or wasting disease at the age of three and was buried in Westminster Abbey. Regular, unpredictable infant mortality was a sad fact of Tudor deliveries and was no respecter of rank; in many families, rates of survival could be as low as 50 per cent, although some families suffered fewer losses. Those dying at birth or within a week were known as 'chrisom children', still wearing the white baptismal cloth, while those surviving the dangerous first months could still be prey to all manner of dangers. It is impossible to know, across time, exactly what factors contributed to specific deaths but undeniably traumatic deliveries, illness, poor hygiene, malnutrition, cot death, accidents and imperfect understanding of childcare were contributing factors. In spite of their grief, Henry and Elizabeth knew their daughter had been in receipt of the best available care. In addition, Elizabeth was three months pregnant again. Her next child, Princess Mary Rose, was born at Richmond on 18 March 1496.

While the arrival dates of most of Henry and Elizabeth's children are carefully recorded, some controversy surrounds the arrival of a short-lived prince named Edward, with at least one historian suggesting his birth must have occurred towards the beginning of the marriage, in 1487 or 1488, rather than its usual placing, somewhere between 1499 and 1502. Given the intervals of her subsequent conceptions, of ten months after her second child Margaret and then three months after Henry, her third, Elizabeth's fertility appears strong. The lengthening gaps between the births of her subsequent children are consistent with patterns of dwindling conceptions experienced by aristocratic and noblewomen married comparatively young and producing larger families. Typically, a rapid number of children were born in the years following marriage, before fertility tailed off and accelerated the arrival of the menopause in the mid-thirties. Elizabeth's childbearing record and advancing age, by the standards of the time, may have affected her fertility. After the birth of Mary, she did not conceive again for over two years. Perhaps the pilgrimage to Walsingham she undertook in the summer of 1497 was related to conception; it had certainly been a difficult period, with the presence of the pretender Perkin Warbeck at court and the great fire that had razed Sheen Palace to the ground that Christmas. Payments made in 1498 by Henry to Elizabeth's physician, Master Lewis, and her surgeon, Robert Taylor, may have been related to a pregnancy or birth: certainly by May that year, she had fallen pregnant again.

At the relatively advanced age, in Tudor terms, of thirty-three, she went into confinement for the sixth time at Greenwich in February 1499. Although this pregnancy went to term and the little Prince Edmund was apparently healthy, something had caused deep concern in those attending the queen. The Spanish ambassador reported that there had been 'much fear for her life' but in the end, the delivery proved straightforward. Perhaps she had experienced a more difficult pregnancy or her age and general health provoked doubts: she had just passed her thirtieth birthday when she delivered Mary back in 1496 and those three extra years may have been considered significant. Possibly these fears combined with political and dynastic dangers: her confinement coincided with the culmination of years of threat from pretender to the throne Perkin Warbeck. In the event, however, the delivery proved comparatively easy and another male heir was welcomed and celebrated. Sadly though, the little prince died at fifteen months and was buried at Westminster: perhaps he was weak or underweight from the start or Elizabeth's unrecorded complications during the pregnancy gave grounds for concern at the time. Alternatively, he may have fallen prey to any one of the infantile illnesses of the age, unpredictable and often untreatable with contemporary medicine. His death may have coincided with the conception of the mysterious Edward, putting this child's delivery date somewhere in the summer of 1501; otherwise he may have pre-dated his brother in birth and death, arriving in 1497 or 1498. Perhaps the very closeness of these pregnancies lay behind the concerns for the queen's health. However, by 1500, Elizabeth was strong and well again and looking forward to the new century.

8

Imposters, Edward VI and Richard IV, 1487–1499

I saw a son of England
Called Richard of York
Who they said was dead
And eaten up in the earth,
Endure great suffering;
And by noble deeds,
Live in good hope that
He would be king of the English.[1]

In May 1487, news of another Coronation shocked the Westminster court. At Christ Church Cathedral in Dublin, a young boy of ten had been crowned as Edward VI, under the direction of the Irish Government, headed by Lord Kildare. His supporters insisted he was the son of George, Duke of Clarence, and therefore the direct male descendant of the Yorkist line, with a better claim to the throne than Henry. Worse still, he was actively supported by Elizabeth's own aunt, Margaret, Duchess of Burgundy, who was raising an army to invade England and place her 'nephew' on the throne.

It had seemed that the arrival of Henry Tudor and his marriage to Elizabeth of York would put an end to decades of recent warfare. Hall recorded the common hope that the union would bring a lasting peace: 'surely that the day was now come, that the seed of tumultuous factions and the fountain of civil dissension should be stopped, evacuate and clearly extinguished'. Yet the supporters of Richard III would not let his sudden death be forgotten so quickly. In 1486, a minor skirmish, led by Lord Lovell, had been easily suppressed, although Richard III's former Chief Butler escaped abroad, to stir up further discontent. The following year, a second rebellion posed a far more serious challenge to the new regime. The ten-year-old crowned at Dublin is better known to history as Lambert Simnel, the low-born son of a baker, joiner or shoemaker, who had been trained to impersonate first Richard, Duke of York, and then Clarence's son Edward. Henry could be certain that the child was an imposter for one key reason: the real Edward, Earl of Warwick, aged twelve, had been imprisoned in the Tower of London since the victory at Bosworth. As the newly anointed king, he had always been aware of the potential threat to his throne by the existence of a Yorkist heir as well as the speculation caused by the disappearance of the Princes in the Tower. To try and disprove the pretender's claim, Henry temporarily released the twelve-year-old Warwick from confinement, parading him through the streets of London to St Paul's where he was allowed to speak with various 'important people'. However, the child only ever had been a figurehead. Further news arrived that a Burgundian army of mercenaries had landed in Ireland, joining forces with John de la Pole, Richard's nephew and designated heir. At twenty-four, Pole was a far more formidable claimant and a very real threat.

Henry was on the wrong side of the country. Anticipating that the Burgundians would cross the North Sea, he had ridden up into Norfolk to patrol the coastline and make a pilgrimage to the shrine of the Virgin at Walsingham. When he learned they had circumvented him entirely, he hurried west and made his headquarters at the Midlands stronghold of Kenilworth Castle. John of Gaunt, his great-great-grandfather, had developed the Norman keep into a palace, with the addition of a great hall influenced by that at Windsor Castle, grand staircase, towers, kitchens and a luxurious series of apartments. Later, Henry V had hunted in the castle's grounds and built a retreat by the lake. It was here that Henry summoned his mother and 'dearest wife' to wait with him until it was time to meet the rebels. For Elizabeth, familiar fears may have resurfaced. Memories of her mother's trials may have led her to wonder whether her own future would be as unstable. The crises of the past decades of civil war were not yet over; the nature of Richard's accession, rule and death, would create a number of ghosts which would resurface throughout Henry's reign. As they waited at Kenilworth Castle for news of the rebels' progress, Elizabeth's recently found security as a wife, mother and queen must have seemed fragile. Among the most difficult aspects of the rebellion must have been the support her aunt, Margaret of Burgundy, gave to the pretender; Bacon went as far as to claim that Margaret hated Elizabeth for being the means by which Henry ascended the throne. Early in May, the foreign troops arrived in Ireland to be headed by John de la Pole, Earl of Lincoln. Pole had been named by Richard as his heir and was a far more serious opponent that the puppet Simnel; he had, until recently, been prominent at the English court, taking a role in the christening of Arthur, but had fled to Margaret that March; quite possibly his intention was to claim the throne for himself once the invasion had been successful. The combined Burgundian and Irish armies landed in England in early June and Henry set out to meet them. Elizabeth and Margaret Beaufort waited together for news.

Fortunately, they did not have to wait long and when news came, it was good. An initial skirmish at Bramham Moor gave the rebels cause to hope and they marched southwards, encountering small pockets of resistance through Sherwood Forest. On 16 June 1487, at around nine in the morning, the armies clashed at Stoke in a decisive victory for Henry. The Yorkists, initially, had the advantageous high ground but surrendered it in order to attack. The Irish troops were ill-equipped for the battle and their lack of body armour meant they quickly sustained heavy losses from the royalist archers, leaving the rebels dependent on their combination of German and Swiss mercenaries. Hall describes them as 'after the manner of their countrey almoste naked' yet fighting hardly and valiantly, but being 'stryken downe and slayne lyke dull and brute beastes'; their destruction 'was a great discouragynge and abashment to the rest of the companye'.[2] After three hours of fighting, Lincoln and many of his supporters were dead; Lovell disappeared and the young Simnel was captured and put to work turning the spit in the royal kitchens, after which he prospered, becoming the king's falconer and dying in 1525. Henry could afford to be merciful: Hall paints him as an 'innocent pore soule, a very chylde'. Of the remaining enemies, Sir Thomas Craig said 'there was not one left to piss against the wall' although Margaret of Burgundy was apparently 'very sorye' at the plan's failure and began to scheme some other way to 'vexe and perturbe' Henry.[3] In the interests of historical tidiness, the Battle of Stoke has been considered the culmination of the Wars of the Roses. It was certainly a crucial victory for Henry, after which he was considerably more secure on the throne, although it was not to be the last challenge to his kingship; in response, he began to develop a network of spies and informers that would serve him well in the future. The king returned triumphantly to London and proceeded to St Paul's where he prayed and gave thanks for his victory: Elizabeth and her mother-in-law watched his progress from a house in St Mary Spittel, in modern Spitalfields.

Henry had successfully seen off one challenger but a more dangerous one was about to emerge.

The victory was seen by many, including himself, as a vindication of Henry's rule. Contemporary beliefs in superstition and divine judgement were strong and the king, in particular, took such signs seriously, to help explain and make sense of events. Writing to Pope Innocent VIII that July, he explained how one rebel, a man named John Swit, had been punished for spreading false rumours about the king's defeat.

> On pronouncing these words he instantly fell dead upon the ground, and his face and body immediately became blacker than soot itself, and shortly afterwards the corpse emitted such a stench that no one soever could approach it. Verily we give thanks to Almighty God, who, of his ineffable mercy has exhibited in our kingdom so great a miracle concerning the Christian faith.[4]

The 'real' or scientific causes behind Swit's fate can only be guessed at by the modern reader. To Henry and his contemporaries, though, this was an unambiguous act of divine punishment which would have carried significant weight. Henry went on to explain recent events to the Pope and asked for his intercession in more usual, formal methods of punishment against those who had threatened his realm:

> As some of the prelates of Ireland, namely, the Archbishop of Dublin, the Archbishop of Armagh, and the Bishops of Meath and Kildare (Darnensis), lent assistance to the rebels, and to a certain spurious lad, whom victory has now delivered into our hands, they pretending that the lad was the son of the late Duke of Clarence, and crowning him as King of England, we implore your Holiness to cite them as having incurred the censures of the Church, and proceed against them at law.[5]

Yet such methods would not prove sufficient to deter another pretender from the lure of the English throne.

The young man known to history as Perkin Warbeck certainly looked as if he was a member of the Yorkist royal family. With similar good looks to Edward IV and George, Duke of Clarence, his image survives in a later sketch of a portrait from the 1490s, showing a fair young man with small features and a heavy chin. Bacon called him 'a curious piece of marble', with a 'crafty and bewitching fashion both to move pity and induce belief'. One Venetian nobleman described him as noble in manner and looks and the later chronicler Vergil agreed he was 'of visage beautiful, of countenance demure'. To Hall, he was a 'doll', to Fabyan, an 'unhappy imp' and poet Bernard André called him a butterfly, with all the associated connotations of manipulation and insubstantiality. Warbeck certainly managed to work his way through the European courts of the day, although this was less a reflection of his true identity than contemporary political expediency. So who was this imposter who claimed to be more entitled to the English throne than its reigning king and queen? Was there any truth in his contention? His very existence can only have raised uncomfortable questions for Elizabeth of York, whether or not she believed, or hoped, there was any substance to the claim that now threatened her position and family. On balance, the evidence suggests Warbeck was not her younger brother returned from the dead, but the circumstances of his death would never allow her any degree of certainty. Even if she were convinced of Richard's death back in 1483, her feelings at the exploitation of his identity cannot have been straightforward.

Later investigation suggested that Warbeck had been born around 1474, the son of customs collector John Osbeck, also known as Jehan de Werbecque, and his wife Catherine from Tournai: his name may have been Piers

Osbeck or Webecque. At the age of nine, he was apprenticed to a merchant in Tournai, Zeeland and Portugal and later, possibly, with a man called Brampton, who called him Piris. Brampton was certainly in favour with Richard III; he was paid £350 for services unspecified in July 1483, soon after the princes went into the Tower. In 1484, he was granted an income of £100 a year for twenty years, from customs revenue, but he kept away from England after Richard's death. If Warbeck needed assistance in impersonating a member of the royal family, Brampton and his associates could have been in a position to help him. Did he have some connection or knowledge about what happened to the real princes, or was he at least placed to have an understanding of courtly manners and something of the boys' lives? By 1491, Warbeck was working for a Breton merchant Pregent Meno who took him to the loyal Yorkist Cork in Ireland. There, he impressed the locals with his looks, dress and manners, striding about the town draped in expensive silks like a mannequin, which could have been the intention, to display these sumptuous wares to potential customers. However, they would have not found many customers. Silk was very expensive at the time and mostly used in small quantities for lace and ribbons; it suggested royal status as sumptuary laws decreed that no one below the rank of a knight was supposed to wear it. The Irish decided he must be important.

Soon after this, Warbeck was able to enlist French backing too. Henry's youthful exile had embroiled him in politics across the channel. Having spent many years in Brittany, which was then independent from the main body of France, he had been supporting Anne of Brittany in her war against King Charles VIII. The French king had married a reluctant fourteen-year-old Anne in 1491 but was still disposed to support any potential enemies of Henry and welcomed Warbeck to his court. Action was needed. In October 1492, Henry headed an army to France, where Calais was still a significant English territory, from which he could lay siege to Boulogne. He did not intend an invasion or full-scale war but the threat was enough. His expenses show that he stayed at the Swan, where he was entertained by various minstrels and his Spanish fool; recompense was made to his sailors, 10s went on hiring 'chapel stuff' and 6s 8d to 'one that had corn trodden down'.[6] His presence was enough to deter Charles from supporting the pretender. Writing to the Pope that December, Henry cannily expressed his 'surprise': 'contrary to all expectation, a peace was proposed to us by the French, with such conditions as to make it appear that no Christian and Catholic prince could be capable of refusing them', while boosting his own reputation as a compassionate and pious king: 'We therefore accepted this peace, both in order to attend to other matters and to avoid shedding Christian blood.'[7]

On 3 November, England and France signed a treaty of peace at Etaples, by which Charles promised not to give any assistance to pretenders to the English throne. The French king seemed keen to halt the potential invasion: Henry also benefited to the tune of £159,000, doubling his income, in return for withdrawing support for Brittany's rebels. Warbeck hastily left.

By 1493, Warbeck had tried out a number of identities. It had been proposed that he was the illegitimate son of Edward IV or Richard III but by 1493, as Henry VII stated in a letter, he had settled on the identity of Richard, Duke of York, the younger of Elizabeth's two brothers who had disappeared in the Tower, and was claiming to have certain hereditary marks on his body that marked him out as such. With his options in France running out, he had one potential ally still to try. Margaret of Burgundy had already been heavily implicated in the Simnel rebellion; now she accepted Warbeck as her nephew, wanting the restoration of the house of York. Writing to Isabella of Spain in 1493, she stated that her family had 'fallen from the royal summit' and their only hope lay in a 'male remnant' who could retake the throne 'usurped by this most iniquitous invader and tyrant'. It has also been suggested that Warbeck may even have been the illegitimate son of Margaret herself, now a widow involved with the lives of her step-children. It was more likely that she saw him as a substitute child, having been unable to bear children herself. He was treated with great favour at the Burgundian court, and in 1493 attended the funeral of Emperor Maximilian III in Vienna as representative of England. Henry sent envoys to his wife's aunt in 1493, 1494 and 1495 to try to end the alliance but his descriptions of Warbeck as a base-born potboy merely served to inflame her passion to dethrone him in favour of the youth. In 1494, Warbeck had his own gold coins minted, carrying the legend 'God Save the King' and symbols of crowned roses, lions and fleur-de-lys; he also had his own seal and signet which used part of the royal arms of England, in a move calculated to assert his own authority and inflame the indignation of the king. Still, questions remained as to how the ten-year-old Richard of York had managed to escape the Tower when his brother was murdered and where he had been since.

Around this time, Warbeck wrote his own explanation of his identity, in a letter to Isabella of Spain. A transcription, preserved in the Calendar of State Papers of Spain, is worth quoting in full:

His elder brother the Prince of Wales, son of King Edward, had been assassinated. He had himself been delivered to a gentleman who had received orders to destroy him, but who, taking pity on his innocence, had preserved his life, and made him swear on the sacraments not to divulge, for a certain number of years, his name, birth, and lineage. That being done he had sent him away under the care of two persons, who were at once his jailors and governors. Had led a wandering life, in the midst of perils and misery, for the period of nearly eight years, during which time his governors had kept him in concealment in different parts of the world, until at last one of them died, and the other returned to his own country. Was left alone while still almost a child. Passed some time in Portugal, then went to Ireland, where he was recognised and joyfully welcomed by the Earl of Ormond and the Earl of Kildare, his relatives. Was equally well received by many of the chief men.

The King of France then sent for him, promising him aid against Henry Richmond, usurper of the Crown of England. Was shown the greatest honour by the King of France, but the promised aid was not given. Went, therefore, to the Duchess of Burgundy, sister to his father, who, moved by her humanity and virtue, welcomed him with open arms. The King of the Romans, his son, the Duke of Austria, the Duke of Saxony, and the Kings of Denmark and Scotland, received him in the same way, and sent ambassadors to him, proffering him friendship and brotherhood. Many of the chief personages in England, whose indignation had been roused by the iniquitous conduct of the usurper, Henry Richmond, had done the same in secret. Hopes Queen Isabella, who is not only his relative, but also the most just and pious of Princesses, will have pity on him, and intercede on his behalf with her husband, entreating that assistance may be given him. Promises that if he regain his kingdom he will be grateful, and a better ally of theirs than King Richard had been.[8]

By 1494, Henry was expecting an invasion of England with Margaret's help. He sent out a network of spies as well as knights and troops to patrol coastland; a fleet was readily waiting to repel foreigners at Orwell in Suffolk and an inspection was made of ports on the south coast. His direct appeals to Philip of Burgundy, who had succeeded Margaret's late husband Charles the Bold, had no result and the trade embargo which Henry then put in place injured English trade. Henry chose this time to reassert the claims of his own family. The three-year-old Prince Henry was invested as Duke of York, to provide a legitimate alternative claimant to the title. Three days of tournaments were held at Westminster, beginning on 9 November, which Henry and Elizabeth watched from a specially erected house covered in blue cloth of arras, embroidered with gold fleur-de-lys, hung inside with cloth of gold. The challengers wore the Tudor colours of white and green, with the queen's blue-and-murrey crest on their helmets; their prizes were awarded by Princess Margaret. As the horses charged down the lists in all their finery and the little prince took centre stage before the cheering crowds, the pretender must have seemed very far away. Within weeks, though, he would make his presence felt in sight of Henry's kingdom.

Warbeck wasn't ready to invade until early 1495. He sailed in July and landed in Deal on the south Kent coast, where he hoped he could summon some local support. However, the men of Kent had been warned of his arrival and hid behind the dunes to lull the arrivals into a false sense of security. Once they had set foot on shore, Warbeck's men were attacked and about 150 were slaughtered on the beach: their leader could do little from his ship but watch. Some were captured and taken to London, to a commission set up at Westminster to interrogate them, with a group of nine sent up to Fotheringhay to be questioned by Henry himself. A few Englishmen had joined Warbeck and their bodies were displayed in coastal areas as deterrents; by contrast, loyal locals were rewarded for resistance to the rebels. Canterbury accounts list drink payments for 300 men going off to fight Richard and the city received a letter of thanks afterwards. Henry's network of spies was also uncovering treason close to home; in 1495, a number of executions, including that of William Stanley, the king's own chamberlain of the household, eradicated the pretender's support base in England. Then in February 1496, the *Magnus Intercursus* treaty was signed, restoring trade between Henry VII and Philip of Burgundy, who had given up on Warbeck after his failed invasion at Deal. By then, though, the young pretender had already moved on; having failed to lay siege to Waterford, the 'untaken city', he headed to Scotland that October and received a warm welcome from James IV. As traditional enemies, England and Scotland had always been swift to support each others' enemies; it would be quite a coup for James if he was able to manoeuvre this latest thorn in Henry's side onto his throne.

Soon after his arrival at the Scottish court in January 1496, Warbeck was married to Lady Catherine Gordon, daughter of the Earl of Huntly. The speed of this raises questions: was it a love match or a diplomatic one; did Catherine herself have a choice? Aged about twenty-two and only a younger daughter by a third wife, she may have been married by royal command, a useful pawn to offer to a pretender. James gave Warbeck a gown of white damask silk to wear, costing £28, for the wedding held at Edinburgh, which was followed by feasting and jousting where the groom wore purple brocade on his armour. He was also given an annual Scottish pension of £1,200, which James could ill afford. Hall describes him 'swellyng with joye that he after his awne phantasye had made the Scots to be his partakers'. In order to raise an army against the Scots, Henry imposed heavy taxes, which provoked resistance at the other end of his kingdom.

In the later spring of 1497, an army of around 15,000 disaffected Cornishmen marched to London. They hoped to unite with Kentish rebels, but the anticipated support did not materialise so the remnant of the army pitched their tents on Blackheath, near Greenwich. This huge open space had traditionally been associated with unrest. Wat Tyler had rallied his revolting peasants there in 1381, as had Jack Cade in 1450. As the rebels were so close to the capital, Henry took steps to protect his family, moving

Elizabeth and the children into apartments at the Tower. The Venetian archives contain the receipt of letters from their ambassador, stating that the Duke of York had 35,000 followers in England. Apparently, Henry had placed 'the queen, and his eldest son in the very strong castle on the coast, and had prepared there certain barks (ships), that he may be able to remove them in case of need'.[9] This vastly overestimates Warbeck's support and the action of Henry. As far as is known, he never considered sending Elizabeth and Arthur abroad or sent them to a coastal castle for their safety. It became clear that the royal troops vastly outnumbered the rebels, who had apparently lost focus and were unclear about their demands beyond the general dissatisfaction of harsh taxation. They were easily defeated at the Battle of Deptford Bridge that June, their leaders hanged and more harsh penalties imposed upon the unlucky Cornish. Henry's actions during the Cornish uprising are representative of his considered, effective approach. Diplomacy and negotiation were his preferred methods and the unravelling of Scottish events soon made this possible, without further bloodshed. However, the tide had already begun to turn against Warbeck there.

The following September, Warbeck and James launched border raids on England, anticipating English rebel troops from Northumberland would join them. None came. The Scots became restless and embarked on a campaign of pillage and chaos, which upset Warbeck and resulted in disagreement with James. The warm welcome had cooled. Warbeck's failure to launch a successful invasion against England and his perceived squeamishness in the raids made him an awkward guest, especially as Henry VII was pushing for a peace treaty with Scotland and offering the hand of his eldest daughter Margaret in marriage. The advantages to James of an English match far outweighed any benefit of continuing to support Warbeck. Equipping him with a suitably named boat, the *Cuckoo*, with all its connotations of usurpation, James bid his burdensome guest goodbye in the summer of 1497 and that July signed the Treaty of Ayton, making peace with England. In September, Warbeck landed in Cornwall near Land's End, where locals were still smarting from their failed rebellion. Here, he was more successful in raising support and was declared Richard IV on Bodmin Moor before an impromptu army who then laid siege to the city of Exeter. However, things went quickly wrong when Henry reacted to the threat. As news reached the pretender that the king's scouts were at Glastonbury, he panicked and deserted his troops, fleeing for sanctuary at Beaulieu Abbey in Hampshire, where he was captured. His wife, Catherine, was taken at St Michael's Mount; both were brought to London. The brief blaze of glory was over.

Soon, the news spread around Europe. It could only serve to enhance Henry's reputation. The Milanese ambassador Soncino reported that the 'sage' king had won two victories, the first against the Cornish, 'who, some 10,000 in number, took up arms under a blacksmith, saying they would not pay the subsidy', the other against the King of Scotland, who raised his camp 'not very gloriously' in support of Warbeck. He also wrote how the Tudor succession was secure through the existence of the virtuous and distinguished Prince Arthur, whom the rulers of Spain must be pleased to welcome as a son-in-law. The removal of Warbeck could only clear the way for this 'matrimonial alliance, which I am told is in negotiation, as this kingdom is perfectly stable'. Soncino was impressed by the king's wisdom, 'whereof every one stands in awe'; and his king's wealth, 'for I am informed that he has upwards of six millions of gold'. In all, he was so impressed that he added 'it is publicly reported that the king is under the protection of God eternal'.[10] After all Henry's victories against his enemies since his arrival in England in 1485, it must have appeared to many a superstitious contemporary that their monarch did indeed have divine approval. Now he returned to his capital, with his prisoner, needing to decide what to do with him. His predecessors would have exacted a swift and deadly penalty but Henry was more cautious and, perhaps, more lenient.

Waiting in London was Elizabeth of York. The meeting with Warbeck, having been mere theory for years, was coming ever closer. No record of her response to him survives but his existence must have been a powerful reminder to her either of her younger brother's death or the possibility of his survival. There seems to have been little doubt in Henry's mind from the start that Warbeck's identity was a sham and most likely that Elizabeth was influenced by this. Her response reopens the question of her beliefs regarding the original boy's fate; if she had reason to believe him dead back in 1483, Warbeck's claims were impossible, yet they may have stirred her indignation or sorrow that his identity was being exploited. She was always keen to remember those who had served her family, sending Richard's old nurse 3½ yards of cloth for a dress in 1502 and rewarding her father's servants. Yet in spite of it all, the glimmer of hope must have presented itself in her mind, even if logic and common sense worked against it; at the very least she must have been curious. Bacon describes the interrogation of Sir James Tirrell, one of the surviving suspects regarding the princes' fates, which convinced Henry of their deaths, although he did not later make public this evidence. Tantalising reference is made to it in a 1493 speech by William Warham as 'set testimonies' which the king 'hath upon record, plain and infallible' regarding the death of Duke Richard.[11] Bacon suggests this urged Henry with greater 'diligence' to uncover the pretender's true identity, by sending spies into Flanders to uncover this 'fable'. It can never be ascertained whether Henry was in possession of conclusive proof regarding the princes but his actions suggest his belief in their decease; if he had been, undoubtedly he would have shared this with his queen, their sister.

Additionally, was Elizabeth aware of her husband's response to Catherine, the pretender's wife? Later chroniclers were keen to state her personal charms and Henry's appreciation: Hall describes him wondering 'at her beautie and countenaunce' and, thinking her a 'praye (prey) more mete (fitting) for the chiefe capitaine than for the meane souldiours', he 'began then a lytle to phantasie her person'. Bacon repeated the king's impression of her 'excellent beauty' and compassionate response, wishing her 'to serve as well his eye as his fame'. She was apparently described as the 'White Rose', in reference to her husband's claims, but there is no reference to how Elizabeth felt as the image's previous embodiment. Catherine was sent to London, became a favourite of Elizabeth and entered her household, where she was provided for long after the death of her husband. She would go on to marry a further three times. Nicholas Nicolas, the Victorian author of the memoir prefacing the Privy Purse records of 1502–3, wrote that 'from the moment in which Elizabeth of York became Queen of England her life loses its political interest'. Perhaps, though, it intensifies its personal fascination. As the moment of their meeting drew closer, the interface of her political and personal identities was hardly more challenging than during the autumn of 1497.

When they met, it would have been at the old manor house of Richmond. Elizabeth had recently returned from pilgrimage to Walsingham, which may have been a response to these challenging personal circumstances or may have been related to conception or pregnancy. By the time Warbeck reached the capital, in Henry's custody, he had already made a full confession about his true identity and pretensions to the throne. As they arrived, late that November, Warbeck walked ahead of Henry, unfettered, leading a courtier by the arm.[12] By now, the young man was accustomed to the jeers of the crowd, having been brought through the streets of London where onlookers shouted curses and jibes; the performance was repeated at court on almost every occasion where he appeared in public. Bacon claims this was so he 'could better tell what himself was'. Soncino describes him as almost enjoying the atmosphere, pausing to look in the windows of shops at Cheapside and making a 'spectacle for the world'.[13] When and where Elizabeth first encountered him is not known; perhaps she watched from a window as they approached or sat graciously on her throne of estate as Warbeck was presented to her. In that initial moment, the first time she set eyes on him, there must have been a frisson of expectation as she traced the outline of his face in search of something familiar. Even given his confession, she cannot help but have wondered what her own brother would have looked like had he survived to maturity, and thus measured the young upstart accordingly. Perhaps it was her influence that led to Henry's leniency towards Warbeck; his failure to punish him at once was, in part, due to the promise he had made in order to extract him from sanctuary but may also have been indicative of the way he perceived the young man's threat. Henry kept his enemy close, making him sleep in an antechamber close to hand and denying him the opportunity to sleep with his wife. He was attended by unarmed 'servants' not guards. Warbeck was kept under house arrest almost like an entertainment, an odd figure of curiosity or fool to remind those who would challenge the king of his ultimate power. It was a situation that could not last, though.

Warbeck was at Sheen when it was engulfed by flames soon after Christmas 1497. It would present a neat, dramatic anecdote for the historian if the dissatisfied Warbeck, champing at the bit of his confinement, had seized the moment and attempted to burn down his rival's palace about his ears, yet no such scenario occurred.

Despite the efforts of some modern writers to build a case for his involvement, contemporary sources are adamant there was no conspiracy. Warbeck was clearly uncomfortable though, as by the following summer he was seeking to escape. On 9 June 1498, he succeeded. He had been sleeping between two guards in the Wardrobe department of Westminster Palace and had climbed out of the window at midnight. From there, he sought sanctuary at the Charterhouse, Sheen, but was soon recaptured and taken to the Tower. This time, Henry would be less lenient. A year later he was implicated in a plot with Edward, Earl of Warwick, Elizabeth's cousin. It appears possible that this was set up in order to provide a pretext for the removal of both threats to the realm, with the two men housed within a proximity that facilitated rather than hindered their contact. Both were executed in November 1499. Finally, Henry and Elizabeth could feel secure that their position was no longer under threat. Warbeck's wife Catherine remained at court, where she was favoured by Elizabeth and went on to remarry.

Contemporary descriptions of Henry and Elizabeth at this juncture give an impression of their presence and majesty. Venetian ambassador Trevisan described how the 'king received him in a small hall, hung with very handsome tapestry, leaning against a tall gilt chair, covered with cloth of gold. His Majesty wore a violet-coloured gown, lined with cloth of gold, and a collar of many jewels, and on his cap was a large diamond and a most beautiful pearl.' After the meeting, 'the ambassador was taken into a hall where dinner had been prepared, and there he dined with four lords; and after dinner the king gave him private audience, which lasted two hours'. Trevisan concluded that 'the king is gracious, grave, and a very worthy person'. He also saw Elizabeth, 'whom he found at the end of a hall, dressed in cloth of gold; on one side of her was the king's mother, on the other her son the prince. The queen is a handsome woman.'[14] The removal of Warbeck and Warwick meant that the royal family could look forward to a new chapter of security and stability. It also facilitated the arrangements for matches with Scotland and Spain, as Elizabeth saw her children growing up and emerging on the European marriage market. As a new century approached, the queen, now in her mid-thirties, had much to look forward to.

9

The Spanish Princess
1501–1502

Intimate and dissoluble.[1]

The early years of the next century saw exciting developments in international terms. As a result, Elizabeth's horizons expanded considerably, with a new continent discovered and more alliances becoming possible. The Silk Road and spice trade had already opened up much of the East; Mediterranean cities supplied the wealthy merchant ships that sailed up the Thames carrying their loads of herbs, silks, spices, drugs and incense. However, the fall of Constantinople in 1453 meant that land access was denied to Christians, forcing them to seek alternative routes across the sea. This initiated a new age of exploration that pushed the boundaries of existing knowledge regarding the size and scale of the world. The Italian 'Fra Mauro' map, a *mappa mundi* (world map) made by a Venetian monk in 1450, only depicts the continents of Africa, Asia and Europe, which were at that time well known. The Atlantic, though, remained largely unexplored. Developments in ship design in the mid-fifteenth century meant greater distances could be travelled in the new Portuguese 'caravel', whose lightweight frame and lateen sails allowed for greater manoeuvrability. Additionally, the publication of charts of the stars over set periods of time helped navigation, like the 1496 *Almanach Perpetuum* drawn up by Abraham Zacuto, royal astrologer to the King of Portugal. In 1492, Christopher Columbus reached the West Indies, funded by Ferdinand and Isabella of Spain, and founded a settlement in present-day Haiti. The native Americans he took as prisoners back to Spain made a significant impact at court. By the late 1490s, Henry VII had become interested in the expeditions to the New World, just at the time that John Cabot was looking for funding.

John Cabot and his son Sebastian were Venetian explorers who travelled to London in search of funding for an expedition to the New World. In March 1496, they received fifty nobles from Italian bankers in London and Henry's backing to 'find, discover and investigate whatsoever islands, countries, regions or provinces of heathens or infidels ... which before this time were unknown to all Christians'. Setting sail in the *Matthew* from Bristol, with enough supplies for seven or eight months, Cabot's exact discovery is unclear; he may have landed on the north-east coast of America in the summer of 1497, where letters of the crew members suggest they found evidence of fire and human tools, although they did not explore or make contact with any natives. On his return, Cabot presented his findings to Henry, who rewarded him with £10 'to hym that founde the new isle'; Soncino described him being fêted in silks at court. Did he regale the royal family with stories about his findings? Perhaps Elizabeth and her children gathered round to listen as he described what the New World was like and the difficulties of months cooped up on board the ship as the provisions depleted. It must have been an exciting time for the family, with the approach of a new century coinciding with discoveries that pushed the limits of contemporary understanding of the world as they knew it. New tastes arrived too, with the Spanish bringing turkeys from the New World to England in around 1500, Columbus bringing back corn and the influx of Arabian spices raising the heat of more familiar dishes. A letter written by a Venetian merchant living in London, Lorenzo Pasqualigo, described the new-found land as being called Grand Cham or Cam. Here, apparently, Cabot

> coasted for 300 leagues and landed; saw no human beings, but he has brought hither to the king certain snares which had been set to catch game, and a needle for making nets; he also found some felled trees, wherefore he supposed there were inhabitants, and returned to his ship in alarm.

Pasqualigo added that 'the King of England is much pleased with this intelligence', which would support Henry's award of Cabot's annual pension of £20 that December. He also promised the explorer ten ships in the spring, manned by prisoners, and financed his stay in England until then, 'wherewith to amuse himself'. Cabot seems to have caused a minor sensation wherever he went, spending the winter of 1497 in Bristol with his wife and son. His popularity was high: 'vast honour is paid him; he dresses in silk, and these English run after him like mad people'.[2] Cabot did undertake a second mission the following year. This time, he may have explored the coastline further, entering Spanish-held territories and returning to England in 1500, although his precise destination is unclear.[3]

Sea voyages could be gruelling. Living for weeks, even months, in crowded, unsanitary conditions, sailors frequently lacked provisions and fresh water before sighting land. Apart from the weather, there was also the danger of piracy and the fear of what may lurk in uncharted waters. Elizabeth was to experience these dangers for herself in 1500, when she left home for the first and only time to accompany Henry to Calais. The trip across the Channel was by no means comparable to the lengthy voyages undertaken by Cabot and Columbus – in theory, with the right conditions, the voyage should last only a few hours

– but it gave the queen a taste of travel and a chance to set foot outside her known world. Technically, though, she was not leaving England as Calais would remain an English possession for another fifty years: it was a little home from home, governed and inhabited by her subjects and as such, she was welcomed there as queen.

The purpose of the visit was for Henry to meet Philip of Burgundy, also known as Philip the Handsome, grandson of Charles the Bold by his first wife. He had married Juana of Aragon in 1496, the elder sister of Catherine, whose hand Henry was hoping to secure in marriage for his eldest son Arthur. No records survive suggesting Juana was present at the meeting, although, given Elizabeth's attendance, she may have been. Philip agreed to meet Henry outside the town at the church of St Peter and the details were recorded by the Calais Chronicle. The accommodation was certainly fit for a king. The church was hung in rich cloths of arras and the Lady Chapel decorated with fine cloth telling the story of Assuerus and Esther and hung in scarlet with the king's arms. The duke's chamber was strewn with roses and lavender and other sweet herbs, hung with rich tapestries depicting the Siege of Troy and blue cloth embroidered with fleur-de-lys. A chamber on the south side was set aside for Elizabeth's use, with the little vestry as her 'secret' chamber. The church's belfry and a house by the steeple were used for catering. Vast quantities of food were ordered, including seven 'horse loads' of cherries with cream, strawberries with sugar, baked venison, spiced cakes, wafers, wine, beer and hippocras (spiced wine) besides a 'yonge kyddes' and 'an Engleshe fatt ox … the plente was so moche that the peple cowed not spende hit that day'. Henry, with his rich company, including the Duke of Buckingham and other nobles, wore gowns of cloth of gold, embroidered and hung with gold chains and topped with white ostrich feathers. All was accompanied by music played by the queen's minstrels.[4] It must have been a festive and splendid occasion.

The removal of recent threats to throne made the Spanish rulers Ferdinand and Isabella more willing to conclude the proposed marriage treaty between Arthur and Catherine of Aragon. With Warbeck's and Warwick's executions in 1499, Ferdinand and Isabella were relieved that the kingdom was now safe, paving the way for this union and that of Princess Margaret with James IV of Scotland. Elizabeth had been corresponding with the teenage Catherine, advising her to learn French as she knew no English at all and extending the warmest wishes to her as her future daughter-in-law. The match had been mooted for years but it had, hitherto, advanced as slowly as the princess's English. Now events moved more quickly. On 19 May 1499 a proxy wedding took place between Arthur and Catherine at Tickenhill Palace, Bewdley, Worcestershire, which had been newly re-glazed and modernised specially. The Spanish ambassador Dr Rodrigo de Puebla stood in for the bride, repeating her vows alongside the young Tudor prince. Such marriages or betrothal agreements were often made in the absence of one or both parties, with only their representatives present, especially in the case of international relations. A further document was drawn up and signed by Arthur at Ludlow in November 1500, making the match 'lawful and indissoluble'. This marked a huge step forward; now it was just a case of waiting until the pair came of age.

Preparations were made almost at once. Isabella of Castile wrote to Puebla that she had heard 'much money would be spent upon her reception and wedding'. Although this delighted her as it showed the 'magnificent grandeur' of Henry and was in honour of her daughter, she asked him to keep the celebrations modest – 'rejoicings may be held but we ardently implore him that the substantial part of the festivities should be his love' – and that Catherine should be treated by him and Elizabeth as their 'true daughter'.[5]

Henry wanted her to sail to Gravesend or London, but Isabella stated that the most important consideration was her daughter's safety and a sea route to the south-west coast, near Southampton, would be swiftest as it was supposedly the safest harbour in England. After that, her company would proceed through the countryside, staying in inns and small villages. She would be accompanied by a small retinue, as Isabella knew she would be 'well attended' by the English but still believed it 'desirable' for her to have Spanish companions. For Henry's part, letters were sent out to all the nobility of England requesting their presence in London to welcome the princess; all foreign knights and nobles would be 'hospitably received' and pay 'nothing for their living'. A huge joust was to be held in the capital, which place was 'perfectly healthy at present', with no threat of plague or the sweat. All towns, villages and seaports were to be made ready to receive and entertain her, with Southampton and Bristol expecting to house the Spanish fleet. Again the old legends were alluded to: 'the 230 knights of the round table will again assemble … In olden times, King Arthur … presided over the round table …' as one of the king's secretaries wrote to his nephew in Spain.[6] The Scottish ambassador recorded that Henry, Elizabeth and Arthur were well 'and occupied with nothing else except putting all things in order for the Princess of Wales'. The Scottish ambassador proudly claimed that no Spanish visitors would die of hunger during the coming celebrations: 'if they die, it shall be from too much eating. Such a stock of provisions is laid in, that nothing shall be wanting.'[7]

The fifteen-year-old Catherine arrived in England in October 1501. Her departure had been delayed a little by a 'rebellion of the Moors' in Spain's 'most inaccessible mountains', which had taken her parents' attention and prevented them accompanying her to La Coruna, from where she would sail.[8] In his desire to see her off,

Ferdinand pardoned the rebels instead of subduing them by force, then fell prey to a fever while Catherine herself suffered from an 'ague', so the departure was set back further. Her fleet made one attempt to sail in September but the weather was so bad they were forced to turn back and wait for it to improve. In the end, she made a smooth crossing and landed at Plymouth not Southampton, where she was met by welcome parties and celebrations along the way before being formally received at Exeter. One Spanish witness described the scene to Isabella: 'She could not have been received with greater rejoicings, if she had been the saviour of the world.'⁹ Still, it must have been a daunting and slightly overwhelming experience for the teenager whose life, until then, had been spent among the Moorish palaces and exotic heat of Spain, with all its African trade and dramatic landscapes. She must have been aware that she was completely alone, a royal ambassador for her country, who would need to adjust to this green, new land and damp climate. She would never see her parents or homeland again. Her future lay in England. From Exeter, she embarked on her slow progress towards London. Those first seeing her admired her beauty and her 'agreeable, dignified manners'. Here, she would meet her future parents-in-law although Spanish custom dictated that she would not set eyes on the young man that was to become her husband until she stood at his side before the altar.

Henry and Arthur, however, had other ideas. Hearing of her arrival, they set out to meet her, encountering the cavalcade at Dogmersfield, in Hampshire. Elizabeth remained behind at Richmond to await her arrival. The Spanish were scandalised by their intrusion. Initially Catherine's ladies wouldn't allow them access, insisting that the princess was resting in bed, but Henry overrode their concerns by stating she was on English soil now and had to obey English customs. The king visited her first and Catherine wisely bowed to his wishes, before Arthur was introduced and they conversed in a mixture of Spanish and Latin. The men were pleased by their first sight of the Spanish princess, despite her unusual foreign clothing; she was short and pretty with long red-gold hair and the powerful, regal manner of her upbringing. When they returned to Richmond, the pair described the new bride in warm terms to Elizabeth before the royal family travelled on to Baynard's Castle, close by St Paul's, where the wedding was to take place. Here preparations were made, including new clothes for the English princesses; the five-year-old Mary had a dress of crimson velvet while her elder sister Margaret was to wear cloth of gold.

Catherine approached London from St George's Fields, where she was met by a welcome party headed by the eleven-year-old Prince Henry. Her procession was paired with English escorts, with each Spaniard partnered with their social equivalent, although the manner of riding side-saddle meant that the ladies were riding back to back. This caused onlookers to comment that they must have quarrelled and incited remarks about the appearance of the foreigners, with their unusual fashions and differing ideals of beauty. Catherine herself, though, was universally praised as she demurely rode her mule and acknowledged the crowds. She wore a little hat like a cardinal's cap, held in place with gold lace and a red undercap, below which her hair hung down long and loose. Sir Thomas More was highly complimentary: 'she thrilled the hearts of everyone; she possesses all those qualities that make for beauty in a very charming young girl'. However, her ladies in black with lace mantillas appeared a little funereal and provoked rude comments, even from the saintly More, who called them 'hunchbacked, undersized, barefoot pygmies'!

Heralds led the party to London Bridge, where the mayor met them and conducted them into the city on a highly symbolic journey. Six elaborate pageants had been set up around London to celebrate the royal arrival with their coded messages drawn from mythology, iconography and legend. The first was in the middle of the bridge itself, with its centrepiece as a Catherine wheel, typical of the visual allusions and parallels made. Some pageants were multi-storied with layers of religious, astrological and heraldic beasts or devices; special effects were created with staircases, lanterns and machinery. Speeches, poems and songs were recited as the party paused before each one. If Catherine, with her poor English, did not understand all the references, she could at least appreciate the scale of her welcome and the splendid spectacle designed to celebrate her arrival. As the city's future queen, she was the subject of intense scrutiny. Henry, Elizabeth, Arthur and Margaret Beaufort watched her pass from the house of a merchant, called Whiting, on the Strand. The procession ended at St Paul's, with the last pageant situated at the gates to the churchyard, where gifts were presented to the princess by the mayor and other leading Londoners. A choir sang and Catherine dismounted to make an offering to the city's own St Erkenwald, before she passed through the church to the newly re-glazed Bishop of London's palace, where she was staying.

The day before the wedding, Elizabeth met Catherine at Baynard's Castle. The queen must have been a comforting figure to the young girl, finally able to put a face to the name at the bottom of the letters she had been receiving for years. Elizabeth was her parallel in many ways; born into royalty and propelled into the limelight by her marriage, her experiences would have made her a valuable ally who understood the pressures Catherine was to face as a wife, mother and queen. In the impressive house on the bank of the Thames, close to St Paul's, with its four wings encircling a courtyard, the two women met and communicated as best they could. Ironically, this house was later to be given to Catherine as a wedding present by her second husband, then the eleven-year-old Prince Henry. But in 1501, all that lay in the future. The two women spent the evening together but nothing about their encounter was recorded; perhaps Elizabeth imparted some motherly advice or explained to her the proceedings she would follow the next day; perhaps she went further and told her what to expect as a married woman. It may have been Elizabeth who suggested the girl's personal motto, 'humble and loyal', which was not too far removed from her own 'humble and reverent'. Whatever passed between them, Catherine retired for the night to the bishop's palace knowing she would meet Elizabeth again as the Princess of Wales.

The wedding took place on 14 November 1501 at old St Paul's Cathedral. It was a huge building with a 489-foot spire, standing on the same spot as the present building. Work on the existing structure had begun in 1087 but three previous churches had stood on the site and improvements continued to be made for the next 300 years. By 1501, it was one of the longest and tallest cathedrals in Europe and annually drew thousands of pilgrims to the pyramid-shaped shrine of St Erkenwald, adorned with jewels, silver and gold. None of this original building survives, having been buffeted by the Reformation and Civil War, before being completely destroyed in the 1666 Great Fire of London. But as Catherine approached it that November, the medieval cathedral, renowned for its beauty, was decked out in fine silks and arras to mark the occasion. Catherine herself was dressed in white satin, her bodice and skirt folded with lots of pleats, in the Spanish style that was later to be known, in English, as the farthingale. Her hair hung long and loose under a veil of white silk embroidered with gold thread and pearls, as befitted her virginal status. Arthur was also clad in white satin; they must have formed an impressive sight as they mounted the platform covered with scarlet cloth, high enough for all the gathered nobility to witness. Henry and Elizabeth watched them from behind a lattice, so as not to distract attention from the young couple, but Prince Henry played a more active role in giving the bride away. After the mass had been performed, the king wrote to Ferdinand and Isabella that 'although the friendship between England and Spain has been most sincere and intimate before this time, it will henceforth be much more intimate and dissoluble'. Their daughter had found 'a second father, who will ever watch over her happiness and never permit her to want anything he can procure for her'. Arthur wrote to them that he had never felt so happy as when he 'beheld the sweet face of his bride' and promised to make a good husband.[10]

The subsequent celebrations lasted for weeks. As the couple left the cathedral, a pageant by the west door featured a strange collection of plants, trees and rocks of coral, amber and jet in the form of royal heraldic symbols such as the dragon, lion, greyhound and white hart, alongside a fountain running with wine. The wedding breakfast was held in the bishop's palace, with feasting continuing until late in the afternoon, when the couple headed to Baynard's Castle for the formal bedding and wedding night. In the following days, a tournament was held at Westminster, with lists set up before the hall and a tilt gallery for the court on the south side. Part of the decorations included a 'tree of chivalry', a colourful and impressive place for the escutcheons and shields of the competitors to be displayed. Inside, disguisings were performed in Westminster Hall, where William Cornish showcased a new type of mobile stage. On 19 November, the entertainment featured a castle centrepiece filled with singers, pulled by four heraldic beasts; a golden lion, a silver lion, a hart with gilt horns and an ibex. These must have been something like a modern pantomime horse, comprising two men in costume. There was also a ship in sail gliding in on hidden wheels, from which eight knights emerged to dance with ladies from the castle, the maiden remaining inside representing Catherine. Figures of Hope and Desire descended and the knights attempted to gain admission, upon which the ladies were compelled to surrender. It was one of these occasions that provided the anecdote of young Prince Henry dancing with his sister Margaret and throwing off his jerkin to the delight of his parents. Later, the Parliament Chamber hosted a great banquet, where a giant white lantern, set with windows covered in fine lawn, contained twelve beautiful ladies lit by 100 tapers. Still the celebrations continued and the pageantry became even more impressive. On 25 November, twelve ladies and twelve gentlemen entered the hall on pageant carts in the forms of mountains, linked by a golden chain, symbolising England and Spain, while the last day of festivities saw a pageant made to resemble a chapel, two stories high, drawn by three seahorses, filled with singing children, who set free baby rabbits and a flock of white doves. At the end of the month, it was time for the Spanish retinue to return home. No doubt they took some impressive tales back with them. Arthur and Catherine stayed for a while at Tickenhill Palace then departed to Ludlow, the prince's seat in Wales, to begin their married life.

10

A Year in the Life
1502–1503

Who feast the poor a true reward shall find
Or help the old, the feeble, lame and blind.[1]

The best-documented year of Elizabeth's life was her last. Surviving Privy Purse records of 1502–3[2] enable us to see her movements and expenses and give the most detailed impression possible of her daily life. She emerges as a devout, compassionate figure; an individual behind the façade of queenship that necessitated the maintenance of a constant public image. Here at last we really see Elizabeth the woman, in her gratitude to the poor who bring her gifts, as she rewards her father's old servants and buys new bonnets and socks. She began the year at Richmond, where the royal family spent the New Year; soon afterwards Henry moved to Westminster for the opening of Parliament. Elizabeth may have accompanied him for a while, but the spring saw her back at Richmond, whence she departed on 2 April. This marks the first appearance of her royal bargeman, Lewis Waltier, who conveyed her to Greenwich in a barge pulled by twenty-one rowers. Another constant figure in the accounts is Richard Justice, page of the robes, who was reimbursed 6d the same month for travelling from Greenwich to London to collect a stole (shawl) belonging to Elizabeth and a further 6d for running an errand to her goldsmith, John Lybert. It was while the royal couple were together at Greenwich, early in April, that terrible news arrived: it 'sodeynly happened a lamentable chaunce and lachrimosable losse to the king, queen and all the people'.[3]

On 4 April, a messenger arrived at Greenwich after riding solidly for two days from Ludlow. The Privy Council received him and, upon hearing his news, sent Henry's confessor to the king to break the news that Prince Arthur had died. A local outbreak of the sweating sickness had taken hold in the late spring, a painful disease that would dispatch most sufferers within days. Both Arthur and Catherine fell ill. While she survived, he succumbed and the sixteen-year-old Spanish princess became a widow after only four and a half months of marriage. The official record of his funeral related that a long-term disease may have been the underlying cause: 'a pitiful disease and sickness' of 'deadly corruption did utterly vanquish and overcome the (healthy) blood', which Victorian commentators interpreted as testicular cancer, although the sweating sickness is equally likely. The terrible sweat was universally feared. Hall describes an outbreak that struck London early in Henry's reign: victims were vexed with a terrible heat which 'infested the stomach and head grievously', making them cast off clothing and bedclothes and unable to quench an insatiable thirst. Death was fairly inevitable and followed very soon after: 'ther was not one emongst an hundredth that escaped'.[4]

Henry immediately sent for Elizabeth, who did her best to comfort him as they took 'the painful sorrow together'.[5] After she left him, she gave vent to her private feelings and was in such distress that her ladies sent for Henry to come and comfort her in turn. Elizabeth was no stranger to loss; her life had been punctuated by a string of family deaths but her grief for the sixteen-year-old first-born son, who had been so carefully groomed for the throne, must have been overwhelming. While their status meant that distance had been an unavoidable factor in their relationship, with Arthur raised at Ludlow, as well as the ever-present threat of child mortality, the couple's grief cannot be considered to be less comparable to that of modern parents. Twentieth-century historians suggested that past parent-child relations were less affectionate, that parents had more offspring and invested less emotion in them because of high rates of infant death. Henry and Elizabeth's reactions do not suggest this. Of the seven children born to them so far, Arthur was the fourth to die. In terms of the succession, they had lost three sons and only one, Prince Henry, remained. While Elizabeth had the comfort of her religion and her duties as queen, such losses must have affected her deeply in her primary role as a mother.

Elizabeth's loss may have been a factor in the volume of religious donations she made that April. Payments were recorded for offerings to a number of shrines dedicated to our Lady at Eton, Cockthorpe, Caversham, Worcester, Walsingham, Sudbury, Woolpit, Ipswich and Stokeclare. Apart from her established devotion and the appeal of her motherhood, the Virgin Mary was a significant figure for Elizabeth in her role as *mater dolorosa*, the mother grieving for her son. By associating herself closely with this figure, Elizabeth, like her mother, was leading a national cult and providing a connection with her female subjects. Since early medieval times, Mary had been held in particular affection in England. She featured heavily during the ritual year: Lady Day, 25 March, the old New Year's Day, was the day of her visitation by Gabriel and the conception of Christ; Candlemas, 2 February, was her purification, or churching, six weeks after having given birth; 15 August was Our Lady of the Harvest, when rural processions paraded sheaves of corn through the streets and 8 September was the feast of her nativity. At the time of the Reformation, there were in excess of sixty shrines across the country in her honour, displaying images, statues and stained glass depictions of the mother of God. The cult was also spread through word of mouth and popularly accessible through numerous ballads, prayers and songs: 'A Song to the Virgin'; 'The Five Joys of the Virgin'; 'A Prayer to Our Lady'; 'A Prayer to the Virgin'; 'Compassion Mariae'; 'Assumptio Mariae' and Wace's poem *Vie de la Vierge Marie* were among many in circulation: John Lydgate had completed a *Life of Our Lady* in 1411. She was also accessible in the many performances of cyclical miracle plays, frequently as a midwife, assisting an actor who was heaving and groaning in supposed labour, before producing a doll in swaddling clothes from between their legs.[6] She was a recognisable, regular feature in processions, often with guild members dressed in female robes carrying a doll, to symbolise Jesus, through the streets to the church altar, like at Beverley in Yorkshire.[7]

As Catholic sovereigns, Henry and Elizabeth were both involved in the religious lives of their subjects. Typical of this was the letter of July 1488, one of many which the king wrote to Pope Innocent VIII regarding the practice of papal dispensations. These allowed individuals freedom from particular religious laws or practices, like exemption from fasting or release from a vow or permission to marry within the forbidden degrees of consanguinity or blood relation if the couple were cousins. Henry wrote on behalf of his subjects who 'require dispensations and cannot afford to go to Rome or to send thither', asking that the Pope's representative, John de Giglis, be given the power to issue such privileges in England. The same summer, Robert the Englishman was sent by Henry to the Pope regarding similar matters. Lorenzo de' Medici supported this, adding his voice to the request for Innocent to grant him an audience, particularly because 'the Queen (of England) has written very warmly on this matter'.[8]

Like her mother, Elizabeth was deeply devout; her motto, 'humble and reverent', appears to have been carefully chosen. The pilgrimage she made to Walsingham in the summer of 1497 may have been in response to issues of fertility and childbirth but it was equally part of a wider pattern of her pious behaviour. Walsingham seems to have been a particular favourite: it lay at the centre of the East Anglian cult of the Virgin Mary, founded in 1061 by Richeldis de Faverches, widow of the Lord of the Manor of Walsingham. Erasmus described the shrine there as surrounded on all sides with gold, silver and gems, shining brilliantly; Mary's statue was draped in fine silk set with precious stones, with a lace veil edged in pearls, gold and silver. It also supposedly contained prized phials of what was claimed to be the Virgin's milk. Hundreds of visitors, of all ranks, made regular pilgrimage to the site, removing their shoes at the slipper chapel and walking the last mile or so barefoot. Although by the time of Elizabeth's visit the shrine had already passed its peak of popularity, it was still associated with particularly female complaints and was arguably the most renowned shrine in the country. Elizabeth also owned a number of religious texts, inscribed with her name, including Books of Hours and Prayers; she also made gifts of such texts to women of her court and was a joint sponsor, with Margaret Beaufort, of Caxton's 1491 edition of St Bridget's prayers. In 1497, Elizabeth paid £6 3s 4d for the celebration of mass at the Charterhouse at Sheen for a year, a Carthusian establishment she also particularly favoured.

Mary's status as a grieving mother must have particularly appealed to Elizabeth in 1502 but it also connected her with her female subjects. Most parish churches across England contained some iconography in celebration of the Virgin as mother, especially those dedicated to her, of which there are many although the biggest concentration is to be found in the east. However, the cult was national and a particular English favourite. An imposing Anglo-Saxon sculpture of the Virgin and Child over the interior door of St Mary's priory church at Deerhurst near Gloucester would have been seen by those entering, as would one on the southern exterior of St Mary and All Saints' in the Cheshire village of Great Budworth. The imagery continued inside, in windows such as those found in the tiny, disused parish church of North Stoke, West Sussex, depicting the Coronation of the Virgin, dating from around 1290. This theme can still be found in many surviving church windows and wall paintings. In Aldermaston, Berkshire, the church of St Mary the Virgin contains two thirteenth-century roundels of the Virgin's Coronation and a lady chapel, dedicated as late as 1530. Medieval stained glass depicting the Virgin and Child and the Coronation of the Virgin can still be found in the nave at Fordwich, Kent and in the village church at Fladbury, contemporary with the nearby abbey and shrine at Evesham. Murals survive on the walls of St Mary the Virgin in Tarrant Crawford, Dorset, as do carvings like that on the rood screen at Elsing, Norfolk, which must have been typical of the many stopping points along the pilgrim route to Walsingham. Elizabeth's subjects saw these and by correlation thought of their queen daily.

The Marian cult was more than a reassuring symbol or a simple channel to the divine: it was an objective correlative for female experiences, accessible to all classes. Julia Kristeva[9] explores childbirth as an 'unveiling of meaning', a crucial moment where meaning is 'born on the edge of nothingness', in a world where women are traditionally excluded from religion. Worshipping the medieval cult of the Virgin Mary, allied with their experiences of childbirth, afforded women a powerful sense of validation and identity in religious and social terms. It must have been an empowering experience for a grieving mother to feel that she had Mary 'on her side', helping make the inexplicable and terrifying less so: offering in Kristeva's words 'a combination of power and sorrow, sovereignty and the unnameable'. Christianity placed a special emphasis in women's dignity and the cult of Mary celebrated and encouraged childbearing. It was certainly a defining feature of Elizabeth's identity.

The queen did not neglect other religious observations. Gifts in 1502–3 were given to individuals who undertook these journeys for her, such as Sir William Barton, for going on pilgrimage for the queen at 10*d* a day and to Richard Milner, for offerings made on her behalf at Crowham, Canterbury, Dover, Barking and Willesdon among other places. Favoured saints and locations also received donations, such as Hailes, which held the legendary holy blood, which her son's commissioners would later claim was nothing more than the blood of a duck. In the early summer, Elizabeth gave the sum of 5*s* to the Fraternities of St George at Southwark, St Corpus Christi at St Sepulchre, London; by August, when she knew she was pregnant again, she gave 20*d* to St Frideswide at Oxford, whose traditional association with the cure of female conditions attracted women pilgrims in numbers that outweighed their male counterparts two to one. The same month, the queen made more offerings to Our Lady, particularly on Assumption Day, as well as 12*d* to the rood at Northampton and 2*s* 5*d* to Our Lady at Linchelade. The regular saints' days through the Catholic calendar were observed: Elizabeth paid 5*s* for offerings on the Feast of the Ascension, 20*s* at Pentecost, 5*s* at Trinity, 5*s* at Corpus Christi, 20*s* for offerings on the Feast of the Nativity of St John the Baptist, the Apostles, St Thomas and on Relic Sunday. In this, she was typical of men and women of her era, in responding to the perceived abilities of saints to intercede for them in spiritual issues. Her record was consistent: that December she was recorded as having honoured the days of St Nicholas and St Andrew with 5*s* each; on Twelfth Night 1503, she donated the same amount but the Eve of the Conception of the Virgin elicited a gift of 6s 8d.

The year's accounts also show that Elizabeth was generous when it came to charitable giving. Regularly, old women, the unfortunate and past servants appear as the beneficiaries of her generosity. As was traditional, she gave alms to thirty-seven poor women on Maundy Thursday 1502, totalling 64s, while the London tailor, Richard Smith, received payment for 61 yards of cloth for their clothing. A Nicholas Grey, clerk of the works at Richmond, received 60s when his house burned down, followed by 11s jointly to nuns in an almshouse and an old woman servant, then 6s 8d to an Agnes Metingham in alms. That June she gave 20d to a poor man in an almshouse who had been a servant of Edward IV; other old servants received 6s 8d in July, 6s 4d in November and 3s 4d to a past servant, Henry Langton, that December. In July she gave 12d to a hermit and 4d to a poor man who guided her to him, while in November, 20d was her gift to an anchoress at Gloucester. She also gave 8s to the clerk of St John's for the burial of men hanged at Wapping. It was certainly within a medieval queen's remit to represent the compassionate face of royalty; some of Elizabeth's gifts may have been in response to the supplications of individuals, while others may have been of her own initiative. She certainly looked after her current staff, paying for the lodging of Ann Saye, one of her gentlewomen who had fallen ill at Woodstock that autumn, for eight weeks at 16d a week. The page of the her bedroom, William Paston, was given 40s to buy wedding clothes while her apothecary John Grice's servant, Leonard Twycrosse, received 16s towards his wedding gown. Certainly those who had been loyal in the past or who served her well during the year were rewarded, either on a regular basis or as one-off recipients. Elizabeth's kindness was also extended to her newly widowed daughter-in-law, Catherine, whom she received at Westminster Palace once she was well enough to travel to the capital.

Elizabeth's final year was spent close to home in London. The court continued to move, with Henry's itinerary showing he was frequently to be found on business between Westminster, Windsor, the magnificent Richmond and Woodstock in Oxfordshire. Elizabeth travelled less. That spring, when the records began, she had just celebrated Easter at Greenwich on 6 April and received the bad news about Arthur. It was during this stay, mere weeks after the couple's loss, that the queen conceived again; she was certainly pregnant by the time she left the palace for the Tower. On 29 May, her bargeman, Lewis Waltier, was paid 4*d* for carrying the queen by barge upriver from Greenwich, with additional payments made for tallow dressing, ropes and other necessaries for the her barge and the transportation of her gowns to the Tower. By July she was at Windsor, where she was enjoying the gardens and made trips across the river at Datchet, the traditional crossing used by royalty to and from London. She may also have visited the medieval church of St Mary's, which still stands there, as she paid 3*s* 4*d* to a ferryman at Datchet that month. This could have been the Hamlet Clegg who received the same amount that November for providing the same service. In August, preparations were being made at Elizabeth's lodgings in Westminster, in anticipation of her arrival and that of some imminent guests. John Browne, her groom of the beds, was recompensed his costs for carrying 'certain stuff' from Baynard's Castle to Richmond for the visit of the Hungarian ambassadors. More of her servants' travel costs were also covered, like when one Henry Roper, page of the beds, travelled from Greenwich to London to visit the goldsmith John Libert and was rewarded for fetching things and carrying messages for the queen. Lewis Waltier was busy again in November, rowing Elizabeth from Richmond to Westminster and receiving payment of 30s 4d for a great boat to carry the ladies and gentlewomen of the court and one for the princesses. Elizabeth continued to travel regularly throughout the winter; Waltier brought her to Richmond for Christmas before she embarked on her final journey to the Tower on 26 January.

As the court moved between its royal residences, the task of providing for its large retinue fell increasingly on the local population. The establishment could run to thousands, all of whom needed to be fed and sheltered; they would systematically eat their way through an area's resources and move on, leaving the area to replenish itself ready for the next visit. Dependent upon seasonal produce, Elizabeth was often the recipient of gifts to supplement her main diet. These came from subjects ranging in status from the Abbess of the Minories, who received 6s 8d for bringing the queen rose water, to 8d given to the poor woman who brought a gift of butter and chickens. Clearly this was a reciprocal arrangement with payments given for what could range from a little fresh produce that a family might spare to more specialist luxury items. Among other gifts Elizabeth received that year, she paid 12d to John Goose for bringing her a carp, 3s 4d to a girl for bringing almond butter, 12d to a poor man who brought apples and oranges to Richmond, 3s 4d to Lady Bray for puddings and 6s 8d to one who brought her June roses. Later in the year she received cherries, apples and pears, followed by venison and bucks, woodcocks, tripe for 3s 4d and wild boar for 10s, puddings and pork at 2s and she rewarded a Spaniard who brought oranges to court. In December 1502, Brice, 'yeoman cook to the queen's mouth', was paid 2s 8d for larks and chickens while her fool, Patch, received a reward for bringing her pomegranates, oranges and other fruits. The following January brought her offerings of orange confiture, cheese and baked lampreys; 2s was paid to a servant of the Archbishop of Canterbury for sending a cheese to the queen at Richmond and 2s to a servant of the Abbess of Syon who sent rabbits and quails. These would have contributed to the general expenses of the kitchens when preparing for the royal family's daily diet as well as the ceremonial and exotic food they enjoyed on feast days and key dates in the Catholic calendar. On average, they might feed several hundred people a day and often more. At Christmas, 6s 8d was paid to the waffry (waffles and wafers), 10s to Thomas Hunt in the confectionary, a high-status department preparing sweet treats for the elite, and 10s more to children of the privy kitchen. The queen's kitchen also received payments for pots, new bowls, basket, flowers, for heating water in the kitchen and transporting the same stuff to London from Richmond.

Elizabeth appears to have enjoyed being outdoors. Tudor garden design could be splendid and ceremonial, extending the motifs and structures of interior décor out into sculpted and painted arenas of formality and pleasure. Walled, designed gardens were separate from a palace's wider grounds, where hunting, archery and other sports might take place, such as exercising the queen's greyhounds, who were cared for at a cost of 2d a day by Thomas Woodnot. They were little havens of relaxation and cultivation, where the royal family could unwind and for high-ranking women, like Elizabeth, flowers as well as culinary and medicinal herbs were grown. Most famously, the intricate but useful knot gardens have survived, recreated at several contemporary properties but the elaborate structures of gardens enjoyed by Elizabeth and her family at the turn of the century were a further mark of their status. By all accounts, the queen herself was involved in their design. In July 1502, Henry Smith, clerk of Windsor, was paid 4s 8d for making an herbour, a sweet-scented arbour, in the garden, as a venue for a banquet held by Elizabeth. Also payments to the king's painter, Fyll, for the 'making of divers beestes and other pleasires' for the queen, similar to those currently standing in the 2009 Chapel Court Tudor garden at Hampton Court, gilded and painted heraldic creatures, mounted on the tops of poles, bearing flags. At her favourite palace of Greenwich, the old Palace of Pleasaunce was gradually being transformed. Work started in 1498 but by 1502, the king's mason, Robert Vertue, was working from a plan made by Elizabeth herself. Those improvements dating from 1502–4 had been designed by the queen, who had included new walls, gardens, gallery, kitchen and tower, as well as fresh painting. Necessary expenses were also incurred that year for developments undertaken at Baynard's Castle, including interior door locks, bolts for the hall and locks for the garden door: a mason was paid 2s for four days' work, setting the iron on the windows.

Her other entertainments followed the usual pattern. Rewards of 26s 8d went to minstrels that played at Richmond, 11s to the king's minstrels playing shawms and to those who played for her daughter Margaret. A Spanish dancing maid, possibly from the retinue of Catherine of Aragon, received 4s 4d. Cards and dice were still favourites; Elizabeth lost 13s 4d playing at dice at Ewelme and enjoyed a game of cards on St Stephen's Day. The Christmas celebrations of 1502 were also enlivened by William Cornish setting a carol to music for 13s 4d, children in chapel choir, the Lord of Misrule, various fools and two gallons of Rhenish wine. Additionally, impressive costumes were made that year for elaborate drama. A considerable 56s 8d went to coppersmiths for making spangles, star drops and silver points, plus gold for the garnishing of jackets to adorn costumes for the disguising in June, while in December, the tailor, Robert Machene, received 22s for making costumes for the festive disguisings; coats of white and green sarcanet for the king's minstrels and trumpeters. As with her other servants, Elizabeth took care of her family's entertainers when they were ill. That summer, a William Worthy was paid for the board of William, the king's fool, for three months at 6s, plus 4s for his food.

The accounts allow us to peek inside the queen's wardrobe for 1502. Elizabeth's clothing expenses include her small-scale domestic needs like the 12d paid for the making of a night bonnet and her November payment for seven pairs of socks to a Thomas Humberston at 6d per pair. Set beside this are the details of her regal clothing. To Henry Byran, London mercer, she paid £32 6s for silks and 7s for making a black damask cloak, plus 4s for lining the cloak with black sarcanet and 17s 2d in black velvet for bordering it. One William Botery received a total of £6 11s and 9d for black tinsel satin to edge a gown of black velvet, black satin to edge a gown of crimson velvet, seven yards of green satin from Bruges, sarcanet of eight different colours to make girdles, tawny green and russet sarcanet. A Friar Hercules supplied gold damask, Venice gold, Venice silk, lace and buttons to make a garter for 50s; Robynet the embroiderer got 30s 4d in May, while 12d was paid for the fur and a half of a fox for a russet gown. In June, Robert Ragdale was paid for making scarlet and linen petticoats for the queen and sheets for hemming kirtles and making white sarcanet sleeves.

Not all Elizabeth's clothing was new. Richard Justice, her page of the robes, received 4s for turning the hem of her damask kirtle, 4d for mending a crimson velvet gown, 4d for mending a black velvet gown and expenses for travel between palaces to collect various clothing items. Frequently some garment was required that had remained in the department of the Royal Wardrobe. Richard Justice was paid in July for fetching a gown of cloth of gold, hiring a boat from Richmond to London, and then from Westminster to London, to fetch Princess Margaret's orange sarcanet sleeves. That November, Justice received 2s 4d for conveying furred gowns from London to Westminster and in August, Thomas Woodnot and John Felde, grooms of the queen's chamber, were paid 8s 6d for transporting her jewels between several residences.

A few intimate glimpses of Elizabeth can be caught through the Privy Purse accounts. When the royal bedroom doors of Elizabeth's many palaces closed for the night, the person of the queen can be glimpsed, from her night bonnets and socks, to the bed she slept in. That October, work began on a new bedstead and hangings, possibly for her use during her approaching lying-in. It would have been an impressive and sumptuously regal piece of furniture, beginning with the payment of 4s to William Hamerton for an iron bedstead. The following month, London mercer Thomas Goodriche supplied 60 yards of blue velvet for £31 10s and Robynet and his team of embroiderers began to work it in gold and silk, for which they received a series of payments. A John Warreyn then furnished the bed in crimson velvet, with blue panels and red thread, and supplied great rings for the curtains and fine white thread for curtains and white fringe at 46s 4d. By the time Elizabeth went into confinement the following January, her new bed must have been ready; perhaps she delivered her final child there; perhaps she died in it. She paid her apothecary John Grice's bill that summer for £9 24s 4d and again in September for 'certain stuff' of his occupation totalling £10 19s 11d. She also reimbursed William Stafford 2s for providing 'divers stuff for the king in the night' and a considerable 40s 4d to London tallow chandler, John Henstead, for rolls of wax in November. A touching picture of the queen emerges in her night cap, tucked up under embroidered covers in red and blue, sipping one of her doctor's cures by candlelight.

Through these accounts, the picture of the real woman emerges, subject as she was to her times and status. At the age of thirty-six, Elizabeth was a long-established queen, wife and mother who had faced many challenges and seen her fortunes fluctuate. The loss of Arthur early in the year was undoubtedly a terrible blow for her personally as well as for the dynasty but these records show that life went on and her determination to do her duty did not waver. Her support for her husband 'behind the scenes' shows that Elizabeth of York was not the passive figure historians have suggested; instead, her charity and humanity provided an important human face to late fifteenth-century monarchy, as half of a successful partnership. In this, she was not only conforming to contemporary ideals of queenship, but excelling at them. Above all, she personified the female virtues of tactfulness, piety, motherhood and compassion but she also proved her strengths as a survivor. The extent of her value can perhaps be seen most strongly in the years following her death, when her influence was removed from her husband, a period that was to shape his later reputation as an introvert and miser.

11

Surprised by Time
1503

In child-bed lost she her sweet Life;
Her life esteemed so dear
Which had been England's loving Queen
Full many a happy year.[1]

Early in 1502, Elizabeth's eldest daughter was finally married. The famous union of the thistle and the rose, between England and Scotland, had been mooted since 1497 but the involvement of James IV with the pretender Perkin Warbeck had delayed the scheme, as had the bride's age. At the time, Margaret had been nine years old, while her prospective husband was a man in his twenties with a reputation for licentiousness, having already fathered at least five illegitimate children. Nor was it his first engagement. In 1486, he had been betrothed to Cecily of York, Elizabeth's younger sister, although this match had come to nothing and Cecily was then married to a half-brother of Margaret Beaufort. When it came to arranging the match, the queen and Margaret worked together; neither wanted her to be married too young – reports suggest she was 'very young and very small for her years'[2] – and the women insisted the ceremony should be delayed until the onset of her puberty. Such marriages were common among the aristocracy; Elizabeth had been present at the wedding of her brother Richard, aged four years old, in 1478. In such circumstances, the bride would usually be sent to live with her husband's family, until the ages of consent were reached. Margaret's first-hand experience of early motherhood must have been a factor in this case, as was the belief that the Scottish king was not to be trusted to wait before consummation took place. According to a letter Henry sent to Ferdinand and Isabella of Spain, the king appreciated that 'the queen and my mother are very much against this marriage ... we should be obliged to send the princess directly to Scotland, in which case they fear the King of Scots would not wait, but injure her, and endanger her health'.[3] By late 1501, though, the girl was approaching her twelfth birthday and Scottish ambassadors arrived in London to take part in the celebrations of Arthur's wedding. There, the final negotiations were made.

On 25 January 1502, the proxy wedding was held at Richmond Palace in the queen's great chamber. It was common for ceremonies to go ahead without one or both parties being present although, by delegating a representative, the vows were just as binding. The Earl of Bothwell stood in for James IV, wearing the regal cloth of gold and, following the mass, the rites were performed in all the attendant splendour of the new palace. Elizabeth and Margaret, now two queens of equal standing, dined together, sharing one 'mess' or set of portions, as a symbolic gesture of her new status. Later that day there was jousting, dancing, pageants and a banquet; London celebrated with wine and bonfires. Despite being a married woman, Margaret was to remain at Westminster a little longer, at the insistence of her mother. The 1502 accounts detail some of the preparations that would ultimately lead to her departure. A pair of crimson state bed curtains embroidered with red roses of Lancaster were prepared and various 'stuff' was bought for her including pewter bowls, washing bowls, a fire pan, basket and bellows carried to Westminster from London by a Henry Roper, at £6 10*d*. 10*s* was paid for strings for her lute and 14*s* for furring of her gown of crimson velvet and other details; she appears to have been particularly fond of her pair of orange sarcanet sleeves.

Margaret would finally leave London with her father as her escort in June 1503. Writing to celebrate the union, the Scottish court poet, William Dunbar, praised her as the softening rose to tame James' 'awful' thistle:

> The fresche roiss, of cullour reid and quhyt ...
> so full of blisfull angelic bewty
> Imperiall birth, honour and dignitie.

Her dignity and regality would light the whole country:

> A coistly croun, with clarefeid stonis brycht
> This cumly queen did on hir heid inclois,
> Quhill all the land illumyit of the licht.

Ultimately, Margaret's future would be less clear and bright than the poet suggested. Quickly disillusioned with her new homeland and the many affairs of her husband, she would bear him six children, all of whom died in infancy save one boy. Following James' death at the Battle of Flodden, against English forces, Margaret's controversial remarriages would put her at the turbulent heart of Scottish politics. Her life would prove to be as much one of suffering and instability as those of her grandmother and mother. However, it would be through her surviving son, James V and her granddaughter, Mary, Queen of Scots, that the English and Scottish thrones would finally be united in 1603.

A century before, though, there seemed to be little reason to predict these dramatic twists in the Tudor succession.

Late in 1502, Queen Elizabeth was preparing for her eighth and final confinement. Devastated by their loss of Arthur, the king and queen had consoled each other as best they could, with Elizabeth telling Henry they still had a 'fair, goodly' son and were young enough to have more children. This was no idle promise. Within weeks, she had conceived again, suggesting her fertility was still strong. At thirty-six, she was not old by modern standards, nor even those of the time: after all, her own mother had delivered her final child, Bridget, in 1480 at the age of forty-three. Elizabeth could still bear a strong male child, who could be the 'spare' heir to the new Prince of Wales, Prince Henry. A fortune-teller had recently predicted a long life for her, claiming she would live until the age of eighty.

As Elizabeth prepared for her confinement, two nurses visited her in November, the start of her final trimester, which may have been routine but may equally have indicated that something was amiss. On the fourteenth, a Mistress Harcourt saw her at Westminster and twelve days later she was attended by a French woman at Baynard's Castle, who was paid 6s 8d for nursing her. The new bedding and curtains were almost complete, accounts for the delivery of bed linen were settled and a monk was paid 6s 8d for delivering the girdle of Our Lady of Westminster in mid-December. Right up until the end, Elizabeth was on the move. On 15 December, bread and ale costing 12d was consumed by her servants at Baynard's Castle; Christmas was spent at Richmond among much celebration and on 26 January, Lewis Waltier rowed her to London from Richmond, which was only intended as a temporary visit. By all accounts, the queen intended to deliver her child at Richmond, so planned to return there in the near future. It was a journey she would never make.

While staying in the Tower, Elizabeth was overcome with pain and her labour began. In this event, caught by surprise, she would have to make the best of the situation. Hurried preparations must have been made as her midwife, Alice Massey, rushed to her side. This was, in itself, a departure from the norm as queens usually withdrew a month or so before labour began, allowing for misdiagnosis, preparation and the long hours of 'travail'; it was more common for babies to arrive later, after weeks of waiting. Perhaps she had miscalculated. After delivering seven children already, she may have not considered the danger to be so acute and decided she did not need such an early retirement from public life. Her labour was long and arduous. A daughter, Catherine, was delivered on Candlemas Day, 2 February 1503, leaving her mother very weak. Soon after the birth it became apparent that Elizabeth was seriously ill; possibly puerperal fever had set in or heavy bleeding; perhaps she had sustained an injury during the delivery. She had suffered an 'ague' after the birth of Arthur but this was something else entirely. As her women worked frantically to calm her and restore her to health, a messenger was dispatched into Kent to try to locate a Dr Aylsworth or Hallysworth. Presumably other royal doctors were present but their efforts were in vain. Nine days later the queen was dead.

Most Tudor mothers did not die during childbirth. Surprisingly, the odds of survival were fairly good, providing there were no complications. Estimated figures have suggested a mortality rate of around one in fifty but difficult deliveries could lead to maternal and infant death without preventative action being taken. Many survived the experience only to succumb to infection or heavy bleeding afterwards. The more babies a mother bore, the greater her risk of death and resulting illness, with the increased physical toll on her body. For some, birth complications made their very first pregnancy fatal, while others bore in excess of ten children and survived into comparative old age. If a delivery was straightforward, the mother stood a fair chance of survival, provided she remained healthy afterwards; if complications arose from a difficult presentment or other trauma, her likelihood of coming through decreased with each passing hour. Midwives were instructed to remove babies which became stuck, using metal hooks or whatever means they could, although this usually resulted in infant mortality. Elizabeth's child was delivered alive but died after eight days and its mother rapidly declined. The interval of nine days between the delivery and the queen's death suggest the birth itself was a success but that a subsequent fever took hold or internal damage later caused a haemorrhage. Straightforward hygienic precautions like the washing of hands and transmission of germs were not understood at the time. Whatever caused her death, it came as a terrible shock to her family. Her young son Henry, then aged eleven, would refer to it as the worst news he had ever received; for her husband, it would be an irrevocable blow. To the nation, also, the death of the popular, gentle and devout queen was cause for national mourning.

The semi-deification of Elizabeth began at once, as the news of her loss spread. She had always been popular, as her father's daughter, as well as for her own tumultuous ride to the throne and personal charms. In the country's eyes, she was the epitome of motherhood, correlating with her favoured cult of the Virgin Mary in her devotion and suffering. Henry gave his wife a splendid and dignified funeral, where colour and light were carefully deployed to intensify her sacrifice. Dramatic white banners were laid across the corners of her coffin, signifying the manner of her death, while the main body of it was draped with black velvet surmounted by a cross of white cloth of gold. Two sets of thirty-seven virgins in white linen and Tudor wreaths of white and green lined her route to Westminster, carrying lighted candles and the torch-bearers wore white, woollen-hooded gowns. More than 1,000 lights burned on the hearse and the vaults and cross of the cathedral were draped in black and lit by 273 large tapers. The coffin was spectacularly topped by a wax effigy of the queen, dressed in robes of estate, her hair loose under a rich crown, a sceptre in her hand and fingers adorned with fine rings. Before burial, the effigy with its crown and rich robes was removed and stored in secrecy at the shrine of Edward the Confessor; so this lifelike, regal image of the queen was absorbed into a collection of holy relics and icons, interchangeable with the symbolic objects that assisted her during childbirth. Part of the effigy still exists in the museum at Westminster Abbey, its face, neck and chest painted white, its features regular and serene, unsmiling but beneficent.

A seventeenth-century ballad recorded Elizabeth's loss and Henry's inconsolable grief:

> The Queen that fair and Princely Dame
> That mother meek and mild
> To add more Number to her Joy
> Again grew big with Child:
>
> All which brought comfort to the King
> Against which careful Hour
> He lodg'd his dear kind hearted Queen
> In London's stately Tower.
>
> That Tower that was so fatal once
> To Princes of Degree
> Proved fatal to this noble Queen
> For therein died She.
>
> In child-bed lost she her sweet Life;
> Her life esteemed so dear
> Which had been England's loving Queen
> Full many a happy year.

> The King herewith possess'd with Grief
> Spent many Months in Moan
> And daily sigh'd and said that he
> Like her could find out none:
>
> Nor none could he in Fancy chuse,
> To make his Wedded Wife
> Wherefore a Widower would remain,
> The Remnant of his Life.

Suddenly there was silence at court. The workings of the queen's household ground to a halt as her staff completed their duties and began to seek re-employment, perhaps elsewhere in the service of the king and his children, or else beyond Westminster's walls. The records list the wages for her waiting men and women that were settled in March, as the establishment was being disbanded. These people had played an intimate part in her daily life for years, often unrecorded and behind the scenes; her loss must have been a significant one to them. Elizabeth was particularly known for her kindness to her employees, paying their expenses when they were sick, looking after them in retirement and contributing towards the cost of key events like their weddings. Agnes Dean, her laundress, received 66*s* 8*d*, William Denton, carver of her meat, got £26 13*s* 4*d*, Owen Whitstones, her messenger, was paid 11*s* while her favourite minstrels got 66*s* 8*d*. Oliver Aulferton, the keeper of her goshawk, was paid 40*s* while Alice Massy, her midwife, received £10.[4] The king's court remained in operation but the corresponding apartments and roles were increasingly taken over by his mother, Margaret Beaufort. While the business aspects of court life continued to demand Henry's attention, as did the education and marital prospects of his remaining children, the queen was not easily forgotten. Those outside the court, such as religious establishments and the poor, who had regularly benefited from her charity and kindness, would have keenly felt her loss. As Henry aged, gaining the reputation for miserliness that appeared to divide his identity into contrasting halves, his people genuinely grieved for Elizabeth and redirected their affection towards his teenage son. The joy that greeted the accession of the exuberant and athletic seventeen-year-old prince in 1509 signalled a continuation of the esteem in which the general populace had held his mother and Plantagenet grandfather.

Early in 1504, an indenture was made between Henry VII and John Islip, Abbot of St Peter's, Westminster. As well as the daily masses that were to be said for the soul of Elizabeth and her deceased children, the anniversary of her death on 11 February was to be marked every year of the king's life, when the whole convent would gather in the choir, or later, when it was completed, the Lady Chapel. There, they would solemnly sing a requiem mass, the bells would be rung and 100 tapers of new wax burned in her honour. In keeping with the queen's generosity, alms would be distributed among the 'blind, lame, impotent and most needy'.[5] That same evening, prayers would conclude with the words:

> God save the king oure soveraign lord and founder king Henry the seventh and have marcy on the soule of the moste excellent Princes Elizabeth late Queen of England his wife and the soules of their children and of their issue and of their progenitours and auncestours of the same king oure soveraign lord and all christen soules.[6]

Henry had planned the construction of Westminster's Lady Chapel before Elizabeth's death. The foundations were laid in January 1503, just days before she gave birth and now it seemed to be a fitting mausoleum for his wife where, at some point in the future, he would join her. Thousands of pounds were spent on its construction, which lasted six years, resulting in a chapel to equal the magnificence of any of Henry's palaces. After his death in 1509, Henry's tomb was sculpted by Italian artist Pietro Torrigiano; he also made the joint bronze images of husband and wife still visible in the chapel today. Around the edge of the tomb, erected in the reign of their son, Elizabeth is described as 'his sweet wife (who) was very pretty, chaste and fruitful. They were parents happy in their offspring, to whom, land of England, you owe Henry VIII.'

Barely a decade after her death, Elizabeth's significance for history was being defined as her motherhood of the next Tudor king. Her second son's immense reputation would come to dwarf that of his parents, whose individual characters and lives were already relegated to statuary and legend. For later generations and centuries, the first Tudor family was merely a prelude for the glorious reign of the controversial Henry VIII. No doubt Elizabeth's untimely death and her conformity to the ideals of queenship, womanhood and beauty of her era facilitated this marginalisation. However, the study of her life illuminates a woman of complex emotions, whose difficult life had taught her the essential qualities of compassion and diplomacy that marked her duration as royal wife and mother. The advent of her son Henry was made possible by the strength of his parents as survivors. Together, Elizabeth and her husband had established, defended and founded the most famous dynasty in English history.

Henry VII contemplated remarriage. It was common at the time, especially among royalty. Yet it was probably deliberate that none of his efforts came to fruition, forming instead a wider part of his foreign policy. He observed every anniversary of Elizabeth's death and died a widower at Richmond in April 1509. His wife's influence upon him personally and politically has been much underestimated since. The nature of medieval queenship was one of symbiosis and balance; while men and women were thought to contrast and complement each other, a queen's feminine qualities would balance and temper her husband's manly, warlike nature with compassion. Thus her influence was of a personal nature, to soothe and soften and be an intermediary; in modern terms, the queen was the approachable face of monarchy. One fourteenth-century petition to Anne of Bohemia, wife of Richard II, requested 'let the queen soften royal severity that the king may be forbearing to his people. A woman mellows a man with love; for this God gave her, for this, o blessed woman, may your love aspire.'[7] Thus, the influence of queens has been exerted mostly through their domestic role, as mothers and in the running of their household. Less well-acknowledged, in recent historical study, is the extent of their political influence, specifically warned against in Caxton's *A Game of Chesse*; rather, they have been defined by what they should not be. Their identities exist within, and cannot escape definition from, a wider framework of gender politics, from which not even a crown could offer them freedom. Just as women were subject to men and wives to husbands, queens could not be allowed to dominate their royal partners. They should not be warlike and hard-nosed like Margaret of Anjou or clandestinely espoused and in possession of large ambitious families like Elizabeth Wydeville. They must be obedient and demure and chaste and industrious, just like all fifteenth-century wives should be, except much more visibly and accountably.

Practically, it is impossible to measure or record the intimate influence of queens. The conversations that took place in the bedroom and the subtle balance of power between lovers served to define the female influence differently within each marriage; after five centuries the secrets of Elizabeth and Henry's union cannot now be recovered. In her role as patron of religion and arts, in her piety and compassion and as a figurehead for motherhood correlative with the Virgin Mary, Elizabeth fulfilled her role as queen and her motto of 'humble and reverent'. In 1972, S. B. Chrimes described her as 'a very handsome woman of great ability, as beloved, as a woman of the greatest charity and humanity ... good reason to suppose she was an admirable spouse in the king's eyes'. A decade later, Anne Crawford supposed she was 'probably everything a fifteenth-century Englishman could have hoped for in his queen'. Subsequent chroniclers, and most historians, have idealised Elizabeth as a shadowy figure, with quasi-divine status; in Hall's words, she was 'virtuous and gracious', in the eyes of others, beautiful and submissive. The real Elizabeth remains comparatively inaccessible through the lack of surviving records but her success as a wife, mother and queen cannot be called into doubt. She set the standard of queenship for her contemporaries and possibly also for her son, the future Henry VIII, by which all other consorts could be measured. As the daughter, sister, wife, mother and grandmother of kings and queens, her offspring would inherit the English throne for the next century, after which they would also claim it as the Stuart line and unite the kingdom for another 100 years. In very real terms, Elizabeth was responsible for delivering the future and her legacy long outlived her.

Notes

Introduction

1. A term deriving from the French Annales school of history and anthropology, by which the collective mindsets of groups of people in the past are studied.

Prologue

1. Gairdner, J. (ed.), *Gregory's Chronicle 1461–9* (London, 1876).
2. Riley, H. T (trans.), *Ingulph's Chronicle of the Abbey of Croyland* (London: H. G. Bohn, 1854).

1 The Rising Star, 1466–1469

1. Heywood, T., *The First and Second Parts of King Edward IV*, Field, B. (ed.) (London: Shakespeare Society, 1842).
2. Weir, A., *Lancaster and York: The Wars of the Roses* (Vintage, 1995).
3. Santiuste, D., *Edward IV and the Wars of the Roses* (Pen and Sword, 2010).
4. Falkus, G., *The Life and Times of Edward IV* (Weidenfeld and Nicolson, 1981).
5. Weir.
6. Gairdner.
7. Weir.
8. Riley.

9. More, T., *The History of King Richard III*, Rawson Lumby, J. (ed.) (Cambridge University Press, 1883).

10. Heywood.

11. More.

12. Cornazzano, A., *La Regina d'Ingliterra* (1466–8).

13. Okerlund, A., *Elizabeth Wydeville, the Slandered Queen* (Tempus, 2005).

14. Ellis, H. (ed.), *New Chronicles of England and France in two parts by Robert Fabyan, 1516* (London, 1811).

15. Roud, S., *The English Year* (Penguin, 2006).

16. Hutton, R., *The Ritual Year in England* (Oxford University Press, 1994).

17. Reading Museum collection, object no. 1931.273.1.

18. Falkus.

19. *Ibid*.

20. Okerlund.

21. Weir, A., *The Princes in the Tower* (Vintage, 2008).

22. Clark, J. and C. Ross, *London, the Illustrated History* (Allen Lane, 2008).

23. State Letters and Papers, Edward IV 1468–9.

24. Nicolas, N. H. (ed.) *The Privy Purse Expenses of Elizabeth of York* (London: William Pickering, 1830).

25. The anonymous fifteenth-century author of *Gawain and the Green Knight*, *Pearl*, *Patience* and *Cleanness*.

26. Okerlund.

27. Thurley, S., *The Royal Palaces of Tudor England* (Yale University Press, 1993).

28. Sharpe, R. R., *Memorials of London and the Kingdom* (1894).

29. Okerlund.

30. *Ibid*.

31. Weightman, C., *Margaret of York, Duchess of Burgundy, 1446–1503* (New York: St Martin's Press, 1989).

32. Calendar of State Papers, Venice, June 1468.

33. Croyland.

34. Gairdner, J. (ed.), *The Paston Letters, 1422–1509* (Edinburgh:

John Grant, 1910).

35. *Ibid.*

36. Mortimer, I., *The Traveller's Guide to Medieval England* (Vintage, 2009).

37. Gairdner, *The Paston Letters* (1910).

38. Page, W. (ed.), *A History of the County of Norwich, Volume 2* (Victoria County History, 1906).

2 Reversal of Fortune, 1469–1471

1. Shakespeare, W., *Henry VI, Part III.*

2. Shulman, R., *Sumptuary Legislation and the Fabric Consrtuction of National Identity in Early Modern England.*

3. Hicks, M., *Anne Neville: Queen to Richard III* (Tempus, 2007).

4. *Ibid.*

5. Gairdner, *The Paston Letters.*

6. SLP Milan, Aug 1469.

7. *Ibid.*

8. Gregory, P., D. Baldwin and M. Jones, *The Women of the Cousins' War: The Duchess, the Queen and the King's Mother* (Simon and Schuster, 2011).

9. C 1/66/296, National Archives.

10. Sharpe, R. R. (ed.), *Calendar of Letter Books for the City of London: L. Folios 61–70, March 1469* (1912).

11. Serjeantson, R. M. and W. R. D. Adkins, *A History of the County of Northampton, Volume 2* (Victoria County History, 1906).

12. Gairdner, *The Paston Letters.*

13. Croyland.

14. Ellis, H. (ed.), *Three Books of Polydore Vergil's English History, comprising the reigns of Henry VI, Edward IV and Richard III* (Camden Society, 1844).

15. Southworth, J., *Fools and Jesters at the English Court* (The History Press, 2003).

16. Mead, W., *The English Medieval Feast* (Allen and Unwin, 1931).

17. Gairdner, *The Paston Letters*.
18. Okerlund.
19. Weir.
20. Vergil.
21. Jenkins, E., *The Princes in the Tower* (Hamish Hamilton, 1978).
22. SLP Edward IV, November 1470.
23. Weir.
24. Gairdner, *The Paston Letters*.
25. Bruce, J. (ed.), *Historie of the Arrivall of Edward IV in England and Finall Recouerye of his Kingdomes from Henry VI* (Camden Society, 1838).
26. *Ibid*.
27. Sharpe, *Calendar of Letter Books* (1912).
28. Fabyan.
29. Jenkins.

3 The Life of a Princess, 1471–1483

1. G. Tetzel in Falkus.
2. *Time Team Guide to Burial* (Channel 4, 2012).
3. Snell, M., 'The Medieval Child: Childbirth, Childhood and Adolescence in the Middle Ages', *Medieval History* (Dec. 2000).
4. Falkus.
5. Fortescue, Sir J., *De Laudibus Legum Anglae* (1543), Amos, A. (ed.) (Butterworth & Son, 1825).
6. Baldwin.
7. Falkus.
8. Pisan, C. de, *The Book/Treasure of the City of Ladies or the Book of the Three Virtues*, Brown-Grant, R. (trans.) (Penguin, 1999).
9. Rickert, E., *The Babees' Book or Medieval Manners for the Young* (Chatto and Windus, 1908).
10. *Ibid*.
11. *Ibid*.
12. *Ibid*.

13. Baldwin, D., *Elizabeth Woodville* (The History Press, 2004).

4 Uncle Richard, 1483–1485

1. 'The Ballad of Lady Bessie' in Baird, I. F., 'Poems Concerning the Stanley Family (Earls of Derby) 1485–1520', PhD thesis (University of Birmingham, 1989).
2. Mancini, *The Occupation of the Throne by Richard III* (1483).
3. Lethbridge, C. (ed.), *Chronicles of London* (Clarendon Press, 1905).
4. Holinshed, R., *Chronicles of England, Ireland and Scotland, Vol. 6* (London: J. Johnson, 1807).
5. Okerlund.
6. *Ibid.*
7. *Ibid.*
8. Bruce, J. (ed.), *Historie of the Arrivall of Edward IV, in England and the Finall Recouerie of his Kingdomes from Henry VI, 1471* (Camden Society, 1838).
9. More, T., *The Utopia and the History of Edward V*, Adams, M. (ed.) (W. Scott, 1890).
10. Vergil.
11. 'The Ballad of Lady Bessie'.
12. Croyland.
13. Weir.
14. Okerlund.
15. Gairdner, J., *Elizabeth of York, Queen of Henry VII*.
16. Holinshed.
17. Licence, A., *In Bed with the Tudors* (Amberley, 2012).
18. Weir, A., *The Princes in the Tower* (Vintage, 2008).
19. Okerlund, A., *Elizabeth of York* (Palgrave Macmillan, 2009).

5 A Royal Wedding, 1485–1486

1. Hall's Chronicle (Richard III on Henry VII).
2. *Ibid.*
3. Hammond, P. W. and A. F. Sutton, *Richard III: The Road to Bosworth Field* (Constable, 1985).

4. Vergil.

5. Legg, L. G. W., *English Coronation Records* (Constable, 1975).

6. Harvey Lenz, N., *Elizabeth of York, Tudor Queen* (New York: Macmillan, 1973).

7. Okerlund.

8. Harris, N. (ed.), *Privy Purse Expenses of Elizabeth of York* (London: Pickering, 1830).

9. British Library, Harley 28.

10. Anon., 'The Shrine of Prince Arthur in Worcester Cathedral, England', *The Illustrated Magazine of Art*, 1 (4) (1853), pp. 251–2.

11. Pisan.

12. 'What the Goodwife Taught her Daughter' in Rickert, *The Babees' Book* (1908).

13. Laynesmith, J. L., *The Last Medieval Queens: English Queenship 1445–1503* (Oxford University Press, 2004).

14. *Ibid*.

6 Motherhood, 1486–1487

1. Robbins, R. H. (ed.), *Historical Poems of the Fourteenth and Fifteenth Centuries* (New York, 1959).

2. Henry VII SLP, February 1486.

3. Milford, H. (ed.), *Hali Meidenhad* (Early English Text Society, 1922).

4. For further discussion see Licence, A., *In Bed with the Tudors* (Amberley, 2012).

5. Hughes, Jonathan, *Arthurian Myths and Alchemy: the Kingship of Edward IV* (Sutton, 2002).

6. Okerlund; Wroe, A., *Perkin: A Story of Deception* (Jonathan Cape, 2003).

7. Licence.

8. Mccarthy, J. H., 'The Emergence of Henrician Drama in the Kynges Absens', *English Literary Renaissance*, 39 (2) (2009), pp. 231–66.

9. Mirkus, Johannes, *Mirk's Festival: A Collection of Homilies*,

Erbe, T. (ed.) (Trubner and Co., 1905).

10. Pisan.
11. Elton, G. R., *England under the Tudors* (Methuen, 1955).
12. Kendall, P. M., *Richard III* (Norton and Co., 2002).
13. Penn, T., *The Winter King; the Dawn of Tudor England* (Allen Lane, 2011).
14. Lander, J. R., 'Marriage and Politics in the Fifteenth Century: the Nevilles and the Wydevilles', *Journal of Historical Research*, 36 (94) (1963), pp. 119–52.

7 Married Life, 1487–1500

1. Leland.
2. Bacon, F., *The History of the Reign of King Henry VII* (Hesperus, 2007).
3. See the iconic but anonymous portrait of Henry wearing the order of the Golden Fleece, *c*. 1505. National Portrait Gallery, NPG 416.
4. Walpole, H., *Historic Doubts on the Life and Reign of Richard III* (1768).
5. SLP Spain, June 1488.
6. *Ibid*.
7. *Ibid*.
8. Wroe.
9. Okerlund.
10. Pollard, A. F. (ed.), *The Reign of Henry VII from Contemporary Sources* (Longmans Green, 1913).
11. Mccarthy.
12. Pollard.
13. Okerlund.
14. Thurley.
15. *Ibid*.
16. Okerlund.
17. *Henry VIII: Mind of a Tyrant* (Channel 4, 2009).
18. Okerlund.

8 Imposters, Edward VI & Richard IV, 1487–1499

1. Prophecy by Molinet in Wroe, *Perkin* (2003).
2. Hall.
3. *Ibid.*
4. CSLP Venice, July 1487.
5. *Ibid.*
6. Nichols, J. G. and R. Turpyn (eds), *The Chronicle of Calais in the Reigns of Henry VII and Henry VIII to the year 1540* (Camden Society, 1846).
7. CSLP Venice, December 1492.
8. CSP Spain, 8 September 1493.
9. CSLP Venice, 1497.
10. *Ibid.*
11. Bacon.
12. Wroe.
13. *Ibid.*
14. CSLP Venice, 1497.

9 The Spanish Princess, 1501–1502

1. CSLP Spain, 1501.
2. SLP Venice, 1497.
3. Jones, E. T., 'Alwyn Ruddock; John Cabot and the Discovery of America', *Journal of Historical Research*, 81 (212) (2008), pp. 224–54.
4. Nichols and Turpyn, *The Chronicle of Calais* (1846).
5. CSLP Spain, 1501.
6. *Ibid.*
7. *Ibid.*
8. *Ibid.*
9. *Ibid.*
10. *Ibid.*

10 A Year in the Life, 1502–1503

1. Royal Museums Greenwich website: http://www.rmg.co.uk/tudor-and-stuart-christmas/food-and-feasts/.
2. Nicolas, N. H. (ed.), *The Privy Purse Expenses of Elizabeth of*

York (London: Pickering, 1830).

3. Hall, E., *Chronicle; containing the History of England, during the reign of Henry the fourth and the succeeding monarchs, to the end of the reign of Henry VIII, in which are particularly described the manners and customs of those periods* (Collated with the editions of 1548 and 1550) (London: J. Johnson, 1809).

4. *Ibid.*

5. Perry, M., *Sisters to the King* (Andre Deutsch, 1998).

6. Warner, M., *Alone of All her Sex: The Myth and the Cult of the Virgin Mary* (Weidenfeld and Nicolson, 1976).

7. Hutton.

8. CSP Venice, 1488.

9. Kristeva, J. and C. Clement, *The Feminine and the Sacred* (Palgrave Macmillan, 2001).

11 Surprised by Time, 1503

1. Anonymous seventeenth-century ballad.

2. Spanish Ambassador, cited in Okerlund.

3. Okerlund.

4. Nicolas, *Privy Purse Expenses* (1830).

5. SLP Henry VII, 1504.

6. *Ibid.*

7. Hilton, Lisa, *Queens Consort: England's Medieval Queens* (Phoenix, 2009).

Bibliography

Primary and Contemporary Sources

Bacon, Francis, *The History of the Reign of King Henry VII* (Hesperus, 2007).

Baird, Ian Forbes, 'Poems Concerning the Stanley Family (Earls of Derby) 1485–1520', PhD thesis (University of Birmingham, 1989).

Bird, W. H. B and K. H. Ledward (eds), *Calendar of State Papers, Henry VI, Edward IV, Edward V, Richard III* (1953).

Brown, Rawdon (ed.), *Calendar of State Papers Relating to English Affairs in the State Papers of Venice, 1202–1509* (1864).

Bruce, J. (ed.), *Historie of the Arrivall of Edward IV in England and Finall Recouerye of his Kingdomes from Henry VI* (Camden Society, 1838).

Cornazzano, Antonio, *La Regina d'Ingliterra* (1466–8).

Ellis, Henry (ed.), *New Chronicles of England and France in two parts by Robert Fabyan, 1516* (London, 1811).

Ellis, Henry (ed.), *Three Books of Polydore Vergil's English History, comprising the reigns of Henry VI, Edward IV and Richard III* (Camden Society, 1844).

Fortescue, Sir John, *De Laudibus Legum Anglae* (1543), Amos, A. (ed.) (Butterworth & Son, 1825).

Gairdner, James (ed.), *Gregory's Chronicle 1461–9* (London, 1876).

Gairdner, James (ed.), *The Paston Letters, 1422–1509* (Edinburgh: John Grant, 1910).

Hall, Edward, *Chronicle; containing the History of England, during the reign of Henry the fourth and the succeeding monarchs, to the end of the reign of Henry VIII, in which are particularly described the manners and customs of those periods* (Collated with the editions of 1548 and 1550) (London: J. Johnson, 1809).

Holinshed, Raphael, *Chronicles of England, Scotland and Ireland* (London: J. Johnson, 1807).

Lander, J. R., 'Marriage and Politics in the Fifteenth Century: the Nevilles and the Wydevilles', *Journal of Historical Research*, 36 (94) (1963), pp. 119–52.

Lethbridge, Charles (ed.), *Chronicles of London* (Clarendon Press, 1905).

Mancini, *The Occupation of the Throne by Richard III* (1483).

Milford, H. (ed.), *Hali Meidenhad* (Early English Text Society, 1922).

Mirkus, Johannes, *Mirk's Festival: A Collection of Homilies*, Erbe, T. (ed.) (Trubner and Co., 1905).

More, Thomas, *The History of King Richard III*, Rawson Lumby, J. (ed.) (Cambridge University Press, 1883).

More, Thomas, *The Utopia and the History of Edward V*, Adams, M. (ed.) (W. Scott, 1890).

National Archives.

Nichols, J. G. and R. Turpyn (eds), *The Chronicle of Calais in the Reigns of Henry VII and Henry VIII to the year 1540* (Camden Society, 1846).

Nicolas, N. H. (ed.), *The Privy Purse Expenses of Elizabeth of York* (London: Pickering, 1830).

Pizan, Christine de, *The Treasure of the City of Ladies or the Book of the Three Virtues*, Brown-Grant, R. (trans.) (Penguin, 1999).

Pollard, A. F. (ed.), *The Reign of Henry VII from Contemporary Sources* (Longmans Green, 1913).

Riley, Henry. T. (trans.), *Ingulph's Chronicle of the Abbey of Croyland* (London: H. G. Bohn, 1854).

Sharpe, Reginald R. (ed.), *Calendar of letter books for the city of London: L. Folios 61–70, March 1469* (1912).

Twemlow, J. A., *Calendar of Papal Registers Relating to Great Britain and Ireland, Vol. 14: 1484–92* (1960).

Secondary Sources

Ackroyd, Peter, *London, the Biography* (Vintage, 2001).

Anon., 'The Shrine of Prince Arthur in Worcester Cathedral, England', *The Illustrated Magazine of Art*, 1 (4) (1853), pp. 251–2.

Ashdown-Hill, John, *Eleanor, the Secret Queen; the Woman who put Richard III on the Throne* (The History Press, 2009).

Ashdown-Hill, John, *The Last Days of Richard III* (The History Press, 2011).

Baldwin, David, *Elizabeth Woodville* (The History Press, 2004).

Chambers, E. K., *Notes on the History of the Revels Office under the Tudors* (A. H. Bullen, 1906).

Clark, John and Cathy Ross, *London, the Illustrated History* (Allen Lane, 2008).

Coss, Peter, *The Lady in Medieval England* (Sutton, 1998).

Elton, G. R., *England Under the Tudors* (Methuen, 1955).

Falkus, Gila, *The Life and Times of Edward IV* (Weidenfeld and Nicolson, 1981).

Goodwin, George, *Fatal Colours: Towton 1461, England's Most Brutal Battle* (Weidenfeld and Nicolson, 2011).

Gregory, Philippa, David Baldwin and Michael Jones, *The Women of the Cousins' War: The Duchess, the Queen and the King's Mother* (Simon and Schuster, 2011).

Hammond, P. W and Anne F. Sutton, *Richard III: The Road to Bosworth Field* (Constable, 1985).

Hancock, Peter, A., *Richard III and the Murder in the Tower* (The History Press, 2011).

Harvey Lenz, Nancy, *Elizabeth of York, Tudor Queen* (New York: Macmillan, 1973).

Henry VIII: Mind of a Tyrant (Channel 4, 2009).

Heywood, Thomas, *The First and Second Parts of King Edward IV*, Field, B. (ed.) (London: Shakespeare Society, 1842).

Hicks, Michael, *Anne Neville: Queen to Richard III* (Tempus, 2007).

Hicks, Michael, *Richard III* (The History Press, 2003).

Hilton, Lisa, *Queens Consort: England's Medieval Queens* (Phoenix, 2009).

Hughes, Jonathan, *Arthurian Myths and Alchemy: the Kingship of Edward IV* (Sutton, 2002).

Hutton, Ronald, *The Ritual Year in England* (Oxford University Press, 1994).

Jenkins, E., *The Princes in the Tower* (Hamish Hamilton, 1978).

Jones, Evan T., 'Alwyn Ruddock; John Cabot and the Discovery of America', *Journal of Historical Research*, 81 (212) (2008), pp. 224–54.

Kendall, Paul Murray, *Richard III* (Norton and Co., 2002).

King, Margaret L., *Women of the Renaissance* (University of Chicago Press, 1991).

Kristeva, Julia and Catherine Clement, Catherine, *The Feminine and the Sacred* (Palgrave Macmillan, 2001).

Laynesmith, J. L., *The Last Medieval Queens: English Queenship 1445–1503* (Oxford University Press, 2004).

Legg, L. G. W., *English Coronation Records* (Constable, 1975).

Leyser, Henrietta, *Medieval Women: A Social History of Women in England 450–1500* (Weidenfeld and Nicolson, 1995).

Licence, A., *In Bed with the Tudors* (Amberley, 2012).

Lockyer, R. and A. Thrush, *Henry VII: Seminar Studies in History* (Longman, 1997).

Maurer, Helen E., *Margaret of Anjou: Queenship and Power in Late Medieval England* (Boydell, 2003).

Mccarthy, Jeanne, H., 'The Emergence of Henrician Drama in the Kynges Absens', *English Literary Renaissance*, 39 (2) (2009), pp. 231–66.

Mortimer, Ian, *The Traveller's Guide to Medieval England* (Vintage, 2009).

Myers, A. R., 'The Book of the Disguisings for the Coming of The

Ambassadors of Flanders, December 1508', *Journal of Historical Research*, 54 (129) (1981), pp. 120–9.

Okerlund, Arlene, *Elizabeth of York* (Palgrave Macmillan, 2009).

Okerlund, Arlene, *Elizabeth Wydeville, the Slandered Queen* (Tempus, 2005).

Page, William (ed.), *A History of the County of Norwich, Volume 2* (Victoria County History, 1906).

Penn, Thomas, *The Winter King; the Dawn of Tudor England* (Allen Lane, 2011).

Perry, Maria, *Sisters to the King* (Andre Deutsch, 1998).

Robbins, R. H. (ed.), *Historical Poems of the Fourteenth and Fifteenth Centuries* (New York, 1959).

Ross, Charles, *Edward IV* (Yale University Press, 1997).

Roud, Steve, *The English Year* (Penguin, 2006).

Rutherfurd, Edward, *London* (Arrow, 2010).

Santiuste, David, *Edward IV and the Wars of the Roses* (Pen and Sword, 2010).

Saul, Nigel, *The Three Richards: Richard I, Richard II and Richard III* (Hambledon and London, 2005).

Serjeantson, R. M. and W. R. D. Adkins, *A History of the County of Northampton, Volume 2* (Victoria County History, 1906).

Shakespeare, William, *Henry VI Part III*.

Shakespeare, William, *Richard III*.

Shulman, Rachel, *Sumptuary Legislation and the Fabric Consrtuction of National Identity in Early Modern England* (Illinois Wesleyan University).

Snell, Melissa, 'The Medieval Child: Childbirth, Childhood and Adolescence in the Middle Ages', *Medieval History* (Dec. 2000).

Southworth, John, *Fools and Jesters at the English Court* (The History Press, 2003).

Thurley, Simon, *The Royal Palaces of Tudor England* (Yale University Press, 1993).

Tremlett, Giles, *Catherine of Aragon: Henry's Spanish Queen* (Faber and Faber, 2010).

Walpole, H., *Historic Doubts on the Life and Reign of Richard III* (1768).

Warner, Maria, *Alone of All her Sex: The Myth and the Cult of the Virgin Mary* (Weidenfeld and Nicolson, 1976).

Weightman, Christine, *Margaret of York, Duchess of Burgundy, 1446–1503* (New York: St Martin's Press, 1989).

Weir, Alison, *Lancaster and York: The Wars of the Roses* (Vintage, 1995).

Weir, Alison, *The Princes in the Tower* (Vintage, 2008).

Wroe, Anne, *Perkin: A Story of Deception* (Jonathan Cape, 2003).

Acknowledgements

Thanks go to the team at Amberley for taking a chance on me and continuing to give me wonderful opportunities; to Jonathan Reeve for suggesting Elizabeth of York, Nicola Gale for her constant interest and kindness and Nicki Giles for encouraging and promoting me. Thanks also to all my family for their support, particularly to Tom and the Hunts, to my mother for her invaluable proofreading skills and to my father for his enthusiasm.

List of Illustrations

1. © Ripon Cathedral.
2. © Ripon Cathedral.
3. © Michael O'Donnell.
4. © Ripon Cathedral.
5. © Jonathan Reeve JR1577b4p548 14501500.
6. © Martin Dolby.
7. © Julie Clarke.
8. © David Noble.
9. © David Baldwin.
10. © Lorna Svoma.
11. © Sean Murphy.
12. © Jonathan Reeve JR1565b13p704 14501500.
13. © George Groutas.
14. © Amy Licence.
15. © Amy Licence.
16. © Phil Grain.
17. © Laurence Burridge.
18. © Laurence Burridge.
19. *Richard, Duke of Gloucester, and the Lady Anne* by Edwin Austin Abbey. © Yale University Art Gallery, Edwin Austin Abbey Memorial Collection.
20. © James Nicholls.
21. © Amanda Miller at Amanda's Arcadia. Thanks also to the Reverend Canon of Leicestershire.

Index

About the Author

Amy Licence is the author of *Royal Babies: A History 1066-2013*, *In Bed With the Tudors: The Sex Lives of a Dynasty from Elizabeth of York to Elizabeth I* ('What really went on in Henry VIII's bedroom' *The Daily Express*), *Cecily Neville: Mother of Kings*, *Anne Neville: Richard III's Tragic Queen* and *Richard III: The Road to Leicester*, all published by Amberley. She lives in Canterbury.

Also by Amy Licence

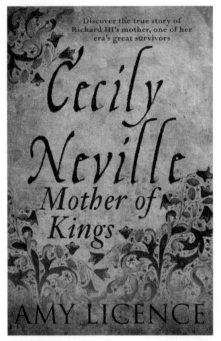

Cecily Neville
Mother of Kings

Discover the true story of Richard III's mother, one of her era's great survivors

Known to be proud, regal and beautiful, Cecily Neville's life spanned most of the fifteenth century. One of a huge family, Cecily would see two of her sons become kings of England but the struggles that tore apart the Houses of Lancaster and York also turned brother against brother. What was the substance behind her claim to be 'queen by right'? Would she indeed have made a good queen during these turbulent times?

£20 Hardback
35 illustrations
256 pages
978-1-4456-2123-4

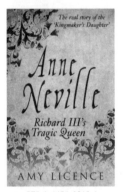

978-1-4456-3312-1

978-1-4456-1475-5

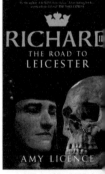

978-1-4456-2175-3

Available from all good bookshops or to order direct
Please call **01453-847-800**
www.amberleybooks.com